福建古厝

FUJIAN ANCIENT BUILDINGS

中共福建省委宣传部　福建省人民政府新闻办公室　编

海峡出版发行集团 THE STRAITS PUBLISHING & DISTRIBUTING GROUP | 福建人民出版社 FUJIAN PEOPLE'S PUBLISHING HOUSE

《福建古厝》编委会

序

《福建古厝》是一本关于福建历史建筑的集萃，包括了从福州华林寺大殿这一有着超过千年历史、中国南方地区最古老的木结构建筑，到建于19世纪末至20世纪前期的鼓浪屿近代建筑群；从体现中国传统文化核心观念的文庙、学宫，到反映福建丰富多样的民间信仰的妈祖庙、慈济宫；从体现门阀世族生活居住形态的三坊七巷，到反映福建客家聚族而居的土楼群；从宗祠到大宅聚落，从佛寺、道观，再到清净寺、礼拜堂、教堂。这些历史建筑，反映了福建作为中华民族文化的重要组成部分的发展与演变过程，反映了福建地方文化的多样性。

文化的形成不仅决定于作为核心部分的精神、观念，而且也受到其所在地理、自然环境的影响，被历史演变过程中的各种事件及各种文化的碰撞、交流与融合所塑造。福建的历史、文化发展清晰地展现了文化发展过程的复杂、深刻、广泛和绚烂多彩的特征。《福建古厝》一书中介绍的这些历史建筑正是福建历史、文化演化过程中文化融合成果的物质载体。通过这些历史建筑能够阅读和认知福建历史、文化的丰富信息。福建是中国大陆地区面对太平洋和印度洋重要的海上贸易和文化交流的区域，在历史上一直保持着与东亚、东南亚、南亚等周边区域，以及更大范围圈层之间的经济、文化交流。这种交流在与中国本土文化的融合过程中，使福建文化形成了鲜明的特征与独特的形态。这也使得福建地区从人类文明互鉴的层面呈现出独特的意义，具有全球性的价值。《福建古厝》一书中介绍的许多建筑遗产本身就是世界遗产的组成要素，或是中国申报世界遗产预备名单上的项目。

《福建古厝》一书中介绍的这些历史建筑，不仅是历史、文化的纪念物，它们当中的许多建筑仍然延续着原有的功能，具有活态遗产的特征。它们的意义不仅体现在作为历史、文化的见证方面，更体现在它们作为一种文化传统与精神的载体在当代社会中所具有的促使人们建立身份与情感认同，形成社会凝聚力的意义与作用上。对这些重要历史文化遗产的保护已成为社会的共识。保护好这些历史遗存，充分展现和实现它们的价值，带动和促进社会的可持续发展也是社会的普遍愿景。《福建古厝》所涉及的内容仅仅是福建丰厚的文化遗产中的一小部分，但它仍然给了读者更深入认识福建文化遗产的可能性。愿所有读者能够喜欢《福建古厝》。

吕舟

清华大学教授

中国古迹遗址保护协会副理事长

2020年7月15日于北京

Preface

Fujian Ancient Buildings is a veritable collection of various styles of historical architecture in Fujian. It is a combination of buildings in old and modern times, ranging from the main hall of Hualin Temple in Fuzhou, the oldest wooden structure in Southern China with a history of more than a thousand years, to modern buildings on Kulangsu dating back to the late 19th and early 20th centuries. And it is a display of key practices of traditional Chinese culture and folk beliefs in a rich diversity of Confucius temples, academies of classical learning, as well as Mazu and Ciji temples. There are also distinctive former official residences such as those in the famous Three Lanes and Seven Alleys, unique earthen dwellings inhabited by Hakka families, in addition to all sorts of ancestral halls, mansions, temples of Buddhism and Taoism as well as mosques, chapels and churches. All these historical buildings reveal the development of Fujian culture as an important part of Chinese culture and its diversity as a unique local culture.

A culture is shaped not only by the local beliefs and concepts as the core, but also by the geographical and natural environment from which it originates, and influenced by various events together with conflicts, communication and integration of different cultures in the process of its historical evolution. The historical and cultural development of Fujian clearly indicates the complexity, depth, width and diversity of this process, which is given tangible expressions in ancient buildings introduced in the book. Through them, we can see and learn more about the rich history and culture of Fujian as a major region for maritime trade and cultural exchange with the outside world, especially areas along the Pacific and Indian oceans. Actually, the province has been historically maintaining close economic and cultural ties with neighboring regions such as East Asia, Southeast Asia, South Asia, and beyond. All these exchanges, integrated with local Chinese culture, have nourished and shaped Fujian culture to give it distinctive and unique features. This also makes Fujian a local example with universal values of human civilizations learning from one another. Many of the heritage buildings included in the book are themselves properties meeting the criteria for World Heritage listing, or items already on China's tentative list for future nomination to the World Heritage List.

Historical houses and buildings collected in the book are not just monuments in memory of history and culture; many of them are still functioning as living heritages. They do not just serve as witnesses of history and culture, but also act as carriers of culture, tradition and beliefs linking the past and the present. They have the attractive power to bring people today together to develop cultural identity and do more for the society. Now the protection of important historical and cultural heritage sites has become a shared awareness of the country and people also hope to promote these sites for the sustainable development of society in general. What is included in the book is only a small part of Fujian's rich cultural heritage resources. It may, however, open up more possibilities for readers to understand Fujian and its cultural heritage deeper and better. I sincerely hope you will like the book and enjoy the reading.

Lyu Zhou

Professor of Tsinghua University

Vice-Executive President of China Association for the Protection of Historical Sites

15 July, 2020, Beijing

(Translated by Chen Xiaowei)

前言

在福州、闽南等地区，人们把房子称作厝。盖房子，称之为起厝。古厝，则是指老房子，即具有一定历史的房屋建筑。

福建古厝数量位居全国前列，总数不下20万座，其中被登记为不可移动文物的有1万多座。本书选录112座古厝，包括被列入全国重点文物保护单位的80处102座古厝；为了全面体现各种建筑文化类型，还收录了9处省级文物保护单位（福州开元寺，三明石壁张氏家庙、陈塘修齐堂、沧海畲族建筑群之龙德堂，莆田大宗伯第，南平下梅大夫第，龙岩芷溪古建筑群之杨氏家庙，平潭上攀古建筑群、五福庙）和1处市级文物保护单位（福州戚公祠）。

福建古厝源远流长。考古资料显示，在三明万寿岩船帆洞遗址发现的距今3万至4万年的人工石铺地面，是人类通过自己的双手改善居住环境最早的案例之一，是房屋建筑的萌芽形态。福州屏山的闽越国宫殿区遗址、武夷山城村的闽越国王城遗址，规模宏大、布局规整、功能齐备，出土的建筑构件规格更是直逼西汉长安皇宫，展现了西汉初期福建房屋建筑的最高成就。汉武帝灭闽越国后，闽地长期处于荒芜、萧条状态，直至唐代才重现辉煌。福建现存的许多寺庙类建筑历史可溯源至唐，就是很好的佐证。这些以木构为主体的早期建筑，历经岁月沧桑，或无存或成遗址，难以完整留存下来，令人惋惜。

宋以来，福建古厝成群成片地得以保留且传承有序，这得益于福建地区长期远离中原战场。我们见到现存最早的福建古厝有两宋时期的福州华林寺大殿、莆田元妙观三清殿、罗源陈太尉宫正殿、永泰名山室祖师殿。顺昌宝山之巅的宝山寺大殿则是元代石质仿木构房屋建筑之精品，其石柱、石梁、石枋、石檩、石椽、石瓦均按木构件正常尺寸、造型而做，既呈现福建石构建筑之成就，又记录着元代木构建筑之技艺信息。明清两朝，以乡土建筑为主体的大量福建古厝则以建筑群形式整体保留，形成了各具特色的历史街区、传统村落。

在多样性文化背景下，建筑风格、建筑艺术的地域性差异成为福建古厝的鲜明特色。以三坊七巷民居为代表的福州、闽东地区建筑，端庄典雅，工艺考究，体现官宦文化的影响；以泰宁尚书第为代表的闽北地区建筑，砖雕精美，灰瓦灰砖马头墙，可见徽派建筑装饰风格的影子；以土楼、土堡为代表的闽中、闽西地区建筑，则是福建地区复杂的自然地理环境对防御性建筑需求的真实写照；以南安蔡氏古民居为代表的闽南地区建筑，红瓦红墙红地板，在红砖建筑鲜艳的主题上配以曲线优美的屋面和多彩多姿的剪瓷装饰，独树一帜。

古厝展现了福建历史文化的深厚积淀，凝聚着福建先民的聪明才智。

何经平

Foreword

People in Fuzhou and some southern parts of Fujian Province call houses cuo and the building of houses "the putting up of cuo". Ancient houses and buildings are time-honored, and have existed for many generations.

The number of ancient buildings in Fujian is in the top rank of China, totaling more than 200,000, among which over 10,000 are registered as immovable cultural relics. Showcasing their best, this book selects 112 ancient buildings; 102 of them in 80 sites have been listed as important heritage buildings under state protection. In addition, 9 ancient buildings under protection at provincial level (Fuzhou Kaiyuan Temple; Sanming Shibi Zhang Family's Ancestral Hall, Chentang Xiuqi Hall, Longde House of the *She* Group in Canghai; Putian Minister of Etiquette's Mansion; Xiamei Dafu Mansion in Nanping; Yang Family's Ancestral Hall of Ancestral Buildings in Zhixi Village in Longyan; Shangpan Ancient Building Group and Wufu Temple in Pingtan), and 1 at municipal level (Sir Qigong Memorial Hall in Fuzhou) are included to better reflect various styles of architectural culture in Fujian.

The oldest ancient building in Fujian dates back thousands of years. According to archaeological literature, there was a stone paving made by manual labor as early as 30,000 to 40,000 years ago, still recognizable in ruins of Sail Cave at Wanshou (Longevity) Rock in Northern Fujian's Sanming, one of the earliest cases of human beings improving their living environment with their own hands, as well as the beginning of housing construction. There are also ruins of Minyue Royal Palace in Pingshan (Screen Hill), Fuzhou, and ruins of Minyue Royal City in Chengcun Village, Wuyishan City. Their magnificent area coverage, well-structured design and full amenities, together with the architectural components excavated that may well rival those found in the ancient Chang'an Royal Palace of the Former Han Dynasty, represent the superb achievement of Fujian architecture in the early days of China's Han historical period. In spite of the fact that there had been a time of depression ever since Emperor Wudi of the Han Dynasty destroyed the State of Minyue, Fujian resumed its life and vitality during the Tang Dynasty. This is evidenced in many extant temples in Fujian built during the Tang Dynasty. Unfortunately many of these early buildings with wooden structure have not survived the time, existing now only in early records or falling into ruins.

Thanks to Fujian's geographical location that keeps it far away from the ancient perennially warring areas in the Central Plains, ancient houses and buildings in Fujian have been well preserved and handed down since the Song Dynasty. We can still see Fujian ancient buildings from the Northern and Southern Song dynasties, such as the main hall of Hualin Temple in Fuzhou, Sanqing Hall of Yuanmiao Temple in Putian, the main hall of Commandant Chen's Temple in Luoyuan, and the Patriarch Hall of Mingshan Temple in Yongtai. Baoshan Temple Hall at the top of Mount Baoshan in Northern Fujian's Shunchang is one of the best examples of the imitation-wood stone buildings of the Yuan Dynasty, with all its stone pillars, beams, columns, purlins, rafters and tiles designed and patterned exactly according to the normal size and pattern of a wooden structure. This not only showcases the super achievements of Fujian stone architecture, but also tangibly records the workmanship of the wooden architecture of the Yuan Dynasty. In the Ming and Qing dynasties, there emerged a large number of local houses and buildings in complexes and clusters, which have grown into today's historical blocks and traditional villages with distinctive characteristics.

Under the backdrop of cultural diversity, ancient houses and buildings in Fujian have grown to feature unique regional diversities in architectural style and artistic appeal. For example, architectures in Fuzhou and Eastern Fujian represented by residential buildings in the ancient Three Lanes and Seven Alleys are famous for their dignity and elegance, with exquisite craftsmanship reflecting the impact of ancient Chinese officialdom culture. The buildings in Northern Fujian exemplified by Shangshu Mansion in Taining are known for their fine brick carvings, with grey bricks, grey tiles and Ma Tau walls (fire walls) , from which we can see traces of the decorative fashion of Anhui-style buildings. Architectures in Central and Western Fujian are best represented by Tulou (earthen dwellings) and Tubao (earthen fortresses), which are vivid reflections of the demands for defense and security in response to complex local natural, and geographical environment. The age-old Cai family's ancient residential complex in Nan'an is a typical example of Southern Fujian architectures. Featuring red tiles, red walls and red floors, the red-brick structure is very unique with its bright theme going along with finely-curved façade and colorful ceramic cutting decorations.

Indeed, reading this book about ancient houses and buildings gives us an exciting experience for the impressive richness of Fujian's history and culture, and the architectural talent and wisdom of Fujian's ancestors.

He Jingping

目　录

Contents

福州古厝

~~~

Ancient Buildings in Fuzhou
~~~

大成殿

华林寺大殿

年代：宋

地址：福州市鼓楼区华林路 78 号

始建于北宋乾德二年（964），原名越山吉祥禅院，明正统九年 (1444) 赐额“华林寺”。现存建筑仅大殿为宋初原构，二十世纪八十年代增建山门、左右配殿和廊庑。华林寺大殿是中国长江以南现存最古老的木构建筑，歇山顶，抬梁式构架，檐下斗拱做双杪三下昂偷心造七铺作。其建筑风格对日本镰仓时期（十二世纪末）的建筑风格如“大佛样”“天竺样”等有着巨大的影响。

Main Hall of Hualin Temple

Period: Song Dynasty

Address: No. 78 Hualin Road, Gulou District, Fuzhou City

This temple was built in 964 during the Northern Song Dynasty; the original name was “Yueshan Auspicious Zen House” but was changed to “Hualin Temple” in 1444 during the Ming Dynasty. After many years, the only remaining building of the original structure dated back from the early Song Dynasty is the main hall. The arch gate, the side halls and a gallery were added in the 1980s. The main hall of Hualin Temple is the oldest extant wooden building south of the Yangtze River in China, and has a gable and hip roof, with post-and-lintel construction, together with double-gong-three-ang combination, stolen-heart seven intermediate sets under the eaves. Its architectural style had a great influence on the architectural styles of the Kamakura period (late 12th century) in Japan, such as “the Great Buddha” and “the Heavenly” temples.

檐下斗拱。（林振寿 摄）
The bracket sets under the eaves. (Photo by Lin Zhenshou)

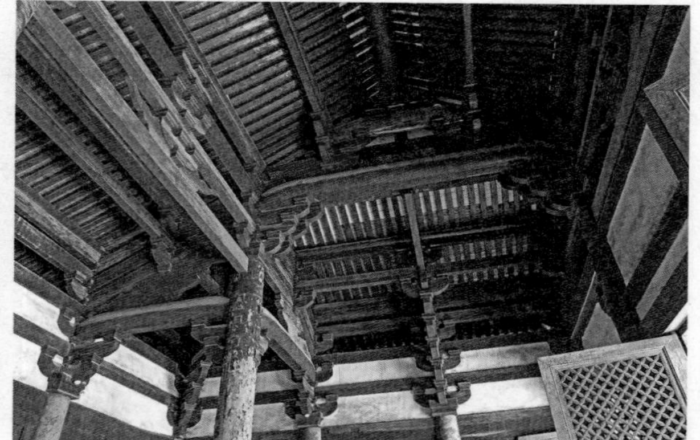

大殿抬梁式构架。（林振寿 摄）
The post-and-lintel construction in the main hall. (Photo by Lin Zhenshou)

华林寺大殿。（林振寿　摄）
The main hall of Hualin Temple. (Photo by Lin Zhenshou)

陈太尉宫

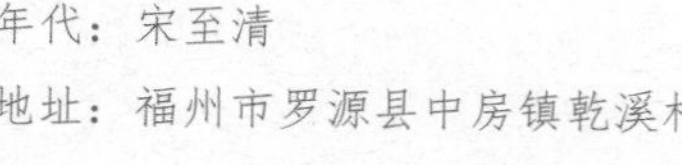

年代：宋至清

地址：福州市罗源县中房镇乾溪村

集宋、明、清建筑艺术风格于一体。原为陈氏宗祠，因祀同族都统伏魔太尉陈庆，南宋嘉定二年（1209）扩建后改称现名。现存建筑有正殿、左右配殿、山门和廊庑。正殿为宋代构造，抬梁式构架，檐下斗拱做双杪双下昂偷心造六铺作。明、清陆续添建左右配殿、戏台、山门。

Commandant Chen Temple

Period: Song to Qing dynasties

Address: Qianxi Village, Zhongfang Town, Luoyuan County, Fuzhou City

This temple has reasons enough to boast of the Song, Ming and Qing architectural styles, all in one building complex. Originally known as Chen family's ancestral hall, the temple was changed to its name after an expansion in 1209 during the Southern Song Dynasty, because the famous Commander Chen Qing was of the same ethnic clan and was honored there. The extant buildings include an arch gate, a main hall, right and left side halls and the gallery. The main hall was built during the Song Dynasty, with a post-and-lintel construction, and double-gong-double-ang combination, stolen-heart six intermediate sets under the eaves. The halls on both sides, the stage and the arch gate were added later during the Ming and Qing dynasties.

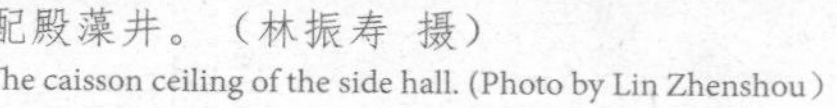

配殿藻井。（林振寿 摄）

The caisson ceiling of the side hall. (Photo by Lin Zhenshou)

正殿内景。（林振寿 摄）

The interior view of the main hall. (Photo by Lin Zhenshou)

戏台。（林振寿 摄）
The stage. (Photo by Lin Zhenshou)

崖壁下的祖师殿（林振寿 摄）
The Patriarch Hall under the cliff (Photo by Lin Zhenshou)

名山室之祖师殿

年代：宋

地址：福州市永泰县大洋镇旗杆村

坐落于高盖山山腰金水洞，坐东向西，完整地保留了宋代抬梁式构架。歇山顶，单开间，进深两间，重拱偷心造六铺作，瓜菱形石柱。室内尚存石须弥座，束腰转角处各立一持刀力士，束腰正面刻有“崇宁二年二月十一日”字样。

The Patriarch Hall of Mingshan Temple

Period: Song Dynasty

Address: Qigan Village, Dayang Town, Yongtai County, Fuzhou City

Located in Jinshui Cave in the Gaogai mountainside, sitting east and facing west, this Patriarch Hall retains the post-and-lintel construction of the Song Dynasty. The hall is one-room wide and two-room deep, with a gable and hip roof, double-gong stolen-heart six intermediate sets and oval stone columns. There are still stone sumeru pedestals in the hall, two strong fierce-looking men with broadswords standing on each side of the doorway and at the waist engraved with the construction date “Lunar February 11th, 2nd year of the reign of Emperor Chongning”.

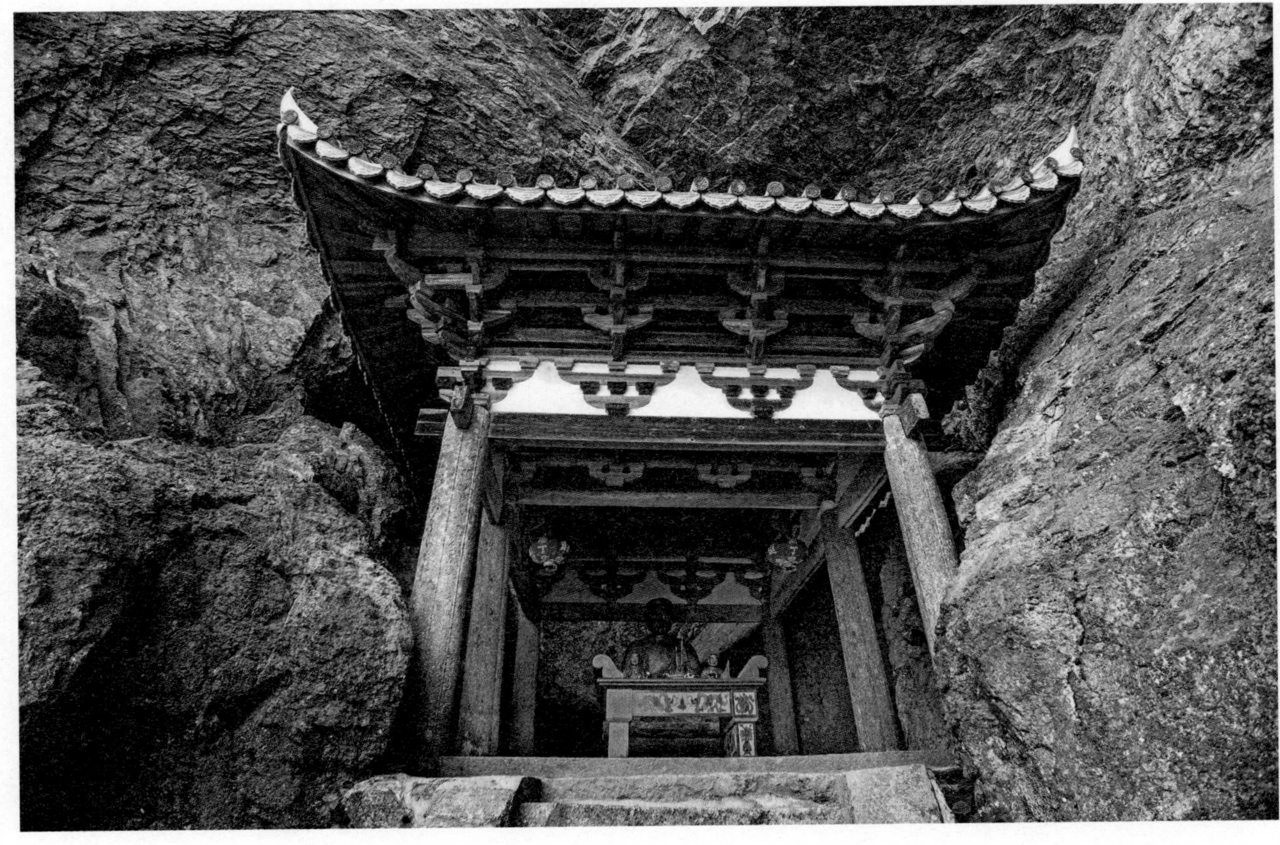

名山室祖师殿。（林振寿 摄）

The Patriarch Hall of Mingshan Temple. (Photo by Lin Zhenshou)

三坊七巷建筑群

三坊七巷起于晋，成于唐五代，至明清鼎盛。以南后街为轴线，西三坊、东七巷，平面呈鱼骨状格局。有“里坊制度活化石”“明清建筑博物馆”“近代名人聚居地”之称。古老的坊巷格局至今基本保留完整，坊巷内保存有 200 余座明清古建筑和庭院园林；自晚清至民国初，从这里走出了林则徐、沈葆桢、严复、林觉民等大量对中国近现代进程有着重要影响的人物，可谓“一片三坊七巷，半部中国近现代史”。

Building Complex in Three Lanes and Seven Alleys

Three Lanes and Seven Alleys kicked off during the Jin Dynasty (265–420), and continued through the Tang Dynasty (618–907), Five Dynasties (907–960) and became prosperous during the Ming and Qing dynasties (1368–1911). Nanhoujie (the South Main Street) acts as the axis, with three lanes in the west, and seven alleys in the east; the layout is in a fish bone pattern. It is known as “the living fossil of the lane system”, “the Architecture Museum of the Ming and Qing dynasties” and “the settlement of modern celebrities”. The ancient lane structure is basically intact, and the alleys have more than 200 ancient buildings and courtyard gardens from the Ming and Qing dynasties. From the late Qing Dynasty to the beginning of the Republic of China, a large number of famous people came from here such as Lin Zexu, Shen Baozhen, Yan Fu, Lin Juemin, all of whom had an important impact on China’s modern development. It has been described as “Three Lanes and Seven Alleys, a half of China’s modern history”.

三坊七巷——“明清建筑博物馆”。（李芳 摄）
Three Lanes and Seven Alleys—an architecture museum of the Ming and Qing dynasties. (Photo by Li Fang)

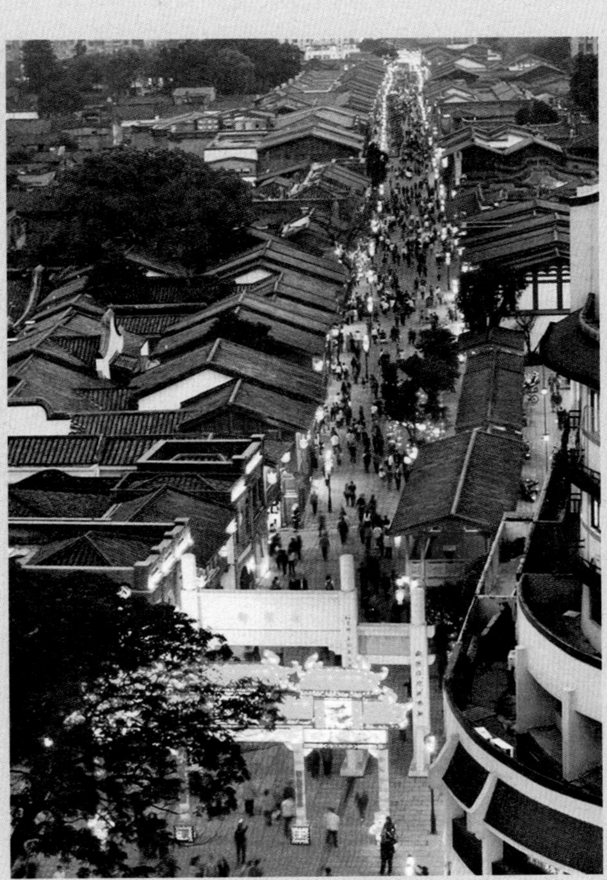

南后街是三坊七巷的中轴线。（俞松 摄）
Nanhoujie (the South Main Street) is the central axis of Three Lanes and Seven Alleys. (Photo by Yu Song)

衣锦坊水榭戏台

年代：明、清

地址：福州市鼓楼区衣锦坊 4 号

水榭戏台位于衣锦坊孙翼谋故居内。大型院落式宅第。坐北朝南，占地面积 2,377 平方米。建于明万历（1573—1620）年间，清道光年间孙氏家族购得此宅后，扩建成为由西落正院、中落别院、东落花厅组成的宅院。因东落花厅的戏台建于水池上，故称水榭戏台。

Water Theater in Yijin Lane

Period: Ming and Qing dynasties

Address: No. 4 Yijin Lane, Gulou District, Fuzhou City

The Water Theater is located in the former residence of Sun Yimou in Yijin Lane. It is a large courtyard-style house, sitting north and facing south, and covering an area of 2,377 square meters. Built from 1573 to 1620 during the Ming Dynasty, this house was later bought by the Sun family during the Qing Dynasty and expanded into a building complex consisting of the west main quadrangle, the central quadrangle and the east parlor and garden. Because the stage in the east garden was built over a pool, it is called the Water Theater.

戏台边的曲水、小桥和亭子。（林振寿 摄）
The winding water, the mini bridge and the pavilion beside the stage. (Photo by Lin Zhenshou)

戏台上正在表演《梁山伯与祝英台》。（彭常通 摄）
The famous opera *The Butterfly Lovers* is being performed on the stage. (Photo by Peng Changtong)

东落花厅。（林振寿 摄）
The east parlor. (Photo by Lin Zhenshou)

严复故居

年代：清

地址：福州市鼓楼区郎官巷 20 号

坐落于郎官巷，分主座和花厅，占地面积 625 平方米。中国近代启蒙思想家、翻译家、教育家严复 1920 年底回到福州，居住于此。主座穿斗式构架，檐柱出三跳插拱，双坡顶。花厅为双层楼，前后走廊、栏杆均为民国时期流行的仿西式建筑纹饰。现辟为严复纪念馆。

Yan Fu's Former Residence

Period: Qing Dynasty

Address: No. 20 Langguan Alley, Gulou District, Fuzhou City

Located in Langguan Alley, and divided into the main section and the parlor, this house covers an area of 625 square meters. Yan Fu, a modern Chinese scholar, translator and educator, returned to Fuzhou at the end of 1920 and lived here. The main section has a column and tie-beam construction and double-slope roofs, with three-tier bracket sets on eave columns. The parlor has two floors, with front and rear corridors and railings which were popular during the Republic of China, imitating a Western-style architectural decoration. It is now a memorial to Yan Fu.

前厅。（林振寿 摄）
The front hall. (Photo by Lin Zhenshou)

大厅。（林振寿 摄）
The main hall. (Photo by Lin Zhenshou)

沈葆桢故居

年代：明、清

地址：福州市鼓楼区宫巷 26 号

坐落于宫巷，始建于明天启年间，清同治初洋务运动重要代表人物沈葆桢任九江知府时购置重修。坐北朝南，总面积 2,000 平方米。前后三进，各进自成院落。最后一列为两层楼，前置覆龟亭与三进相接。西侧为花厅、书斋等。

Shen Baozhen's Former Residence

Period: Ming and Qing dynasties

Address: No. 26 Gong Alley, Gulou District, Fuzhou City

Located in Gong Alley, this house was built from 1621 to 1627 during the Ming Dynasty. Shen Baozhen was an important official of the Westernization Movement. He purchased and rebuilt this residence when he was the governor of Jiujiang government in Jiangxi. It sits north and faces south, with a total area of 2,000 square meters. There are three quadrangles and each quadrangle comprises a courtyard. The rear area has a two-story building and a front pavilion connected to the third quadrangle. On the west side there is a parlor, a reading room and more buildings.

首任船政大臣沈葆桢。（祝闽海 供图）
Shen Baozhen, the founding head of Shipbuilding Agency in the Qing Dynasty. (Courtesy of Zhu Minhai)

位于宫巷的沈葆桢故居。（林振寿 摄）
Shen Baozhen's former residence in Gong Alley. (Photo by Lin Zhenshou)

林觉民故居

年代：明、清

地址：福州市鼓楼区杨桥路 17 号

革命烈士林觉民父辈七户人家聚居处。现存二进厅堂、紫藤书屋、小书斋等，于 1991 年临街增修仿清式门头房。林觉民在辛亥革命中殉难后，林家避祸迁离，房屋售让著名作家谢冰心祖父谢銮恩，冰心幼年时与其祖父曾居于此。

Lin Juemin's Former Residence

Period: Ming and Qing dynasties

Address: No. 17 Yangqiao Road, Gulou District, Fuzhou City

This was the residential home of seven families including Lin Juemin's parents. The original hall in the second quadrangle, plus the "Wistaria Book House" and a small reading room still exist. An arched doorway facing the street was added in 1991, which is an imitation of the Qing Dynasty arched-doorway style. After Lin Juemin suffered martyrdom during the Revolution of 1911, the Lin family fled the disaster and moved away, and the house was sold to Xie Bingxin's grandfather, Xie Luan'en. Xie Bingxin (a famous female writer) lived here with her grandfather when she was a child.

大厅。（林振寿 摄）
The main hall. (Photo by Lin Zhenshou)

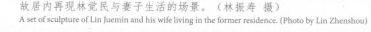

故居内再现林觉民与妻子生活的场景。（林振寿 摄）
A set of sculpture of Lin Juemin and his wife living in the former residence. (Photo by Lin Zhenshou)

紫藤书屋。（林振寿 摄）
The Wistaria Book House. (Photo by Lin Zhenshou)

朱紫坊慢生活。（陈霖 摄）
Leisure life in Zhuzi Lane. (Photo by Chen Lin)

朱紫坊建筑群

依安泰河而筑，沿河古榕垂髯，明清民居鳞次栉比。宋代通奉大夫朱敏功曾居此，朱氏兄弟四人皆登仕榜，满门朱紫，乡人就以朱紫为坊名。坊内有明代内阁大学士叶向高故居，也是萨镇冰、萨师俊、方伯谦、方莹等海军名人聚居地。

Building Complex in Zhuzi Lane

Standing along the Antai River, among the ancient banyan trees with their hair-like sagging branches, these houses from the Ming and Qing dynasties were built side by side. Zhu Mingong of the Song Dynasty lived here, with his three brothers, who all became government officials, so the villagers named this lane "Zhuzi (the color of red and purple indicating fame and honor)". The former house of grand secretary Ye Xianggao of the Ming Dynasty, and the homes of some naval celebrities including Sa Zhenbing, Sa Shijun, Fang Boqian, and Fang Ying, were all in this historic lane.

朱紫坊牌坊。（林志源 摄）
Memorial Arch Gate of Zhuzi Lane. (Photo by Lin Zhiyuan)

芙蓉园

年代：明、清

地址：福州市鼓楼区花园弄 19—23 号

大型府第，自西而东毗连三组建筑，占地面积 1,800 多平方米。原为宋代参政陈韡的“芙蓉别馆”，明代成为内阁大学士叶向高的别墅，清代为藩司龚易图所有。现存建筑为明、清重建，院内错落有致地构建了假山、鱼池、花亭、雪洞、楼台水榭、曲桥回廊等各种园林景致，极富福州园林式民居特色。

Furong Mansion

Period: Ming and Qing dynasties

Address: No. 19—23 Huayuan Lane, Gulou District, Fuzhou City

This is a large-scale mansion, with three groups of buildings adjacent to each other from the west to the east, covering an area of more than 1,800 square meters. Originally, it belonged to the statesman Chen Wei during the Song Dynasty and was called “Furong Villa”; in the Ming Dynasty it became the villa of grand secretary Ye Xianggao; and in the Qing Dynasty it belonged to a provincial official Gong Yitu. The extant buildings were rebuilt in the Ming and Qing dynasties. The courtyard garden is decorated with rockeries, fish ponds, flower pavilions, snow caves, storied buildings, waterside pavilions, winding bridges and corridors, and other garden landscapes, which is a typical characteristic of Fuzhou garden-style residential houses.

芙蓉园是福州园林式民居的代表。（林振寿 摄）
Furong Mansion is a typical example of "Fuzhou garden-style residence". (Photo by Lin Zhenshou)

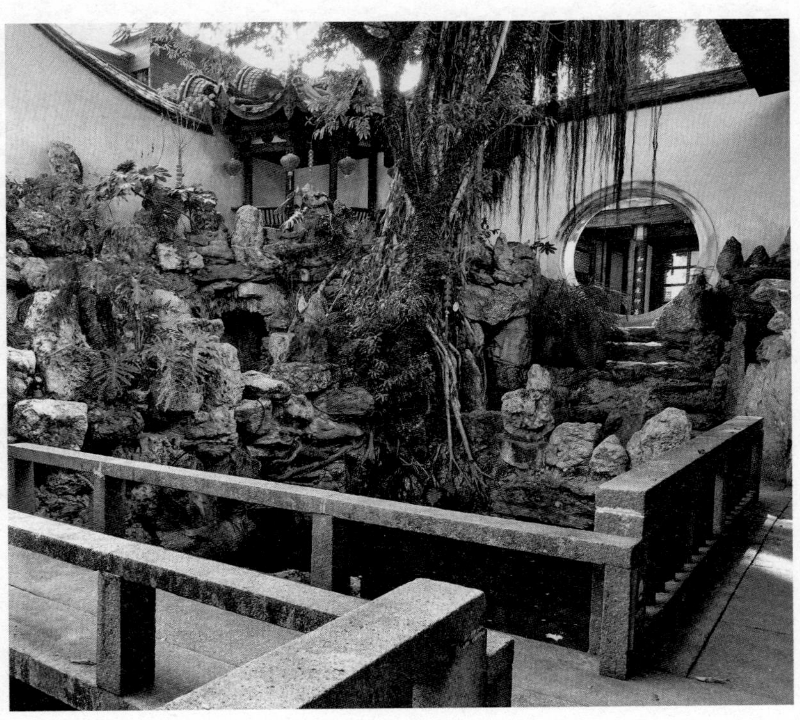

多样景致集于一园。（林振寿 摄）
Diverse views in one garden. (Photo by Lin Zhenshou)

萨氏民居

年代：清

地址：福州市鼓楼区朱紫坊 22 号

三朝海军元老萨镇冰和抗日海军将领“中山舰”舰长萨师俊的宅第。坐南朝北，由主座及其西侧的跨院组成。主座前后共五进。西侧的跨院分为前后两个花厅，花厅内部隔扇饰博古等图案，极其精美。

Sa Family's House

Period: Qing Dynasty

Address: No. 22 Zhuzi Lane, Gulou District, Fuzhou City

This was the house belonging to Sa Zhenbing—the "three-dynasty" navy leader through the Qing Dynasty to People's Republic of China, and Sa Shijun—the naval general of resistance against Japanese aggression and captain of "Zhongshan Warship". The house sits south and faces north, consisting of the main building with a courtyard on its west side. There is a total of five adjacent quadrangles of the main building. The courtyard on the west side is divided into two parlors in the front and rear. The partitions in the interiors of the parlors are decorated with antique patterns which are extremely beautiful.

花厅隔扇装饰博古等精美图案。（林振寿 摄）
Beautiful decorations and patterns are displayed on a partition in the parlor. (Photo by Lin Zhenshou)

萨氏民居内景。（林振寿 摄）
The interior view of Sa family's house. (Photo by Lin Zhenshou)

福州文庙

年代：清

地址：福州市鼓楼区圣庙路 10 号

唐大历七年（772）始建学官，五代王审知置四门学，宋太平兴国年间改为孔子庙，现存建筑为清咸丰元年至四年（1851—1854）重建。坐北朝南，占地 7,552 平方米，由棂星门、仪门、大成殿以及两侧廊庑、官厅、乡贤祠、名宦祠等组成。大成殿为重檐歇山顶，殿内立四根石柱，每根重达 16 吨，用材硕大，为全国现存文庙建筑中所少有。

Fuzhou Confucius Temple

Period: Qing Dynasty

Address: No. 10 Shengmiao Road, Gulou District, Fuzhou City

In the year 772 of the Tang Dynasty a palace was built as the highest educational institution, and was later used as an official school by Wang Shenzhi during the Five Dynasties; during the Song Dynasty it was changed into a Confucius Temple. The extant buildings were rebuilt between 1851 and 1854 during the Qing Dynasty. Sitting north and facing south, it covers an area of 7,552 square meters, consisting of the arch gate Lingxingmen, Etiquette Gate, the Dacheng Hall and galleries on both sides, as well as the Official Hall, the Village Sage Hall and Famous Officials' Memorial Hall and more. Dacheng Hall has a double-eave gable and hip roof with four large stone pillars inside the hall, each weighing 16 tons, and the structure is very large, quite rare among extant Confucius temple buildings in China.

大成殿内举行祭孔仪式。（福州日报社 供图）
A sacrificial ceremony in Dacheng Hall. (Courtesy of Fuzhou Daily)

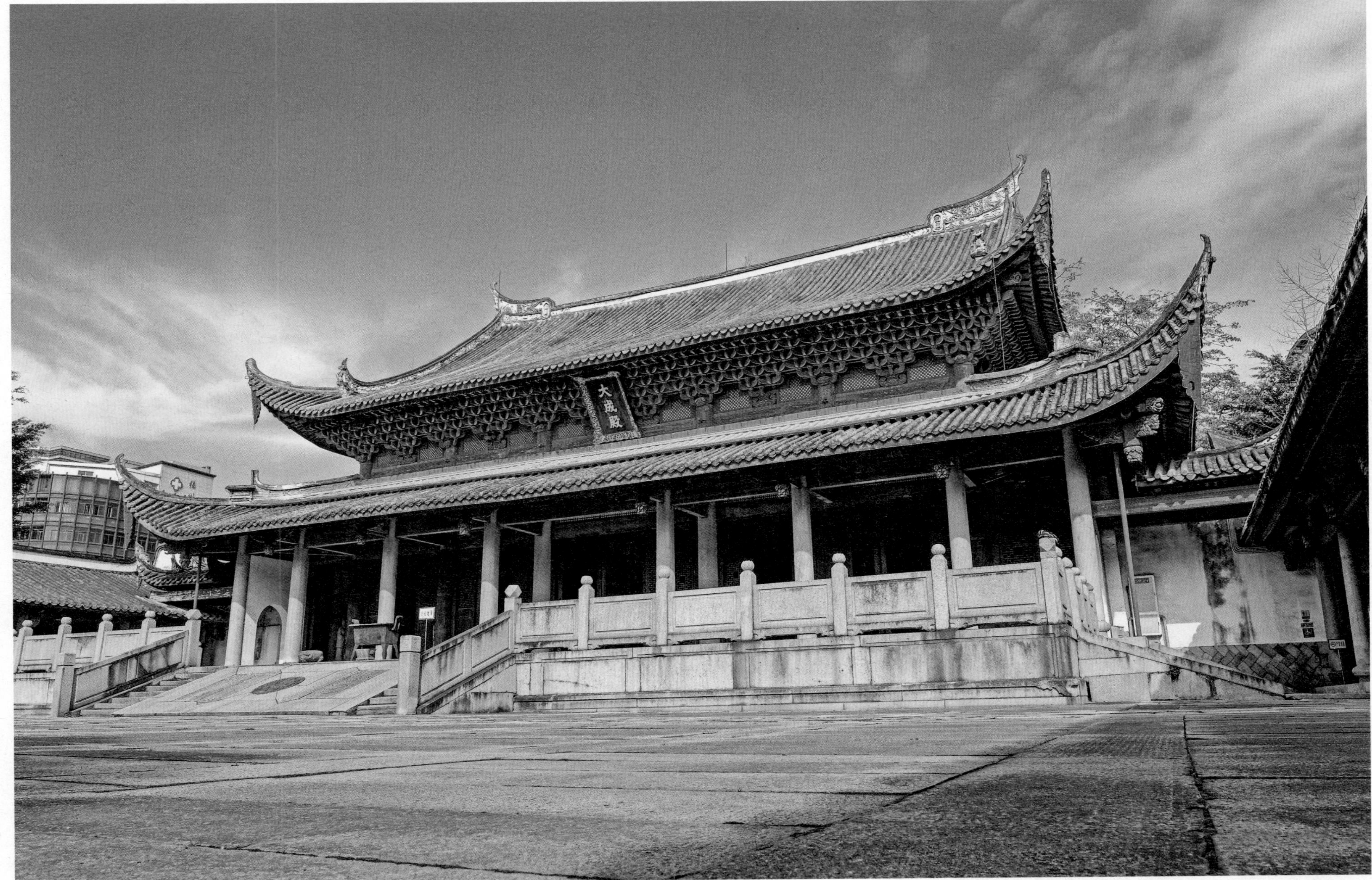

气势恢宏的福州文庙。（林振寿 摄）
Magnificent Fuzhou Confucius Temple. (Photo by Lin Zhenshou)

九头马民居

年代：清

地址：福州市长乐区鹤上镇岐阳村

当地富人建造的大型民居建筑，因宅地中有九块巨石，俗称“九头马”。建筑为五路并排纵向多进式格局，中间轴线上的祖厅为陈利焕于清嘉庆（1796—1820）初建造，左右各两条轴线分别为其四个儿子于清道光（1821—1850）年间所建。五路建筑之间隔有防火墙或夹弄，相互之间又有框门相通，形成一个既独立又完整的建筑群。建筑藻井形式多样，木雕精巧别致，石雕、灰塑、彩画等内容丰富。

Nine Horses Buildings

Period: Qing Dynasty

Address: Qiyang Village, Heshang Town, Changle District, Fuzhou City

This is a large residential building complex built by a wealthy family and is known as the “Nine Horses Buildings” because of nine large boulders located around the compound. The buildings are laid out in five rows of multi-courtyard pattern. The ancestral hall on the central axis was built by Chen Lihuan in the early years during the reign of Emperor Jiaqing (1796—1820) of the Qing Dynasty, and the other four rows of buildings on the left and right were built by his four sons between 1821 and 1850. The five rows are separated by firewalls, with framed doorways connecting them to each other, forming a building group that is both independent and unified. The forms of the caisson ceilings are diverse, the wood carvings are exquisite and stylish, and the stone carvings and color paintings are rich in content.

建筑中有多种藻井形式。（林振寿 摄）
There are various forms of caisson ceilings in the buildings. (Photo by Lin Zhenshou)

老宅中仍住着人家。（陈铭清 摄）
There are still people living in the old buildings. (Photo by Chen Mingqing)

九头马建筑群。（林振寿 摄）
Nine Horses residential building complex. (Photo by Lin Zhenshou)

永泰庄寨建筑群之仁和庄

年代：清

地址：福州市永泰县同安乡三捷村

又称青石寨，是大型防御性民居——永泰庄寨建筑之精品。坐西北向东南，占地面积 3,000 多平方米。外部围以青石砌建的高大寨墙，寨墙上部开窗。大门设有两重门，厚重结实。四个转角处均建有碉楼，防御功能完备。寨内为堂横式民居院落，均隔以封火山墙，梁架和窗花雕工精细。共有房屋 80 多间，水井两口。

Renhe Fortress of Yongtai's Zhuang Fortress Group

Period: Qing Dynasty

Address: Sanjie Village, Tong'an Town, Yongtai County, Fuzhou City

Also known as "Bluestone Fortress", it is a large-scale defensive residential complex and a masterpiece of Yongtai's Zhuang Fortress Group. Sitting northwest and facing southeast, it covers an area of more than 3,000 square meters. The ramparts around the fortress are made of bluestones, with windows in the upper parts. The arch gate is armed with double doors, which are thick and strong. Towers are built at the four corners of the building complex, and the defense function is obvious. The interiors have residential courtyards, separated by firewalls, with fine beam frames and window carvings. There are more than 80 houses and two wells in the fortress.

仁和庄景色。（陈霖 摄）
The views of Renhe Fortress. (Photo by Chen Lin)

规模宏大的仁和庄。（陈成才 摄）
Grand Renhe Fortress. (Photo by Chen Chengcai)

林则徐祠堂

年代：清

地址：福州市鼓楼区澳门路 16 号

祭祀林则徐的专祠，清光绪三十一年 (1905) 由林则徐后裔及门人集资兴建。坐西朝东，占地面积 3,000 平方米，由门墙、仪门厅、御碑亭、树德堂、南北花厅、曲尺楼等组成。祠厅树德堂坐北朝南，面阔三间，进深五柱，内有天井，周以围墙，自成院落。御碑亭内立三方青石碑刻，文为咸丰御赐，碑则是建祠时分别由徐辅敬、陈宝琛、郑孝胥等晚清书法名家所书。

Ancestral Hall in Honor of Lin Zexu

Period: Qing Dynasty

Address: No. 16 Aomen Road, Gulou District, Fuzhou City

This special hall was built to honor Lin Zexu by his descendants and disciples who raised funds and constructed it in 1905. Sitting west and facing east, it covers an area of 3,000 square meters, consisting of an arched gateway, Etiquette Gate, the Imperial Monument Pavilion, Shude Hall, north and south parlors, Quchi Building and so on. The Shude Hall, sitting north and facing south, is three rooms wide and five columns deep, with a patio in the center, and is surrounded by walls. The Imperial Monument Pavilion has 3 stone inscriptions, with the texts bestowed by Emperor Xianfeng, and also inscriptions written by Xu Fujing, Chen Baochen, Zheng Xiaoxu and other famous calligraphers of the late Qing Dynasty.

林则徐祠堂内景。（林振寿 摄）
The interior of Lin Zexu's Ancestral Hall. (Photo by Lin Zhenshou)

林则徐祠堂门墙。（林则徐纪念馆 供图）
The arched gateway of Lin Zexu's Ancestral Hall. (Courtesy of Lin Zexu Memorial Museum)

马江海战昭忠祠

年代：清

地址：福州市马尾区昭忠路 1 号

清光绪十年（1884）七月初三，法国侵略军偷袭马江，福建水师在极不利的情况下仓促还击，英勇奋战，水师将领高腾云等七百多将士壮烈牺牲。为纪念中法马江海战阵亡官兵，同年冬奉旨筹建昭忠祠，光绪十二年（1886）竣工。祠分前后两进，大厅祀 736 名阵亡福建水师烈士灵位，为我国近代反侵略战斗的历史遗迹。

Memorial Hall for the Sino-French Majiang River Naval Battle

Period: Qing Dynasty

Address: No. 1 Zhaozhong Road, Mawei District, Fuzhou City

In 1884, the French invading forces raided up the Majiang River. The Fujian naval division hastened to fight back under extremely adverse circumstances. Unfortunately' General Gao Tengyun and more than 700 martyrs died. To commemorate the officers and soldiers who died in the battle, the local government built this memorial hall that same winter and it was completed in 1886 of the Qing Dynasty. The temple has two quadrangles, with the big memorial hall dedicated to the 736 martyrs from the Fujian naval division. It is an important historical monument of China's modern anti-aggression struggles.

福建水师阵亡将士墓。（林振寿 摄）
The tomb of Fujian naval martyrs. (Photo by Lin Zhenshou)

昭忠祠里奉祀着 736 位福建水师将士灵位。（叶诚 摄）
Memorial Hall for the 736 Fujian naval martyrs. (Photo by Ye Cheng)

福州开元寺

年代：民国

地址：福州市鼓楼区开元路 88 号

南朝梁太清三年（549）始建，初名灵山寺，唐开元二十六年（738）改今名，五代之后寺院规模逐渐缩小，且屡毁屡修。现存铁佛殿、灵源阁、宋塔等建筑。铁佛殿于 1946 年重建，坐北向南，双坡顶，两侧封火墙，面阔三间，进深七柱。殿内一尊铁佛为阿弥陀佛像，佛像高 5.3 米，叠掌盘坐于宝莲之上，外表披泥贴金，螺髻，身披袈裟，敞胸、含口、隆额，眉目慈祥，两耳垂肩。殿前原有明代曾异撰所书“古佛由来皆铁汉，凡夫但说是金身”。

开元寺铁佛。（叶诚 摄）
The iron Buddha in Kaiyuan Temple. (Photo by Ye Cheng)

Fuzhou Kaiyuan Temple

Period: The Republic of China

Address: No. 88 Kaiyuan Road, Gulou District, Fuzhou City

This famous temple was built in 549 during the Northern and Southern Dynasties. Its first name was Lingshan Temple and was changed to Kaiyuan Temple in 738 of the Tang Dynasty. After the Five Dynasties, the temple was gradually reduced in size, and repeatedly destroyed and rebuilt. The Iron Buddha Hall, Lingyuan Pavilion, Song-dynasty Tower and other buildings still exist. Rebuilt in 1946, the Iron Buddha Hall sits north and faces south, with double-slope roofs and firewalls on both sides. It is three rooms wide and seven columns deep. The iron Buddha in the hall represents the Amiable Buddha; the statue is 5.3 meters high, sitting cross-legged on top of a lotus-pattern pedestal. It was gilt, with a body draped by a kasaya. It has an open chest, close mouth, wide forehead, looking kind and nice, with two earlobes drooping to the shoulders signifying wisdom. The hall once had an ancient couplet written by Zeng Yizhuan of the Ming Dynasty, "the ancient Buddha might be a man of iron, but the ordinary people said it has a golden body" .

萧梁古刹——开元寺。（林振寿 摄）
Kaiyuan Temple—an ancient temple from the Northern and Southern Dynasties. (Photo by Lin Zhenshou)

戚公祠

年代：1933 年

地址：福州市鼓楼区于山路 9 号

明嘉靖四十一年（1562），戚继光入闽抗倭班师回浙时，福州官绅、士民在于山平远台设宴饯别，勒碑纪功。1933 年，十九路军将领蔡廷锴等人在此建祠。该祠坐北朝南，建筑面积 120 平方米，面阔三间，进深五柱，双坡顶，马鞍式山墙。内祀戚公戎装塑像。

Sir Qigong Memorial Hall

Period: 1933

Address: No. 9 Yushan Road, Gulou District, Fuzhou City

In 1562 of the Ming Dynasty, when Qi Jiguang (Qigong) withdrew his troops back to Zhejiang after defeating the Japanese pirates, officials and villagers in Fuzhou gave him a farewell dinner in the Pingyuan Terrace on Yushan Hill and built a monument to commemorate his contribution to Fujian. In 1933, Cai Tingkai, general of the 19th Route Army, and others built the hall here. Sitting north and facing south, with a floor area of 120 square meters, it is three rooms wide and five columns deep, with double-slope roofs, and saddle-style gables. Inside there is the statue of Sir Qigong in armor.

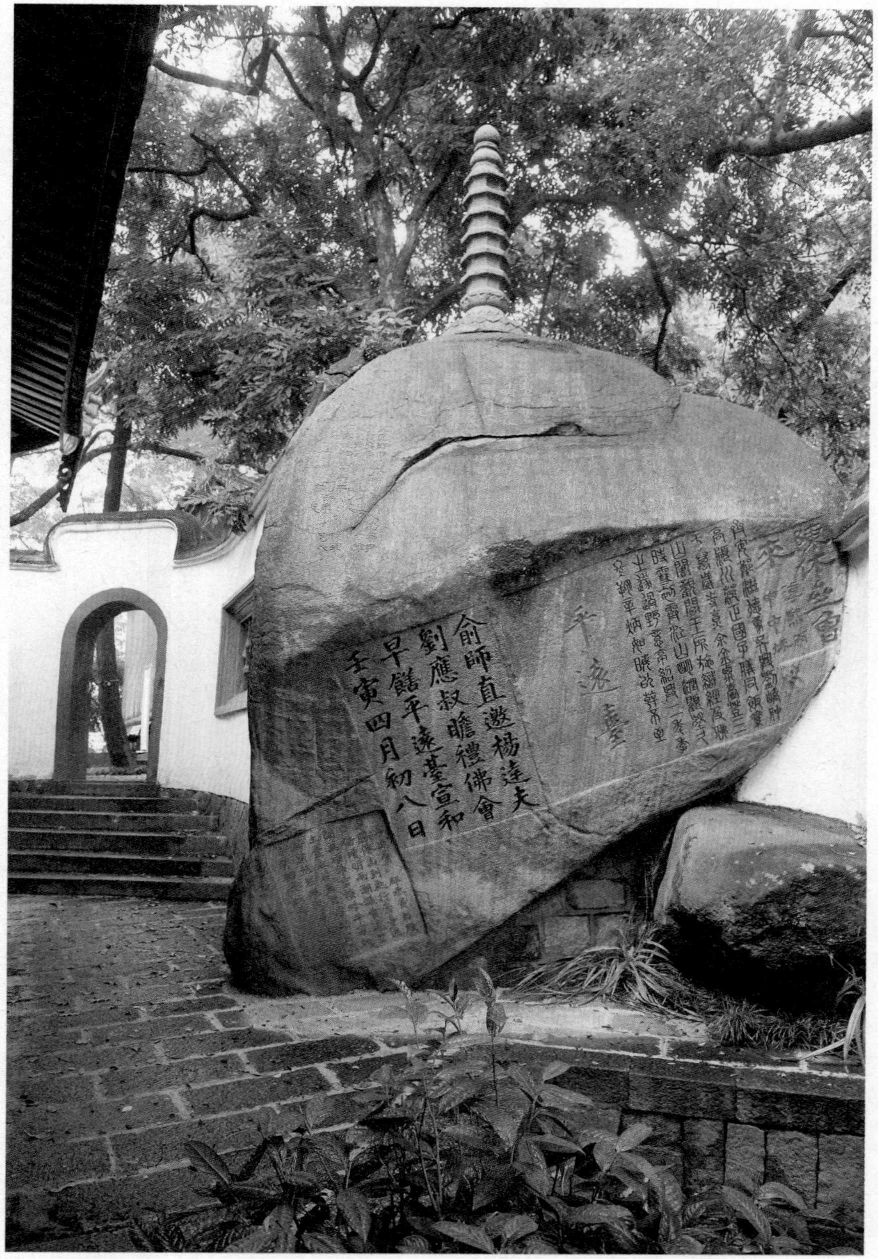

补山精舍内的摩崖石刻。（叶诚 摄）
Stone carvings on the cliff in Bushan House. (Photo by Ye Cheng)

戚公祠内奉祀明代抗倭名将戚继光。（叶诚 摄）
Sir Qigong Memorial Hall in memory of Qi Jiguang, the Ming Dynasty hero against the Japanese pirates. (Photo by Ye Cheng)

厦门古厝

~~~~

Ancient Buildings in Xiamen

~~~~

青礁慈济宫全景。（林广明 摄）
Panoramic view of Qingjiao Ciji Temple. (Photo by Lin Guangming)

青礁慈济宫神兽彩绘。（郑伟明 摄）
A holy beast painting in the temple. (Photo by Zheng Weiming)

两岸信众共祭保生大帝。（郑伟明 摄）
A sacrificial ceremony to worship Wu Tao held by believers across the Taiwan Strait. (Photo by Zheng Weiming)

青礁慈济宫

年代：宋至清

地址：厦门市海沧区海沧镇青礁村

俗称“慈济东宫”，始建于南宋绍兴年间（1131—1162），现存主殿重建于清初，系宋代以来供奉福建名医吴夲的宫祠。建筑坐西朝东，分前殿、正殿、后殿，三殿两侧设廊庑相连。正殿供吴真人神像，重檐歇山顶，殿顶中部设如意藻井。宫内保存大量工艺精湛的石雕、木雕及彩绘。吴夲生前为济世良医，受其恩惠者无数，逝世后被追封为“大道真人”“保生大帝”。明清时期，保生大帝信仰随移民传到台湾和东南亚。

Qingjiao Ciji Temple

Period: Song to Qing dynasties

Address: Qingjiao Village, Haicang Town, Haicang District, Xiamen City

Commonly known as “Ciji East Temple”, it was built between 1131 and 1162 during the Southern Song Dynasty, and the extant main hall was rebuilt in the early Qing Dynasty. Since the Song Dynasty it has been a place to honor the famous Fujian doctor Wu Tao. The building sits west and faces east, divided into the front hall, the main hall, the rear hall, and galleries connecting the three halls on both sides. The main hall has a statue of Wu Tao, and a double-eave gable and hip roof, with a auspicious caisson ceiling in the middle of the hall. The temple has a large number of exquisite stone carvings, wood carvings and color paintings. Wu Tao was a beloved doctor, and countless people were cured by him. He was declared a god of medicine (God Baosheng) by canonization after he died. During the Ming and Qing dynasties, the faith of God Baosheng spread to Taiwan and Southeast Asia by Fujian migrants.

屋顶精美的剪瓷装饰。（郑伟明 摄）

Exquisite decoration with colored porcelain pieces on the roof. (Photo by Zheng Weiming)

鼓浪屿日光岩景区。（林乔森 摄）
Sunlight Rock Scenic Area of Kulangsu. (Photo by Lin Qiaosen)

鼓浪屿近代建筑群

鸦片战争后，厦门被迫开放为通商口岸，西方列强纷纷涌入鼓浪屿，建造了许多公用和民用西式建筑。二十世纪二三十年代，大量富商、华侨也纷纷到鼓浪屿建宅置业，兴建了为数众多的仿西式或中西合璧式住宅，这种建筑风格被称为厦门装饰风格。鼓浪屿也因此被誉为“万国建筑博物馆”。2017年，“鼓浪屿：历史国际社区”被列入《世界遗产名录》。

Modern Building Complex in Kulangsu

After the Opium War, the city of Xiamen was forced to open to the West as a trading port, and Western powers poured into Kulangsu Island, constructing many Western-style buildings. In the 1920s and 1930s, a large number of rich businessmen and overseas Chinese also returned to Kulangsu to build homes, and many large homes in imitation Western-style or Chinese-Western residential style buildings were built at that time. This architectural style became known as “Amoy Deco Style”. Later, Kulangsu became known as the “Architectural Museum of Nations”. In 2017, “Kulangsu: Historic International Community” was added to the World Heritage List.

鼓浪屿金瓜楼。（林乔森 摄）
Golden Pumpkin Villa in Kulangsu. (Photo by Lin Qiaosen)

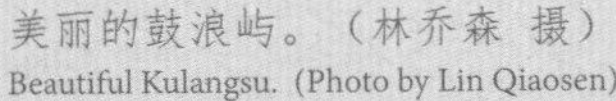

美丽的鼓浪屿。（林乔森 摄）
Beautiful Kulangsu. (Photo by Lin Qiaosen)

美国领事馆旧址

年代：1930 年

地址：厦门市思明区鼓浪屿三明路 26 号

清道光二十四年（1844）美国在鼓浪屿设立“交通邮政办事处”，代行领事馆事务。同治四年（1865）设驻厦领事馆，并在此建办公楼。1930 年由美国工程师设计后翻建成折衷主义建筑。坐东北朝西南，砖混结构，地上二层，地下一层。正立面设置外廊，立有六根科林斯式巨柱；南面设有四根科林斯巨柱支撑三角山墙的突出门廊；两侧清水砖作法采用佛兰德斯砌法。

Former US Consulate

Period: 1930

Address: No. 26 Sanming Road, Kulangsu, Siming District, Xiamen City

In 1844, the United States set up a “traffic and post office” on Kulangsu to act as a precursor for a consulate. Later, in 1865, they set up an official consulate in Xiamen and built an office building here. Designed by American engineers in 1930, it was later turned into a building of eclecticism architecture. Sitting northeast and facing southwest, the building is a brick and stone structure, with two floors above ground and one underground. The outer porch is set up on a facade with six Corinthian columns; the south side features four Corinthian columns supporting the prominent porch with triangular gables; the Flemish Bond style alternating bricks were used on brick walls on both sides of the building.

南面三角山墙突出门廊。（蔡松荣 摄）

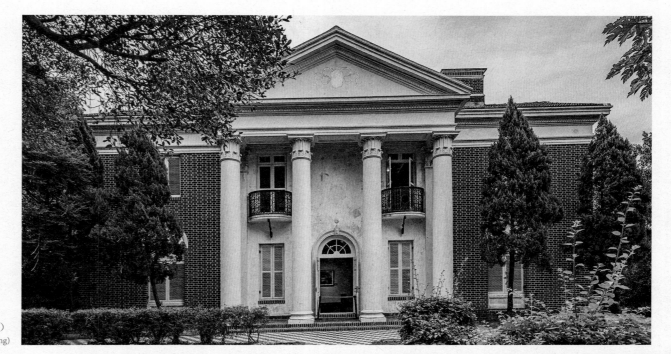

The porch on the south side with a triangular gable. (Photo by Cai Songrong)

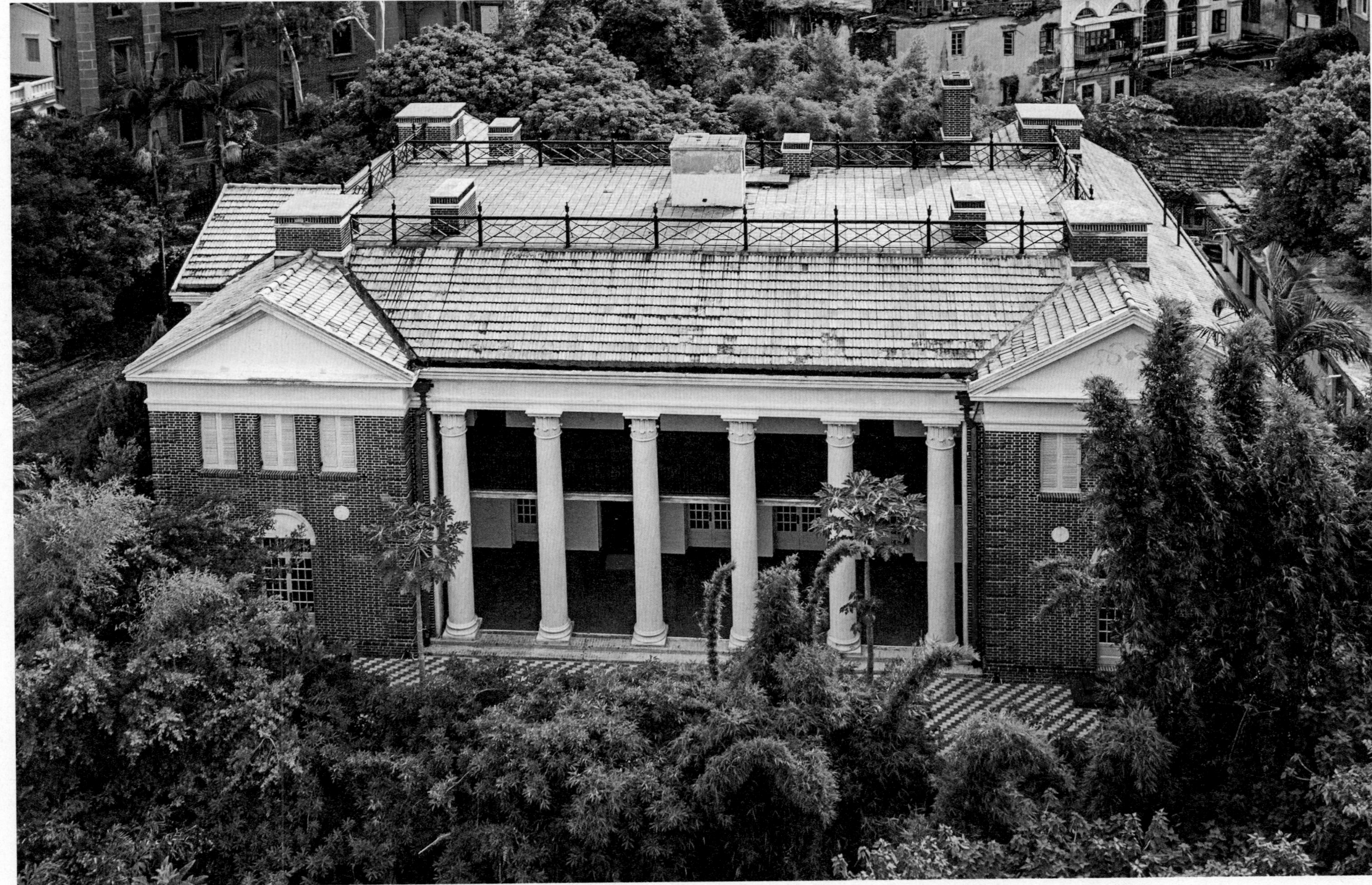

美国领事馆外廊有六根科林斯式巨柱。（林乔森 摄）
The veranda of the US Consulate with six Corinthian columns. (Photo by Lin Qiaosen)

蓝天下醒目的科林斯柱廊。（蔡松荣 摄）
The eye-catching Corinthian colonnades under the blue sky. (Photo by Cai Songrong)

汇丰银行公馆旧址

年代：1873 年

地址：厦门市思明区鼓浪屿鼓新路 57 号

坐落于笔架山东北端悬崖上，由英国怡记洋行所建，名“闲乐居”。1873 年“香港上海汇丰银行”在厦门开设分行，以此为汇丰银行高级住宅。砖石结构，地上一层，半地下一层。建筑三面设廊，科林斯式柱廊，柱基为花岗岩，柱身为红砖，柱头为水泥雕塑的花瓣，典型的欧式别墅建筑。

Former Residence of HSBC's President

Period: 1873

Address: No. 57 Guxin Road, Kulangsu, Siming District, Xiamen City

Located on the cliff on the northeast side of Bijia Hill, this building was built by the former Messrs. Elles & Company, originally called "Leisure and Pleasure Residence". In 1873, the Hong Kong and Shanghai Banking Corporation Limited (HSBC) opened a branch in Xiamen, and used this building as its senior managers' residence. It is a brick and stone structure, with one floor above ground and a half floor underground. The building has three verandas with Corinthian colonnades, the base of each column is made of granite and the body is made of red brick. The top of the pillar has cement sculptured petals, which is a typical European villa style.

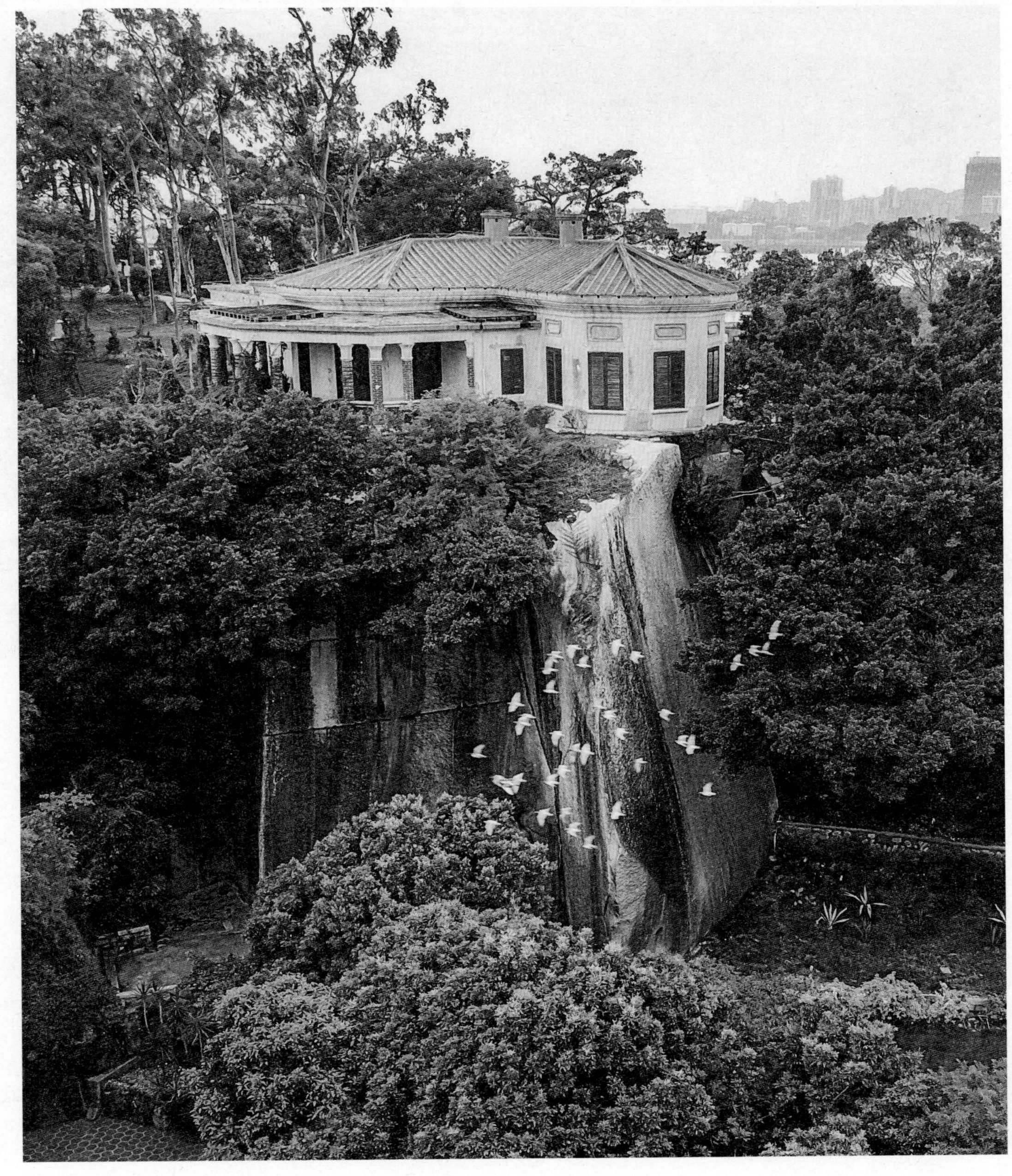

汇丰银行公馆位于一整块大岩石上。（林乔森 摄）
Residence of HSBC's President located on a large rock. (Photo by Lin Qiaosen)

天主堂

年代：1917 年

地址：厦门市思明区鼓浪屿鹿礁路 34 号

西班牙建筑师设计，哥特式建筑。坐西北朝东南，砖石结构，建筑平面采用简单的巴西利卡形式，建筑立面装饰哥特式小尖塔，十字架置于塔顶；窗楣上镌刻“天主堂”及“ECCLESIA CATHOLICA”等字样，玫瑰花窗雕饰精美。建筑后部为礼拜大厅和神坛，两侧立面各开 4 道尖拱形窗，立柱为希腊爱奥尼克式。

Catholic Church

Period: 1917

Address: No. 34 Lujiao Road, Kulangsu, Siming District, Xiamen City

Designed by Spanish architects, this Gothic architecture sits northwest and faces southeast. Using a simple basilica layout, it is a brick and stone structure, with the building facade decorated by a small Gothic pointed tower, and a cross placed on the top of the tower. You can see “天主堂” and “ECCLESIA CATHOLICA” inscribed on the windows, and the carved rose decorations on the windows are amazingly exquisite. At the rear of the building is the chapel and the altar, with four sharp vertically arched windows on each side of the facade, and the pillars in the Greek Ionic style.

鼓浪屿天主堂是厦门地区唯一一座哥特式天主堂。（蔡松荣 摄）
Kulangsu Catholic Church is the only Gothic style Catholic church in Xiamen. (Photo by Cai Songrong)

天主堂钟楼和教堂。（林乔森 摄）
The bell tower and church of the Catholic Church. (Photo by Lin Qiaosen)

八卦楼

年代：1907 年—1913 年
地址：厦门市思明区鼓浪屿鼓新路 43 号

台湾板桥林家族人林鹤寿于 1907 年投资兴建的大型别墅。占地面积近 11,000 平方米，建筑面积近 5,800 平方米，采用西方古典复兴风格。屋顶中央设高达 10 米的红色大穹顶，周有 8 道棱线，八面开窗，故称“八卦楼”。该楼为鼓浪屿救世医院院长、美籍荷兰人郁约翰设计，以回报林鹤寿捐建救世医院的情谊。

Bagua (Eight Diagrams) Mansion

Period: 1907—1913
Address: No. 43 Guxin Road, Kulangsu, Siming District, Xiamen City

Lin Heshou, a member of Lin family from Banchiau, Taiwan, invested in the construction of this large-scale villa in 1907. It covers an area of nearly 11,000 square meters, with a building area of nearly 5,800 square meters, using a Western classical revival style. On the top of the roof is a large red dome, which is up to 10 meters high, with eight arches and eight windows, hence the name “Eight Diagrams Mansion” (from Taoism). The building was designed by John Abraham Otte, the then president of Kulangsu Hope Hospital, a Dutch-American, in return for Lin Heshou’s generosity in donating funds to build Kulangsu Hope Hospital.

占地面积巨大的八卦楼。（林乔森 摄）
Bagua Mansion covers a huge area. (Photo by Lin Qiaosen)

八卦楼标志性的红色大穹顶。（蔡松荣 摄）
The iconic red dome of the Bagua Mansion. (Photo by Cai Songrong)

海天堂构

年代：1920 年—1930 年

地址：厦门市思明区鼓浪屿福建路 34 号、38 号、40 号和 42 号

晋江籍旅菲华侨黄秀烺和黄念忆建造。由门楼与五座建筑组成的大型宅院，总占地面积 6,500 平方米。宅院入口门楼上书“海天堂构”四字。楼群由四座殖民地外廊风格的洋楼和最后建成的中西合璧风格的“中楼”组成，中心建一广场，形成了具有中国传统礼制空间意向的中轴对称、主次分明的总平面设计。

Hai Tian Tang Gou Mansion

Period: 1920—1930

Address: Nos. 34, 38, 40 & 42 Fujian Road, Kulangsu, Siming District, Xiamen City

Hai Tian Tang Gou Mansion was built by Huang Xiulang and Huang Nianyi, overseas Chinese who returned from the Philippines. It is a large complex consisting of an arch-gated enclosure with five buildings, covering a total area of 6,500 square meters. The entrance gate of the house has four Chinese characters “海天堂构”. The complex consists of four veranda colonial style buildings and in the back, a built-up “Central Building” in a Chinese-Western style, with a courtyard built in the center, forming a symmetrical enclosed compound. The layout was clearly designed to follow the traditional Chinese ritual system in symmetry and order of importance.

海天堂构运用了多种中式建筑元素。（蔡松荣 摄）
Hai Tian Tang Gou Mansion adopts a variety of Chinese architectural elements. (Photo by Cai Songrong)

中西合璧的“中楼”。（蔡松荣 摄）
“Central Building” with the integration of Chinese and Western styles. (Photo by Cai Songrong)

中西合璧的“中楼”与洋楼协调共存。（林乔森 摄）
The Chinese-Western style “Central Building” and the Western style buildings coexist in harmony. (Photo by Lin Qiaosen)

厦门海关副税务司公馆

年代：1923 年—1924 年

地址：厦门市思明区鼓浪屿漳州路 9 号、11 号

厦门海关副税务司公馆由副税务司楼和“大帮办楼”两座建筑组成。1865 年和 1870 年厦门海关由英商德记洋行购入别墅两栋。1917 年 9 月别墅毁于一次强台风，1923 年至 1924 年在原址重建。两座建筑均为二层住宅建筑，两侧设外廊，外墙清水红砖砌筑，稍微出挑的平屋顶，具有早期现代风格。

Residence of Amoy Customs Deputy Commissioner

Period: 1923—1924

Address: Nos. 9 & 11 Zhangzhou Road, Kulangsu, Siming District, Xiamen City

The Residence of Amoy Customs Deputy Commissioner consists of two buildings, the Building of Amoy Customs Deputy Commissioner and the "Chief Deputy's Building". In 1865 and 1870, Amoy Customs bought these two villas from Tait, a British business firm. The villas were destroyed by a strong typhoon in September of 1917 but were rebuilt on the original site from 1923 to 1924. Both buildings are two-story residential buildings, with verandas on each side. The red bricks without plastering on the exterior walls and a slightly warped flat roof display an early modern style.

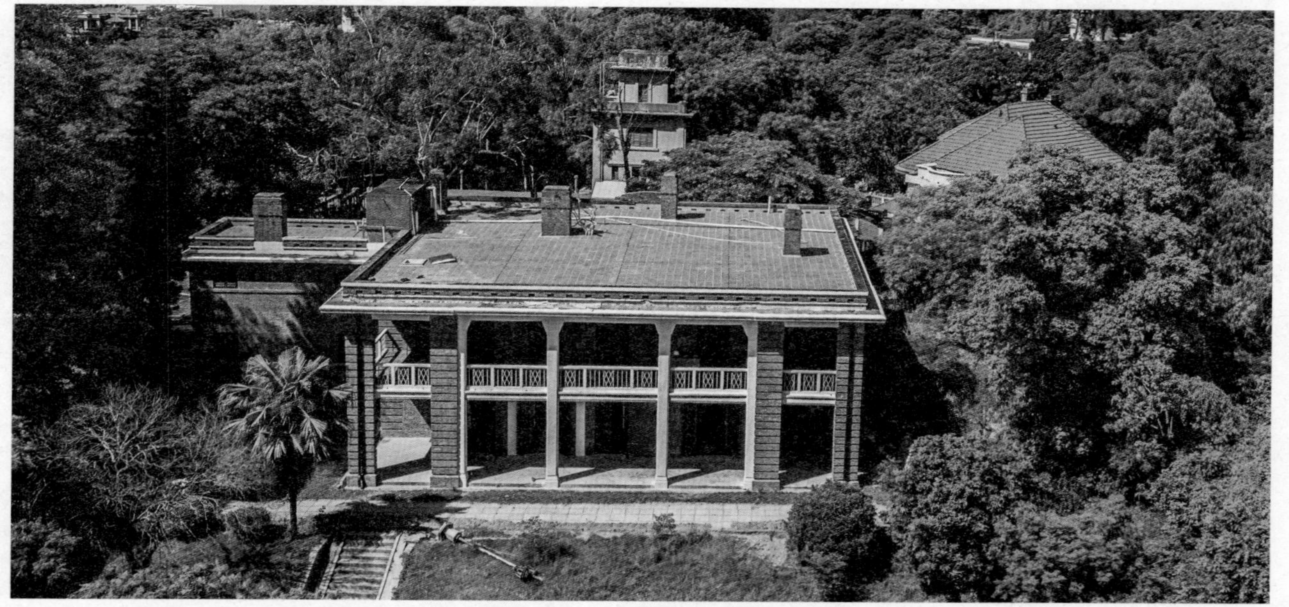

俯瞰“大帮办楼”。（林乔森 摄）
Overlooking the "Chief Deputy's Building". (Photo by Lin Qiaosen)

厦门海关副税务司楼。（蔡松荣 摄）
The Building of Amoy Customs Deputy Commissioner. (Photo by Cai Songrong)

集美学村南侨楼群

年代：1954 年—1959 年
地址：厦门市集美区嘉庚路 8 号

由南侨十三、南侨十四、南侨十五及南侨十六楼四幢组成，是著名华侨实业家、教育家陈嘉庚先生捐资于 1954 年至 1959 年建造。四幢建筑均坐北朝南，砖石木混合结构，依地形而建，呈“一”字形东西向排开。建筑平面呈前廊式，长廊为圆拱券廊；外墙以花岗岩条石为承重墙，清水红砖作镶砌装饰；山花采用齿轮、麦穗、五角星等新式图案，角柱作“出砖入石”状装饰；闽南式大屋顶与西洋式屋身组合。为嘉庚风格建筑的精品。

Nanqiao (Southeast Asian Chinese) Building Compound in Jimei School Village

Period: 1954—1959
Address: No. 8 Jiageng Road, Jimei District, Xiamen City

Consisting of No. 13, No. 14, No. 15 and No. 16 buildings, Nanqiao Building Compound was built from 1954 to 1959 thanks to the famous overseas Chinese industrialist and educator, Mr Tan Kah-kee, who donated funds to build these. Sitting north and facing south, the 4 buildings are brick, wood and stone mixed structures, built according to the terrain, in the shape of a Chinese character "一" from east to west. The building plan is the front-porch style, the porch being a circular arched arcade, and the exterior bearing walls are made of granite, decorated with red bricks without plastering. The pediment utilized patterns such as gears, wheat spikes, five-pointed stars, and the corner columns are decorated in the "brick-out and stone-in" construction style. The buildings have Southern Fujian style roofs on top of Western-style buildings. It is a great example of the unique Tan Kah-kee style architecture.

南侨十三、南侨十四、南侨十五及南侨十六楼。（颜志伟 摄）
Nanqiao Building Compound. (Photo by Yan Zhiwei)

漫步于南侨楼群间的师生们。（颜志伟 摄）
Teachers and students strolling around the Nanqiao Building Compound. (Photo by Yan Zhiwei)

厦门大学建南大礼堂

年代：1952 年—1954 年

地址：厦门市思明区思明南路 422 号

厦门大学的标志性建筑，由陈嘉庚女婿李光前先生为主的福建南安华侨捐资而建。整座楼面宽 47.12 米，进深 69.035 米，建筑面积 5,578 平方米。共有 4,085 个座位（其中一楼 3,122 个座位，二楼 963 个座位），至今依然是全国高校容纳空间最大的会堂。前部为门楼，后部为礼堂主体，石木结构。门楼共 4 层，屋顶为双翘脊重檐歇山顶，脊尾呈燕尾式，屋面铺绿色琉璃瓦。礼堂为西式双坡顶屋面，铺红色机平瓦。中西合璧的建筑形式，为嘉庚风格建筑的精品。

Jiannan Auditorium in Xiamen University

Period: 1952—1954

Address: No. 422 Siming South Road, Siming District, Xiamen City

Jiannan Auditorium, Xiamen University's landmark building, was built with donations from the overseas Chinese from Nan'an, Fujian, mainly by Mr Li Guangqian, son-in-law of Mr Tan Kah-kee. The building is 5,578 square meters, with a depth of 69.035 meters and a width of 47.12 meters. It has 4,085 seats in total, with 3,122 seats on the first floor and 963 seats on the second floor, the largest space capacity among China's colleges. The front is an arched gate building, and the rear is the main structure of the auditorium of stone and wood. The arch gate building is 4 floors. The roof, covered with green glazed tiles, has a double-upturned ridge, double-eave gable and hip roof and the ridge tails are swallowtail-style. The auditorium is a Western-style double-slope roof with red flat tiles. The architectural form combines the best of Chinese and Western styles and is one of the best of the Tan Kah-kee style buildings.

雄伟的建南大礼堂。（吴智庆 摄）
Magnificent Jiannan Auditorium. (Photo by Wu Zhiqing)

厦门大学地标——建南礼堂和上弦场。（厦门大学 供图）
Landmark of Xiamen University—Jiannan Auditorium and Upper String Field. (Courtesy of Xiamen University)

灯光照射下的“金色建南”。（厦门大学 供图）
The “Golden Jiannan Auditorium” with the shining lights. (Courtesy of Xiamen University)

漳州

Zhangzhou

白礁慈济宫

年代：宋至清

地址：漳州市台商投资区角美镇白礁村

俗称“慈济西宫”，为祭祀民间名医吴夲的宫殿式祠堂，与青礁慈济宫（东宫）直线距离仅 2.5 千米。南宋绍兴二十年（1150）高宗皇帝敕建，乾道二年（1166）宋孝宗赐庙号曰“慈济”，淳祐元年（1241）改庙为宫。历代均有修葺，现为清代风格建筑。中轴线上依次为山门、前殿、正殿、后殿，两侧为钟、鼓楼。正殿供吴真人神像，重檐歇山顶，设如意藻井。吴夲去世后敕封“保生大帝”。明清时期，保生大帝信仰随移民传到台湾和东南亚。

Baijiao Ciji Palace

Period: Song to Qing dynasties

Address: Baijiao Village, Jiaomei Town, Taiwan Business Investment District, Zhangzhou City

Commonly known as “Ciji West Palace”, this is a palace-style shrine building dedicated as a memorial to the folk doctor Wu Tao and sits only 2.5 kilometers away on the straight line from the Ciji East Palace. The Gaozong Emperor in the Southern Song Dynasty gave the order to build it, while the Xiaozong Emperor granted the temple name “Ciji” in 1166 and it changed from a temple to a palace in 1241. It has been repaired several times over many generations, and finally became a Qing Dynasty style architecture. Along the central axis, there is the arch gate, the front hall, the main hall, the rear hall, and on the two sides, the bell and drum buildings are in a line one by one. The main hall has a statue of Immortal Wu, with a double-eave gable and hip roof, and is set up with an auspicious caisson ceiling. After Wu’s death, he was conferred with the title of nobility as the “Baosheng God (the God of Medicine)”. During the Ming and Qing dynasties, the faith of “Baosheng God” was introduced to Taiwan and Southeast Asia by Fujian migrants.

华丽的慈济宫内殿。（蔡文原 摄）

Gorgeous Ciji Palace. (Photo by Cai Wenyuan)

白礁慈济宫组照。（洪淑珍 摄）
Pictures of Baijiao Ciji Palace. (Photo by Hong Shuzhen)

关帝庙俯视。（陈瑜 摄）
A bird's eye view of the Temple of Lord Guan. (Photo by Chen Yu)

东山关帝庙

年代：明、清
地址：漳州市东山县铜陵镇风动石风景区

原名关王庙，又称武庙，供奉关帝圣君。始建于明洪武二十二年（1389），现存建筑于康熙十九年（1680）重建。坐西朝东，依山面海，分门楼（俗称太子亭）、前殿、主殿。门楼为单间牌楼式，屋脊有闽南特色的剪瓷雕塑“八仙过海”“八兽图”及唐宋帝王将相造型塑像120尊。主殿为悬山顶，穿斗抬梁混合式木构架，面阔三间，进深六间。庙内木雕、石雕尤为精美。台湾数百座关帝宫庙均奉东山关帝庙为祖庙。

Temple of Lord Guan in Dongshan

Period: Ming and Qing dynasties
Address: Windstone Scenic Area of Tongling Town, Dongshan County, Zhangzhou City

The former name of the temple was “Lord Guan”. Also known as the “Wu (Martial) Temple”, it is dedicated to the Holy Lord Guan. Founded in 1389 during the Ming Dynasty, the extant building was rebuilt in 1680 during the Qing Dynasty. Sitting west and facing east, with its back to the mountain and front to the sea, it includes an entrance building (commonly known as the Prince's Pavilion), with a front hall and the main hall. The entrance building is a single-room memorial-arch building style; the roof ridge is decorated with figurines made up of colored porcelain pieces, including “eight immortals across the sea” “eight beasts” and 120 statues of the emperors, generals and ministers of the Tang and Song dynasties. The main hall has an overhanging gable roof, with a post-and-lintel construction combined with column and tie-beam structure, and is three rooms wide and six rooms deep. The wood carvings and stone carvings in the temple are particularly beautiful. Hundreds of Lord Guan's Temples in Taiwan recognize the Temple of Lord Guan in Dongshan as their ancestral temple.

屋脊上的剪瓷雕塑。（黄志雄 摄）
Porcelain-cut figurines on the roof ridge. (Photo by Huang Zhixiong)

巍然壮观的门楼。（黄志雄 摄）
Spectacular arch gate. (Photo by Huang Zhixiong)

福建土楼

为大型防御性民居建筑，主要分布于福建龙岩、漳州地区。建筑选址注重人与自然的和谐，遵循中国传统的风水观；建筑设计突显“天圆地方”的传统理念，强调家族聚居和防御功能；建筑结构彰显地域特性，围合型土木结构，土质为主体的外墙既是整体建筑的主要承重墙，又是整座建筑的防御墙。福建土楼按照建筑形式，可分为圆形、方形和府第式（又称五凤楼）等类型；按照建筑结构，又可分为内通廊式和单元式两类。

Fujian Tulou

These large-scale earthen defensive residential buildings are mainly distributed in Longyan and Zhangzhou areas. The sites of the building pays attention to the harmony between man and nature, following the traditional Chinese rules of geomantic alignment. The architectural design highlights the traditional concept of “round sky and square earth”; while the architectural function emphasizes the family settlement and its defense; and the architectural structure shows the regional characteristics, with an enclosed civil structure; with an exterior wall made of earth, which serves as the main load-bearing wall of the whole structure, and also as the defensive wall of the whole building. According to the form of architecture, Fujian Tulou can be divided into round, square and mansion-style (also known as five-phoenix-style buildings) and also some other types. According to the inner building structure, they can be divided into generally two types: inner corridor type and unit type.

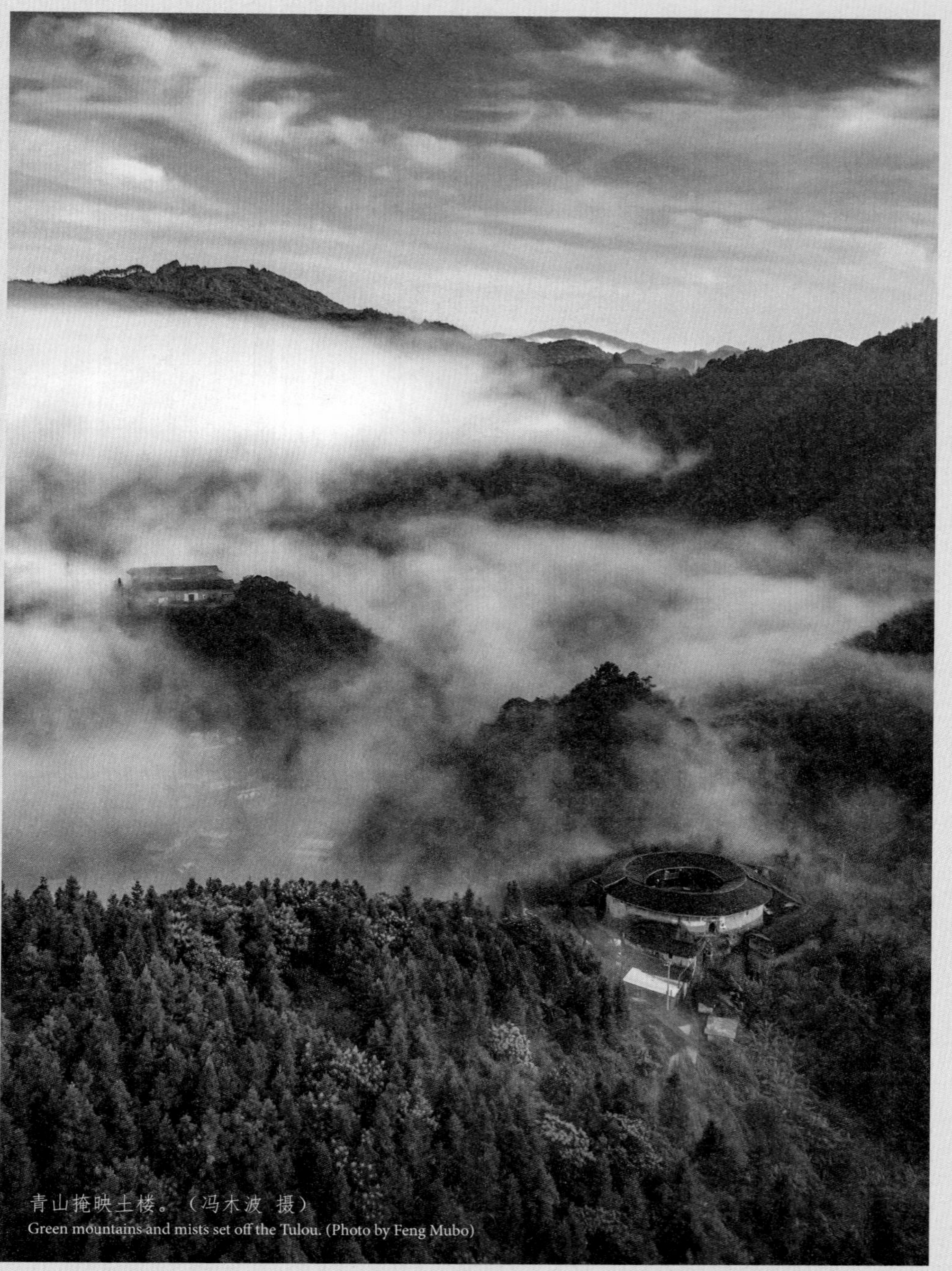

青山掩映土楼。（冯木波 摄）
Green mountains and mists set off the Tulou. (Photo by Feng Mubo)

梯田下的方圆土楼。（王福平 摄）
Tulou under the terraces. (Photo by Wang Fuping)

华安大地土楼群之二宜楼

年代：清

地址：漳州市华安县仙都乡大地村

圆形土楼，前后花30年建造，于清乾隆五年（1740）建成。坐东南朝西北，双环形、内通廊式和单元式相结合，外环高4层，内环单层。占地9,300平方米，外径73.4米，是福建单体最大的双环圆形土楼。整座楼分成16单元，其中4个单元是共用的门、梯道及厅堂；余下的12个单元为住户，自备梯道，相对独立。底层外墙设有12个“之”字传声洞；外环顶层设通廊，将外环楼各单元连成一体，并向外开有56个观察窗和射击窗。内院是公共活动场所，设有两口公用水井。二宜楼建筑装饰简繁有度，内有上千处精美华丽的木雕、彩绘、壁画、楹联等。2008年7月被列入《世界遗产名录》。

Eryilou of Dadi Tulou Cluster in Hua'an

Period: Qing Dynasty

Address: Dadi Village, Xiandu Township, Hua'an County, Zhangzhou City

This round earthen building is a double-ring Tulou which took 30 years to build, and was completed in 1740. Sitting southeast and facing northwest, Eryilou is a combination of inner corridor and unit-style; the outer ring has 4 floors and the inner ring has a single level. Covering an area of 9,300 square meters and with an outer diameter of 73.4 meters, it is the largest double-ring Tulou in Fujian.

The whole building is divided into 16 units, 4 of which serve as doors, stairwells and halls. The remaining 12 units are for households with their own staircases and are relatively independent. The bottom wall is provided with 12 zigzag sound transmission holes. The top floor of the outer ring is provided with a corridor, which connects all the units of the outer ring, and has 56 observation windows for defence. The inner courtyard is a public place with two public wells. The architectural decoration of Eryilou is simple but also complex, with thousands of exquisite and gorgeous wood carvings, paintings, murals, couplets, etc. In July 2008, it was inscribed on the World Heritage List.

西洋风格的壁画。（黄建和 摄）
Western-style murals. (Photo by Huang Jianhe)

丰富的彩雕彩绘。（黄建和 摄）
Rich carvings and paintings. (Photo by Huang Jianhe)

气势雄伟的二宜楼。（黄建和 摄）
Magnificent Eryilou. (Photo by Huang Jianhe)

田螺坑土楼群

年代：清至近代

地址：漳州市南靖县书洋镇上坂村

由方形的步云楼，圆形的振昌楼、瑞云楼、和昌楼和椭圆形的文昌楼共5座土楼组成。步云楼建于清康熙年间（1662—1722），振昌楼建于1930年、瑞云楼建于1936年、和昌楼重建于1953年、文昌楼建于1966年。5座土楼均为坐东北朝西南，土木结构，高三层，内通廊式。步云楼居中，其他4座土楼围绕其四周，依山而建，高低错落，疏密有致，形成了五楼环抱的一道独特风景线。2008年7月被列入《世界遗产名录》。

Tianluokeng Tulou Cluster

Period: Qing Dynasty to modern times

Address: Shangban Village, Shuyang Town, Nanjing County, Zhangzhou City

This group of Tulou consists of the square Buyunlou, the circular Zhenchanglou, Ruiyunlou, Hechanglou and the oval Wenchanglou. Buyunlou was built between 1662 and 1722 in the Qing Dynasty, while Zhenchanglou built in 1930, Ruiyunlou in 1936, Hechanglou in 1953 and Wenchanglou in 1966. The 5 earthen buildings are all sitting northeast and facing southwest, of a typical civil structure, with three floors, and an inner corridor-style. The cluster is located on the slope of the mountain, with the square Buyunlou in the center, and the other 4 circular Tulou around it, which forms a unique landscape. It was added to the World Heritage List in July 2008.

群山环抱土楼群。（冯木波 摄）
The Tulou cluster surrounded by mountains. (Photo by Feng Mubo)

闻名遐迩的“四菜一汤”布局。（冯木波 摄）
Famous “four dishes one soup” layout. (Photo by Feng Mubo)

河坑土楼群

年代：明至近代

地址：漳州市南靖县书洋镇曲江村

由方形的朝水楼、永盛楼、绳庆楼、永荣楼、阳照楼、永贵楼和圆形的裕昌楼、东升楼、春贵楼、晓春楼、永庆楼、裕兴楼及五角形的南薰楼组成。最早的朝水楼大约建于 470 年前，最年轻的永庆楼则建于 20 世纪 60 年代。13 座不同年代、不同类型，但空间结构均为内通廊式的土楼，错落有致地分布于山谷和溪流间，是福建土楼中分布最密集的区域。2008 年 7 月被列入《世界遗产名录》。

Hekeng Tulou Cluster

Period: Ming Dynasty to modern times

Address: Qujiang Village, Shuyang Town, Nanjing County, Zhangzhou City

This set of Tulou buildings is composed of the square Chaoshuilou, Yongshenglou, Shengqinglou, Yongronglou, Yangzhaolou, and Yongguilou, and the round Yuchanglou, Dongshenglou, Chunguilou, Xiaochunlou, Yongqinglou, Yuxinglou and also the pentagon-shaped Nanxunlou. The first Chaoshuilou was built about 470 years ago, while the youngest, Yongqinglou, was built in the 1960s. The 13 Tulou are from different generations, but the spatial structure are all the inner corridor-style. They are scattered in the valley and streams, which is the most densely distributed area of Tulou in Fujian. They were added to the World Heritage List in July 2008.

美丽如画的土楼群。（冯木波 摄）

Beautiful Hekeng Tulou Cluster. (Photo by Feng Mubo)

春贵楼内景。（冯木波 摄）
The view inside Chunguilou. (Photo by Feng Mubo)

和贵楼

年代：清

地址：漳州市南靖县梅林镇

方形土楼。清雍正十年（1732）建于沼泽地上，以200多根木桩打桩、铺垫，高达5层，历经280多年仍坚固稳定，保存完好。坐西向东，设1个大门，内通廊式。四个角落各设一个楼梯，每层楼设28间房屋。内院两边各有一口水井，一口水质清澈甘甜，另一口却浑浊不清，被称为“阴阳井”。内院中间建有面积159.1平方米的“三间一堂”私塾，楼外建有15间平房护厝，形成楼包厝、厝包楼的景观。2008年7月被列入《世界遗产名录》。

Heguilou

Period: Qing Dynasty

Address: Meilin Town, Nanjing County, Zhangzhou City

The square Heguilou was built on the marshes in 1732 during the Qing Dynasty, on top of more than 200 pilings of pine wood, up to 5 stories high. Sitting west and facing east, with an entrance arch gate and inner corridor style, it has remained solid and stable for more than 280 years. There is a staircase in each of the four corners, with 28 rooms on each floor. There is a well on either side of the inner courtyard, one of which is clear and sweet, and the other is dirty, known as the “Yin-Yang wells”. In the middle of the courtyard is an area of 159.1 square meters for a private school called “three rooms with one hall”. Outside the building there are 15 bungalows, forming the landscape of building and bungalows surrounded by each other. It was added to the World Heritage List in July 2008.

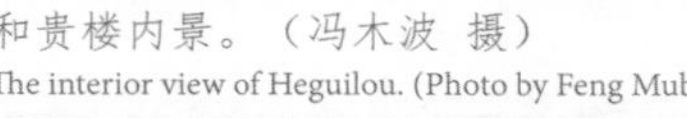

和贵楼内景。（冯木波 摄）
The interior view of Heguilou. (Photo by Feng Mubo)

建在沼泽地上的和贵楼。（胡家新 摄）
Heguilou built on the marshland. (Photo by Hu Jiaxin)

庄上大楼

年代：清
地址：漳州市平和县大溪镇庄上村

又名“庄上城”，建于清康熙年间（1662—1722）。占地面积 34,650 平方米，是现存规模最大、住户最多的土楼。前方后圆，南北间距 220 米，外墙周长达 700 多米。楼内建筑依地势而建，住房建筑分内外 2 环，外环 3 层，高 9 米。共有 142 个单元，单门独院，外环第三层有通廊贯通全楼。楼内尚有祠堂、书斋、宫观等公共建筑物，凿水井 4 口。楼内保存较多的石木雕刻。

Zhuangshang Building

Period: Qing Dynasty
Address: Zhuangshang Village, Daxi Town, Pinghe County, Zhangzhou City

Also known as “Zhuangshang City”, was built between 1662 and 1722 during the Qing Dynasty. Covering an area of 34,650 square meters, it is the largest extant single Tulou building and also has the largest number of residents. Square in the front and round in the rear, with the north-south dimension of 220 meters, it has an outer wall perimeter of more than 700 meters. The buildings inside were built according to the layout of the terrain. The housing buildings are divided into 2 rings inside and outside; the 9-meter-high outer ring has 3 floors. Zhuangshang Building consists of a total of 142 units, each with a single-door courtyard, and are all connected by a corridor on the third floor. The building still has an ancestral hall, study rooms, temple and other communal buildings, plus 4 wells. There are a lot of stone and wood carvings throughout the buildings.

叶氏祠堂。（叶秀林 摄）
Ancestral hall of Ye family. (Photo by Ye Xiulin)

规模宏大的庄上大楼。（叶秀林 摄）
Grand Zhuangshang Building. (Photo by Ye Xiulin)

漳州府文庙大成殿

年代：明、清

地址：漳州市芗城区修文西路 2 号

南宋绍兴九年（1139）始建。朱熹任职漳州时，定期在此讲学。左庙右学，泮池位于庙、学前。明伦堂已毁，仅存基址。文庙由戟门、大成殿、东西两庑等组成。大成殿明成化十八年（1482）重建，清乾隆八年（1743）重修。文庙坐北朝南，重檐歇山顶，面阔五间，进深六间，面积650平方米。大殿的前檐六根廊柱为浮雕蟠龙石柱，鼓形石柱础；其余皆为花岗石圆柱，覆盆式柱础。保留“插柱造”“偷心造”等早期做法。庙内保存有明代以来记录重修文庙的四块石碑。

Dacheng Hall of Zhangzhou Confucius Temple

Period: Ming and Qing dynasties

Address: No.2 West Xiuwen Road, Xiangcheng District, Zhangzhou City

First built in 1139 during the Southern Song Dynasty. When Zhu Xi, the famous philosopher scholar, was an official in Zhangzhou, he lectured here regularly. The left side has a temple and the right side has a school, with a pool located in front. Minglun Hall has been destroyed, leaving only the foundation. The temple is composed of the arch gate, Dacheng Hall, and the east and west wing rooms. Dacheng Hall was reconstructed in 1482 and remodeled in 1743. The temple sits north and faces south, with double-eave gable and hip roof, and is five rooms wide and six rooms deep, covering an area of 650 square meters. The six columns in front of the main hall are embossed with dragon designs, and have drum-shaped bearing stone at the base; the rest are granite columns, in the style of inverted-pots; retaining the ancient style of “pillar-making”. The temple has four stone tablets that recorded the renovations of the temple since the Ming Dynasty.

泮池横跨文庙和明伦堂前。（吴瑜琨 摄）
The pool is across the entire front of the temple and Minglun Hall. (Photo by Wu Yukun)

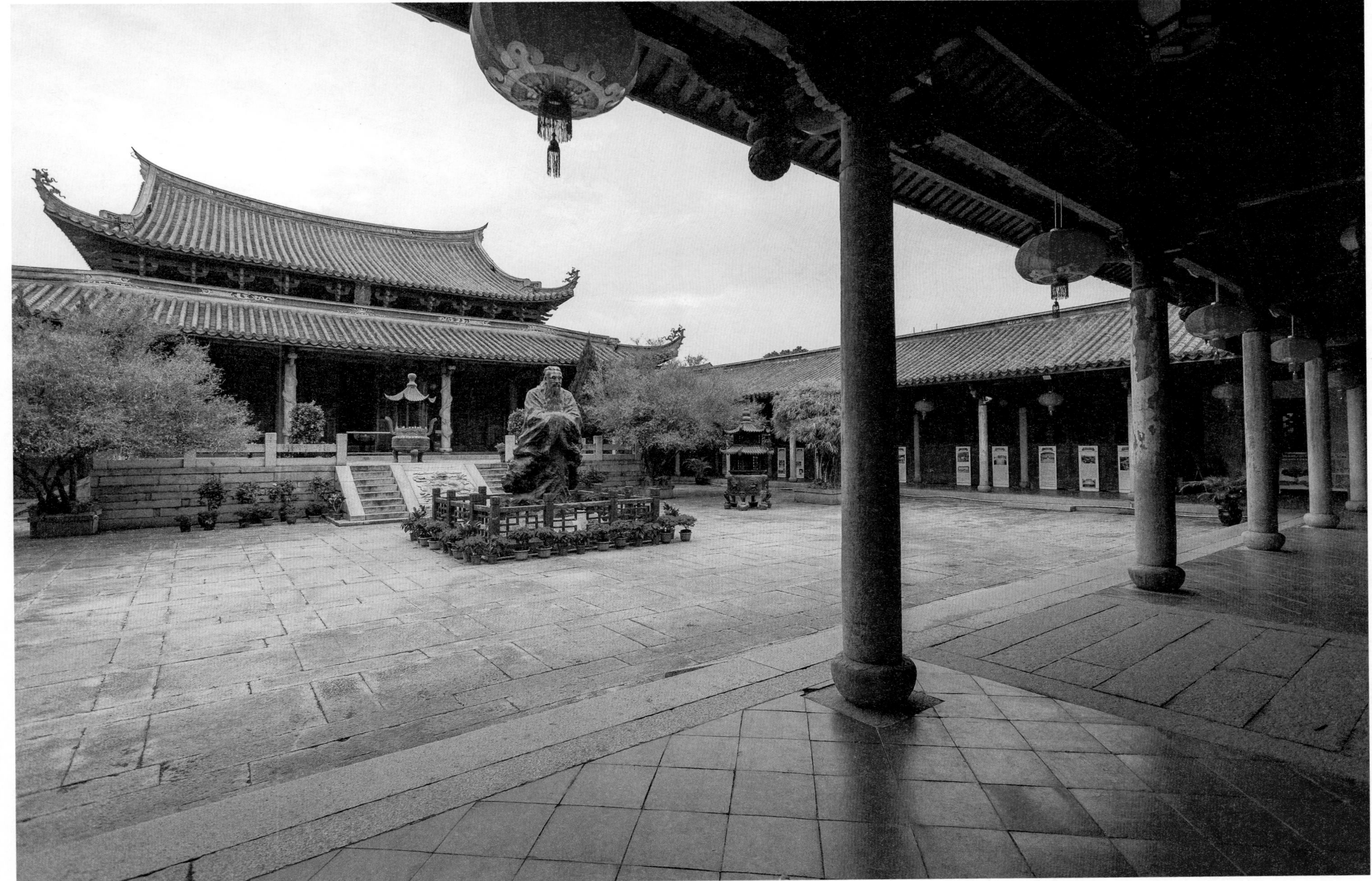

漳州府文庙是闽南大型殿堂建筑的代表。（吴瑜琨 摄）
Zhangzhou Confucius Temple is a typical large-scale temple architecture in southern Fujian. (Photo by Wu Yukun)

赵家堡之完璧楼

年代：明

地址：漳州市漳浦县湖西畲族乡赵家城村

赵家堡，建于明万历年间（1573—1620），是赵宋皇族后裔仿照北宋都城汴京的布局而建。分内外城，完璧楼始建于1600年，位于赵家堡内城，是整个城堡的核心建筑，寓“完璧归赵”之意。完璧楼为三层内通廊式方形土楼，平面呈正方形。外墙为三合土砌筑，一层对外不开窗，二、三层分别有12个和16个石窗，呈喇叭形，外窄内宽。此外楼中还设有射击孔、密室、暗道等防御设施。

Zhao Family's Wanbi Building

Period: Ming Dynasty

Address: Zhaojiacheng Village, Huxi She (Ethnic Group) Township, Zhangpu County, Zhangzhou City

Zhao Family's Castle was built from 1573 to 1620 during the Ming Dynasty, by the descendants of Emperor Zhao and modeled on the layout from the Northern Song Dynasty's capital city Bianjing. It was divided into the inner and outer castles, and Wanbi Building was built in the inner castle in 1600. As the core building of the entire complex, Wanbi Building bears the meaning of "returning safely to the State of Zhao". Wanbi Building is a three-story inner-corridor-style earthen building, built on a square layout. The exterior wall is built with an earthen mixture fill; the windows on the first floor are not open to the outside; the second and third floors have 12 and 16 stone windows respectively, horn-shaped, wide outside and narrow inside. In addition, the building also has shooting holes, secret rooms, hidden escape passages and other defensive facilities.

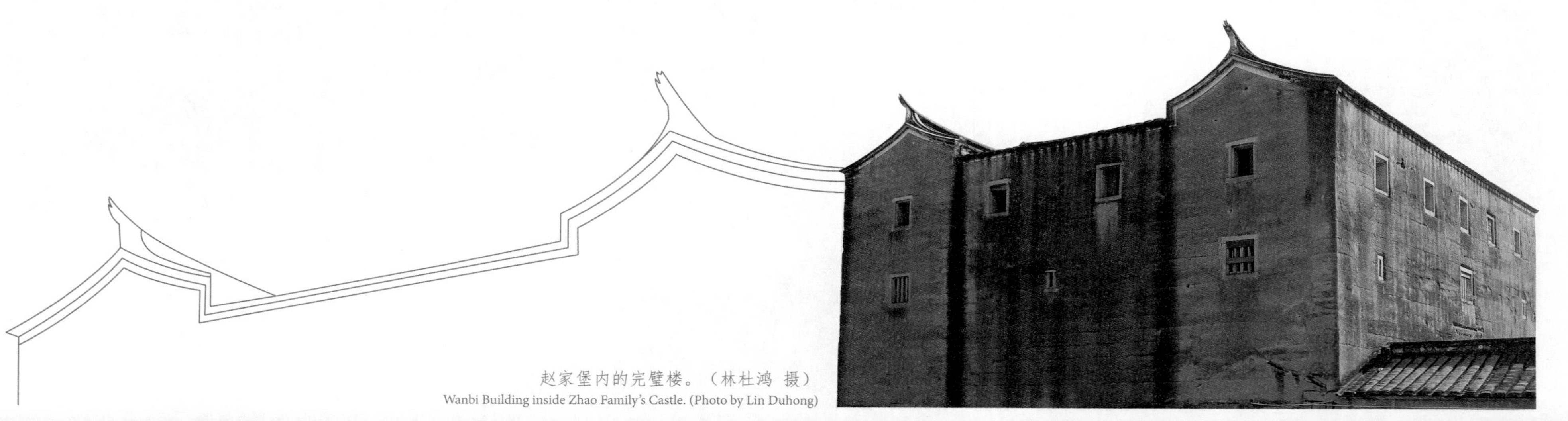

赵家堡内的完璧楼。（林杜鸿 摄）
Wanbi Building inside Zhao Family's Castle. (Photo by Lin Duhong)

赵家堡全景。（林杜鸿 摄）
Panoramic view of Zhao Family's Castle. (Photo by Lin Duhong)

南山宫

年代：明至清
地址：漳州市华安县华丰镇良埔村南

始建于宋德祐元年（1275），明弘治十八年（1505）重建，明、清屡有修葺。为祀奉圣祖大仙和都统舍人之所。坐西向东，重檐歇山顶，面阔五间，进深五间，建筑面积 169.5 平方米。明间置八角旋转式藻井，柱、梁、枋构件和天花板上绘满彩画。

Nanshan Temple

Period: Ming to Qing dynasties
Address: South of Liangpu Village, Huafeng Town, Hua'an County, Zhangzhou City

Founded in 1275 of the Song Dynasty, reconstructed in 1505 during the Ming Dynasty, and repaired again in the Ming and Qing dynasties. It was built for the worship of the local gods. Sitting west and facing east, with a double-eave gable and hip roof, the temple is five rooms wide and five rooms deep, covering a building area of 169.5 square meters. The octagonal swirled caisson ceiling is very special. The columns, beams, girder components and ceilings are covered with colorful paintings.

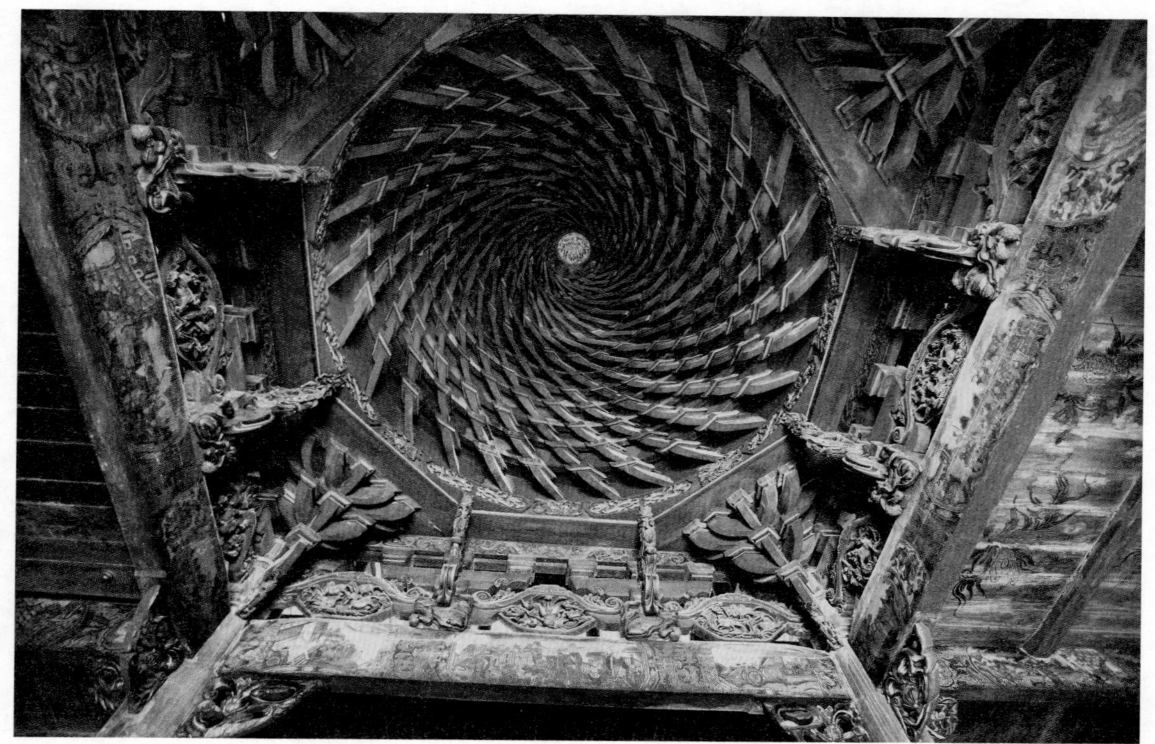

令人称奇的藻井。（黄建和 摄）
Amazing swirl caisson ceiling. (Photo by Huang Jianhe)

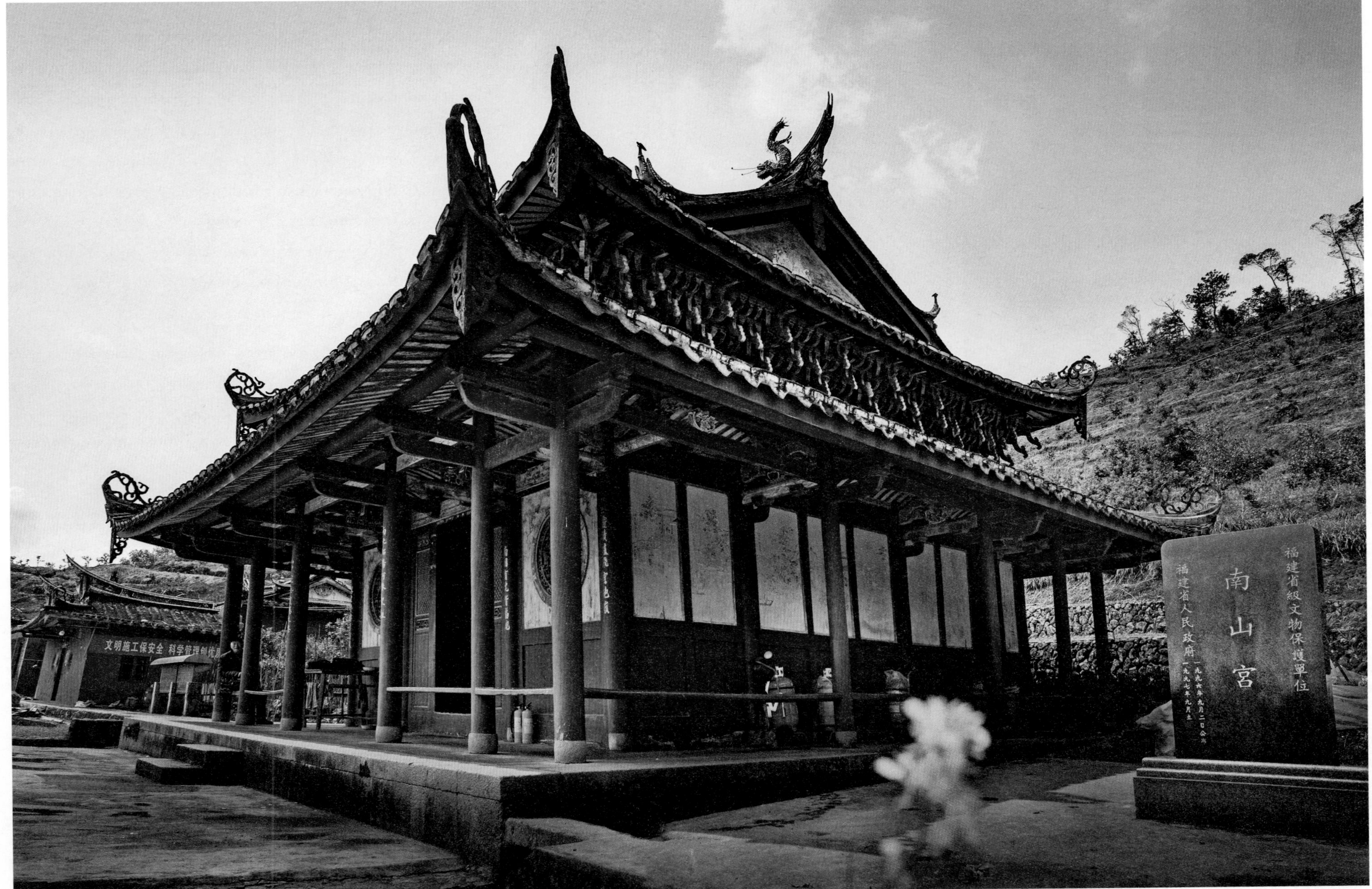

南山宫。（黄建和 摄）
Nanshan Palace. (Photo by Huang Jianhe)

漳州林氏宗祠

年代：明至清

地址：漳州市芗城区振成巷

系漳州七县林姓氏族合建的大宗祠，因供奉林氏始祖比干，又称“比干庙”。始建年代不详，明、清重修。坐北朝南，现仅存大殿（四方殿）和东、西挟屋。大殿重檐歇山顶，面阔三间，进深五间，建筑面积228.72平方米。保留“插柱造”“偷心造”“真昂”等早期做法。

Zhangzhou Lin Family's Ancestral Hall

Period: Ming to Qing dynasties

Address: Zhencheng Lane, Xiangcheng District, Zhangzhou City

Built by the Lin family members from the seven counties of Zhangzhou, it has also been known as the "Bigan Temple" in memory of Lin's ancestor Bigan. It was unknown when it was built, but was reconstructed in the Ming and Qing dynasties. Sitting north and facing south, there is only the main hall (the Square Hall) and the east and west short buildings remaining. The main hall has double-eave gable and hip roof, is three rooms wide and five rooms deep, and covers a building area of 228.72 square meters. It retains several types of early practices in using beams, columns and bracket sets.

大殿梁柱。（吴瑜琨 摄）
The columns and beams of the main hall. (Photo by Wu Yukun)

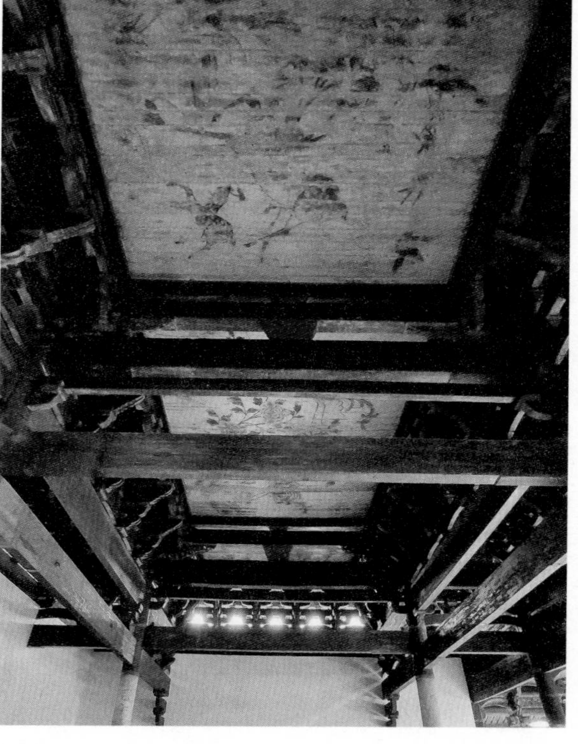

屋顶彩绘。（吴瑜琨 摄）
Roof paintings.(Photo by Wu Yukun)

重檐歇山顶。（吴瑜琨 摄）
The double-eave gable and hip roof. (Photo by Wu Yukun)

漳浦文庙大成殿

年代：明

地址：漳州市漳浦县绥安镇龙湖大道东 154 号

文庙始建于南宋庆元四年（1198），明洪武二年（1369）重建。现仅存大成殿，坐北朝南，建筑面积约 460 平方米。重檐歇山顶，平面近正方形，面阔五间，进深五间，带前檐廊。正金柱柱础直径巨大，用覆莲纹柱础。外檐柱头施单杪双下昂六铺作，天花上为穿斗式草架。弯枋、雀替多用镂花板装饰。脊檩绘双龙戏珠金漆彩画。

Dacheng Hall of Zhangpu Confucius Temple

Period: Ming Dynasty

Address: No.154 East of Longhu Avenue, Sui'an Town, Zhangpu County, Zhangzhou City

This Confucius Temple was built in 1198 during the Southern Song Dynasty and reconstructed in 1369 during the Ming Dynasty. There is only the Dacheng Hall remaining, sitting north and facing south, with a building area of 460 square meters. Dacheng Hall has a double-eave gable and hip roof; the layout is nearly square, with five rooms wide and five rooms deep, and with a front eave colonnade. The diameter of the bases of the hypostyle columns is huge, with lotus-carved bases. The outside bracket sets on the columns are of a unique style, and the ceiling has a column and tie-beam construction. The bending tie-beams and sparrow braces are decorated with engraved flowers. The ridge is decorated with a gold-paint painting of two dragons playing with a pearl.

大成殿。（林杜鸿 摄）
Dacheng Hall. (Photo by Lin Duhong)

精巧的大成殿屋角。（林杜鸿 摄）
Exquisite roof corner of Dacheng Hall. (Photo by Lin Duhong)

德远堂

年代：清

地址：漳州市南靖县书洋镇塔下村

始建于明末清初，为张氏家庙，坐西北朝东南。主堂系一座分前、后厅的悬山顶建筑，两侧带厢房，西南角入口处建有门楼。屋脊为花鸟纹剪瓷脊饰，具有典型的闽南古建筑风格。主堂前为天井和照壁，并辟有半圆形泮池一畦，22 支石龙旗杆环池而立。高过 10 米的石龙旗杆，是为考中举人、进士等学衔的族人竖立，造型各异，且有明确的立杆记事铭文。

Deyuan Hall

Period: Qing Dynasty

Address: Taxia Village, Shuyang Town, Nanjing County, Zhangzhou City

Sitting northwest and facing southeast, this hall is the ancestral hall of the Zhang family. It was founded in the late Ming and early Qing dynasties. The main hall displays an architectural style which has front and back halls with overhanging gable roofs and wing rooms on each side, and the southwest corner entrance has an arch gate. The roof ridge is decorated with beautiful flowers and birds made up of colored porcelain pieces, in the typical Minnan (Southern Fujian) ancient architectural style. In front of the main hall there lies a patio with a Fengshui wall, and a semi-circular pool with 22 stone dragon flagpoles around it. The different-shaped flagpoles, over 10 meters high, were put up to commemorate the ancestors who succeeded in the imperial examinations in ancient times, with a distinct inscription on each pole.

族人祭祖。（冯木波 摄）
Clansmen honor their ancestors. (Photo by Feng Mubo)

德远堂全景。（冯木波 摄）
Panoramic view of Deyuan Hall. (Photo by Feng Mubo)

林氏义庄

年代：清

地址：漳州市台商投资区角美镇杨厝村

清代开发台湾志士林平侯于清嘉庆二十四年（1819）所建的慈善机构。整个院落包括自西而东三落毗连的具有闽南风格的两进大厝，以及花园、院埕、池塘，占地面积7,528平方米。三落建筑均为坐西北朝东南，单檐硬山顶，梁架、斗拱及神龛等木构雕刻精美。居中的永泽堂西侧走廊墙上镶嵌有12块乌石碑刻，记载了林氏义庄的由来、施赈条规等内容。林氏义庄是清代中后期持续了一个多世纪的闽台两地著名慈善机构。

Lin Family's Charity Institution

Period: Qing Dynasty

Address: Yangcuo Village, Jiaomei Town, Taiwan Business Investment Zone, Zhangzhou City

Lin Pinghou, a Taiwanese patriot, established a charity institution here in 1819 during the Qing Dynasty. The entire complex consists of three parts adjacent from west to east, with Minnan-style houses, as well as gardens, courtyards and ponds, covering an area of 7,528 square meters. The buildings are sitting northwest and facing southeast, with single eave flush gable roofs. The wood carvings on the beam frames, brackets and shrines are exquisite. There are 12 stones with inlaid carvings on the wall of the corridor on the west side of the Yongze Hall in the middle of the building, which record the origin of the institution and the regulations for giving relief. It was a famous charity organization in Fujian and Taiwan that lasted for more than a century during the middle and late Qing Dynasty.

精美的木雕。（张奇辉 摄）
An exquisite wood carving. (Photo by Zhang Qihui)

有趣的砖雕。（张奇辉 摄）
An interesting brick carving. (Photo by Zhang Qihui)

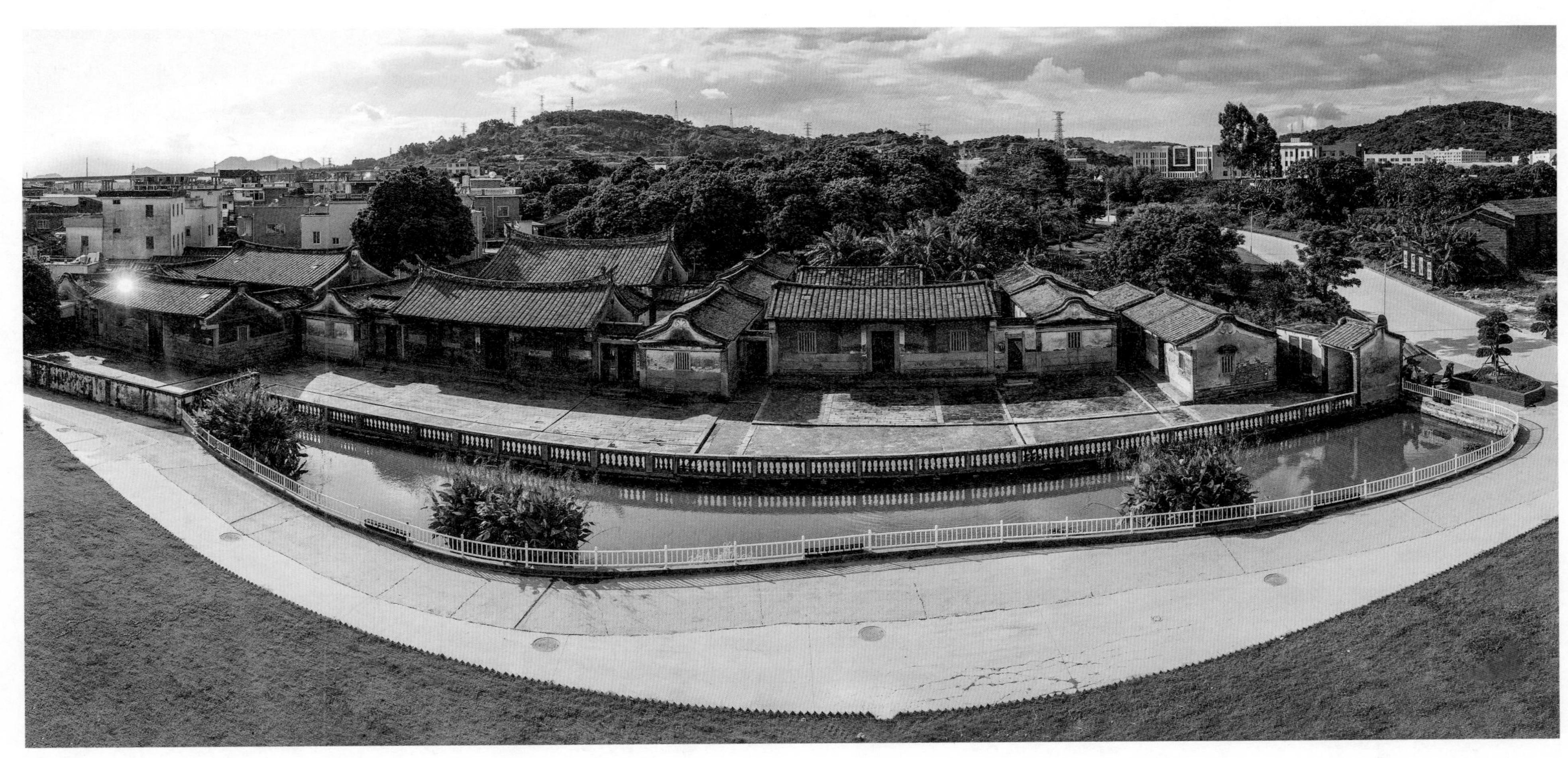

林氏义庄俯视图。（林萍 摄）
Top view of Lin Family's Charity Institution. (Photo by Lin Ping)

《十八层地狱图》（杨诚彬 摄）
Map of Eighteen Levels of Hell. (Photo by Yang Chengbin)

《二十四孝图》（杨诚彬 摄）
Picture of Twenty-four Filial Piety. (Photo by Yang Chengbin)

平和城隍庙

年代：清

地址：漳州市平和县九峰镇东门内侧

始建于明正德十三年（1518），清代重建。以明代理学家王阳明所倡之唐代著名爱国诗人王维为主神。坐西北朝东南，中轴线上依次为大门、仪门、拜亭、大殿、后殿等建筑，两侧连以廊道，山墙围合，形成完整的前后三进廊院式格局。大殿为重檐歇山顶，面阔五间，进深六柱。墙垣、梁架间的多处壁画和彩绘保存完好，其中《二十四孝图》《十八层地狱图》《平和八景图》等壁画尤为珍贵。

Pinghe Temple of the City God

Period: Qing Dynasty

Address: Inside the East gate of Jiufeng Town, Pinghe County, Zhangzhou City

This temple was built in 1518 during the Ming Dynasty and reconstructed in the Qing Dynasty. Sitting in the northwest and facing to the southeast, the temple was built to honor Wang Wei, a famous patriotic poet of the Tang Dynasty, who was later made famous by Wang Yangming, a neo-Confucian scholar of the Ming Dynasty. On the central axis there stands the arch gate, the secondary gate, a worshiping pavilion, the main hall, the rear hall and other buildings; both sides are connected by a corridor and surrounded by a gable wall, forming a complete three part corridor courtyard pattern.

The main hall has a double-eave gable and hip roof, and is five rooms wide and six columns deep. Many murals and color paintings on the walls and beams are well preserved, among which are murals such as the famous "*Picture of Twenty-four Filial Piety*", "*Map of Eighteen Levels of Hell*" and "*Peaceful Eight Scenes*", which are especially precious.

城隍庙内回廊天井。（杨诚彬 摄）
Cloister patio inside the temple. (Photo by Yang Chengbin)

蓝廷珍府第

年代：清
地址：漳州市漳浦县湖西畲族乡顶坛村

清福建水师提督蓝廷珍及其孙江南水师提督蓝元枚的故居。坐西向东，占地面积约 4,400 平方米，通面宽 50 米，纵深 86 米。规模庞大，布局严谨，建筑群左右对称，纵向五落，中轴线是依次为门厅、正堂、后堂（已毁）、主楼与后厢。主楼又称日接楼，两层三合土方楼，木结构毁于火，外墙完整保留。左右两厢为护厝，以“过水廊”相连，形成大合院内套两个小合院的平面格局。

康熙六十年(1721)蓝廷珍出师台湾征战朱一贵义军。平台后，暂理台湾总兵官事务和提督印务，对台湾的治理和开拓，提出了一系列很有远见的建议和措施，对台湾的发展产生了深远的影响。

Lan Tingzhen's Mansion

Period: Qing Dynasty
Address: Dingtan Village, Huxi She (Ethnic Group) Township, Zhangpu County, Zhangzhou City

This is the former residence of Lan Tingzhen, a Fujian navy commander, and his grandson Lan Yuanmei, a Jiangnan navy commander.

Sitting west and facing east, it covers an area of about 4,400 square meters, with a width of 50 meters and a depth of 86 meters. It is a large scale, traditional layout, with symmetrical buildings left and right, forming five quadrangles. Along the central axis there is the entrance hall, the main hall, the rear hall (destroyed), the main building and the rear house.

The main building, also known as Rijielou, has two floors of tabia timber construction, however the wood structure was destroyed in a fire, but the outer wall is still intact. The left and right houses are the guardhouses, connected by a covered corridor, forming the traditional pattern of two small courtyards in the front yard of a grand courtyard.

In 1721 Lan Tingzhen led his forces to Taiwan to fight Zhu Yigui's army. After the recovery of Taiwan, he temporarily managed the affairs there as Taiwan's chief military officer and assisted the governor. He put forward a series of far-sighted measures for the governance and development of Taiwan, which has had a beneficial impact on Taiwan.

主楼日接楼内部。（林杜鸿 摄）

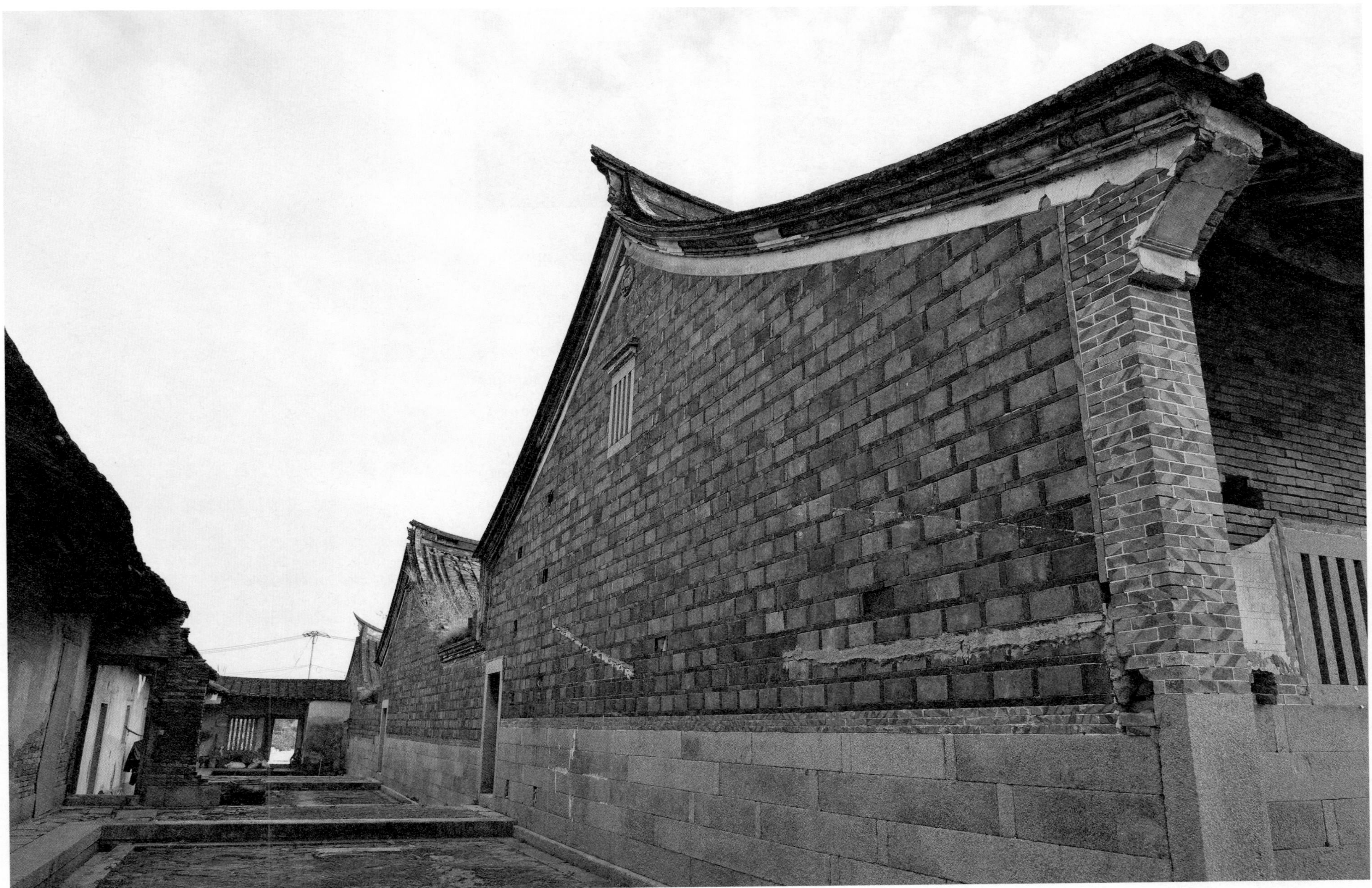

蓝廷珍府一角。（林杜鸿 摄）

A corner of Lan Tingzhen's Mansion. (Photo by Lin Duhong)

天一总局旧址

年代：民国

地址：漳州市台商投资区角美镇流传村

又称“天一信局”，占地面积 11,300 平方米。由旅菲华侨于 1880 年创办，经营时间长达 48 年（1880—1928），是我国历史上规模最大、分布最广、经营时间最长的早期民间侨批机构，时国内外分局达 33 家。1911 至 1921 年，历经十年建成总局楼群。现存办公楼“北楼”、生活区“宛南楼”和休闲花园陶园楼 3 座建筑。北楼面阔 25 米，进深 28 米，为设有天井的中式四合院结构、西式装饰风格的二层楼房，是近代由闽南侨胞建造的中西合璧精品。

The Old Site of Tianyi General Administration

Period: Republic of China

Address: Liuchuan Village, Jiaomei Town, Taiwan Businessmen Investment Zone, Zhangzhou City

Also known as “Tianyi Postal Bureau”, this complex covers an area of 11,300 square meters. Founded in 1880 by overseas Chinese who traveled to the Philippines, it operated 48 years from 1880 to 1928. It was the largest, most widely used and longest-serving early non-governmental overseas Chinese branch organization in China's history, with 33 branches at home and abroad. The General Administration Complex took ten years to build (from 1911 to 1921). There are 3 extant buildings: the office building “North Building”, the residence building “Wannan Building” and the leisure garden “Taoyuan Building”. The North Building, 25 meters wide and 28 meters deep, is a two-story building with a Chinese style courtyard and Western-style decorations—which was typical of Chinese-Western buildings built by overseas Chinese in Southern Fujian.

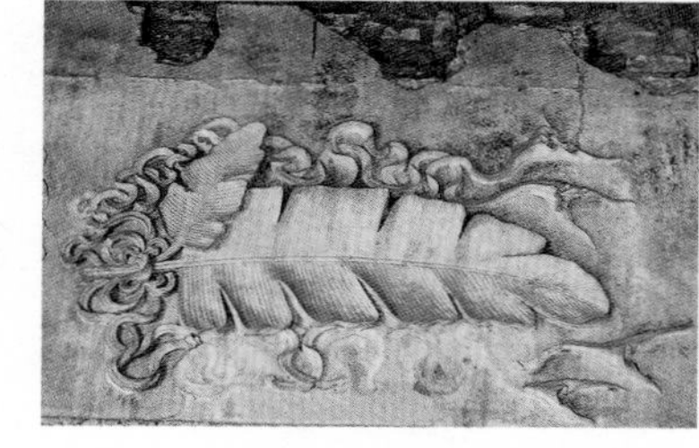

精美的石雕。（李淑芬 摄）
Beautiful stone carvings. (Photo by Li Shufen)

独特的墙饰。（李淑芬 摄）
Unique wall decoration. (Photo by Li Shufen)

天一总局组图。（林宝枝摄）
Pictures of Tianyi General Administration. (Photo by Lin Baozhi)

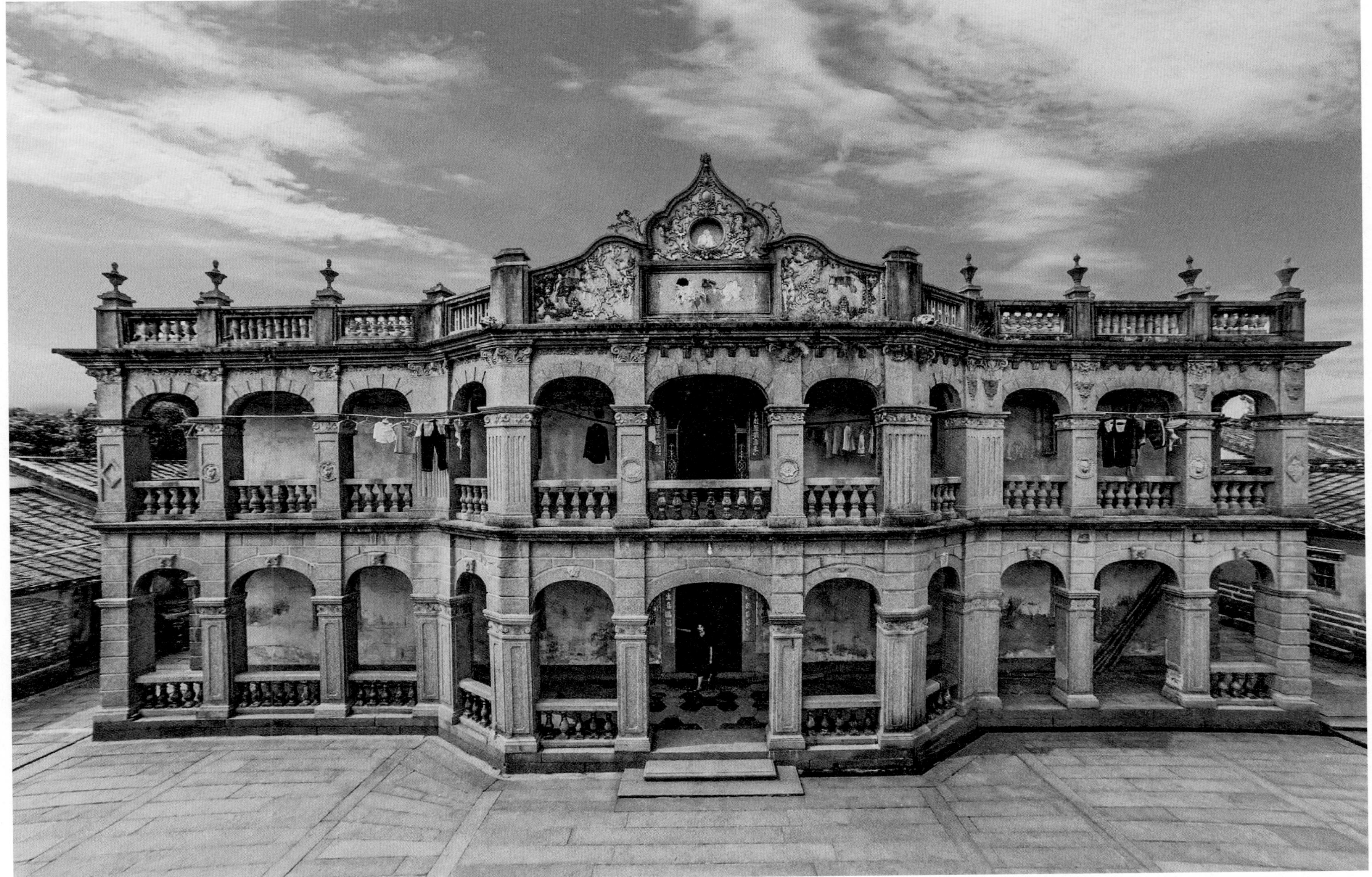

天一总局。（林宝枝摄）
Tianyi General Administration. (Photo by Lin Baozhi)

东美曾氏番仔楼

年代：清

地址：漳州市台商投资区角美镇东美村墩上社

始建于 1903 年，至 1910 年这座大型民居建筑的主体工程方得以完成。坐南朝北，占地面积 5,996 平方米，包括宗祠、中楼、后楼、东大厝、西大厝、西楼、东楼、副楼、打谷房等，拥有房厅 120 间，当地人称“99 间”。楼群以宗祠为中轴线，对称排列，左右各有两条通巷，形成五纵三横的建筑布局。内设三横三纵排水沟，周环护墙。宗祠为闽南传统祠堂建筑风格，两侧大厝融闽南传统民居与西方外廊式建筑元素于一体。群楼前凿大型月池，后造精致花园。

Dongmei Zeng Family's Fanzai Building

Period: Qing Dynasty

Address: Dongmei Village, Jiaomei Town, Taiwan Business Investment Zone, Zhangzhou City

This large residential complex was founded in 1903 and completed in 1910 during the Qing Dynasty. Sitting south and facing north, it covers an area of 5,996 square meters, including the ancestral hall, a middle building, the back building, the east house, the west house, the west building, the east building, the annex building, the threshing building, etc., with 120 rooms and halls, so the locals call this complex “99 rooms”. The building group used the ancestral hall as the central quadrangle, and arranges the others symmetrically around it, each has two alleys on the left and right, forming a five vertical and three horizontal architectural layout. Inside there are three horizontal and three vertical drainage ditches, surrounded by a defensive wall. The ancestral hall is in the traditional architectural style of Minnan (Southern Fujian), with the two sides of the houses combining Minnan traditional residential style with Western porch-style architectural elements, all in one. A large moon pool is built in front and a fine garden is built in the back of the complex.

夜色下的番仔楼人家。（张辉煌 摄）
People at home in Fanzai Building at night. (Photo by Zhang Huihuang)

镜头下的多姿番仔楼。（林宝炔 摄）

The colorful buildings. (Photo by Lin Baozhi)

泉州古厝

Ancient Buildings in Quanzhou

龍山寺
佛
以法自娛

清净寺

年代：宋、清

地址：泉州市鲤城区涂门街 108 号—110 号

始建于北宋大中祥符二年（1009），曾多次重修。现存门楼、奉天坛、明善堂。门楼、奉天坛基本保持了 11 世纪至 14 世纪的阿拉伯建筑风格。门楼通高 12.3 米，基宽 6.6 米，采用花岗岩石和辉绿岩石砌筑，正面从内到外、依次向上砌筑三重穹顶尖拱门式样，东西两壁各砌饰一尖拱壁龛。奉天坛在门楼西侧，为阿訇率穆斯林诵经礼拜之处所，现仅存建筑墙体、柱础及 9 根残柱。门楼、奉天坛、寺围墙等墙体上雕刻古体阿拉伯文《古兰经》共 13 处。明善堂为清代建造的闽南传统建筑。

Qingjing Mosque

Period: Song Dynasty and Qing Dynasty

Address: No. 108—110 Tumen Street, Licheng District, Quanzhou City

This mosque was built in 1009 during the Northern Song Dynasty and has been rebuilt many times. The extant buildings are the arch gate, Fengtian Altar and Mingshan Hall. The arch gate and Fengtian Altar have for the most part maintained the Arabic architectural style from the 11th to the 14th centuries. The arch gate is 12.3 meters high and 6.6 meters wide, made of granite and diabase stone. From the inside to the outside, the top of the triple dome is built in pointed arch in sequences, with the east and west walls decorated with pointed arch niches. Fengtian Altar is on the west side of the arch gate and it is the place where the Imam led the Muslims to recite the prayers. Unfortunately, there are only the original building walls, column bases and 9 residual pillars remaining now. A total of 13 ancient Arabic quotations from the Quran were carved on the arch gate, Fengtian Altar and the enclosing walls. Mingshan Hall is a traditional Southern Fujian style building built during the Qing Dynasty.

门楼穹顶。（李祖耀 摄）
Dome of the arch gate. (Photo by Li Zuyao)

奉天坛。（李祖耀 摄）
Fengtian Altar. (Photo by Li Zuyao)

夕阳与灯火辉映下的清净寺。（陈英杰 摄）
The Qingjing Mosque illuminated by the setting sun and the lights. (Photo by Chen Yingjie)

开元寺

年代：宋至清

地址：泉州市鲤城区西街 176 号

始建于唐垂拱二年（686），开元二十六年（738）改今名。寺院格局定型于宋，明、清多次重修。寺院坐北朝南，规模宏大，格局完整，占地面积 78,000 平方米。中轴线上依次有紫云屏、山门、拜圣亭、拜庭、大雄宝殿、甘露戒坛、藏经阁。大殿东侧有檀樾祠、准提禅林，西侧有功德堂、尊胜院、水陆寺等。大雄宝殿为明代风格，重檐歇山顶，面阔九间，进深六间，斗拱饰飞天乐伎，须弥座和后檐柱有雕刻印度教题材的建筑构件。寺院前部东西两侧分立宋代建造的镇国塔和仁寿塔，五层八角仿木楼阁式石塔。

Kaiyuan Temple

Period: Song to Qing dynasties

Address: No. 176 West Street, Licheng District, Quanzhou City

This famous temple was built in 686 of the Tang Dynasty and was changed to its present name in 738. The pattern of the temple was finally fixed in the Song Dynasty and was rebuilt many times during the Ming and Qing dynasties. The temple sits north and faces south, with a large scale and complete pattern, covering an area of 78,000 square meters. On the central axis there are Ziyunping, the arch gate, Baisheng Pavilion, Worship Pavilion, Mahavira Hall, Ganlu Altar, and Sutra Depository. On the east side of Mahavira Hall, there is Tanyue Hall, Zhunti Chanlin, and on the west side, there is Gongde Hall, Cundi Temple, and Shuilu Temple. The Mahavira Hall is of typical Ming Dynasty style, nine rooms wide and six rooms deep, with a double-eave gable and hip roof. The bracket sets are decorated with Chinese flying Apsaras with instruments. The sumeru pedestal and the back eave columns have components carved with Hindu-theme elements. On the east and west sides of the front part of the temple, there are Zhenguo Pagoda and Renshou Pagoda built during the Song Dynasty, which are both five-story octagonal imitation-wood stone pagodas.

大雄宝殿。（陈英杰 摄）
The Mahavira Hall. (Photo by Chen Yingjie)

斗拱上的飞天乐伎。（陈英杰 摄）
The Chinese flying Apsaras with instruments on the bracket sets. (Photo by Chen Yingjie)

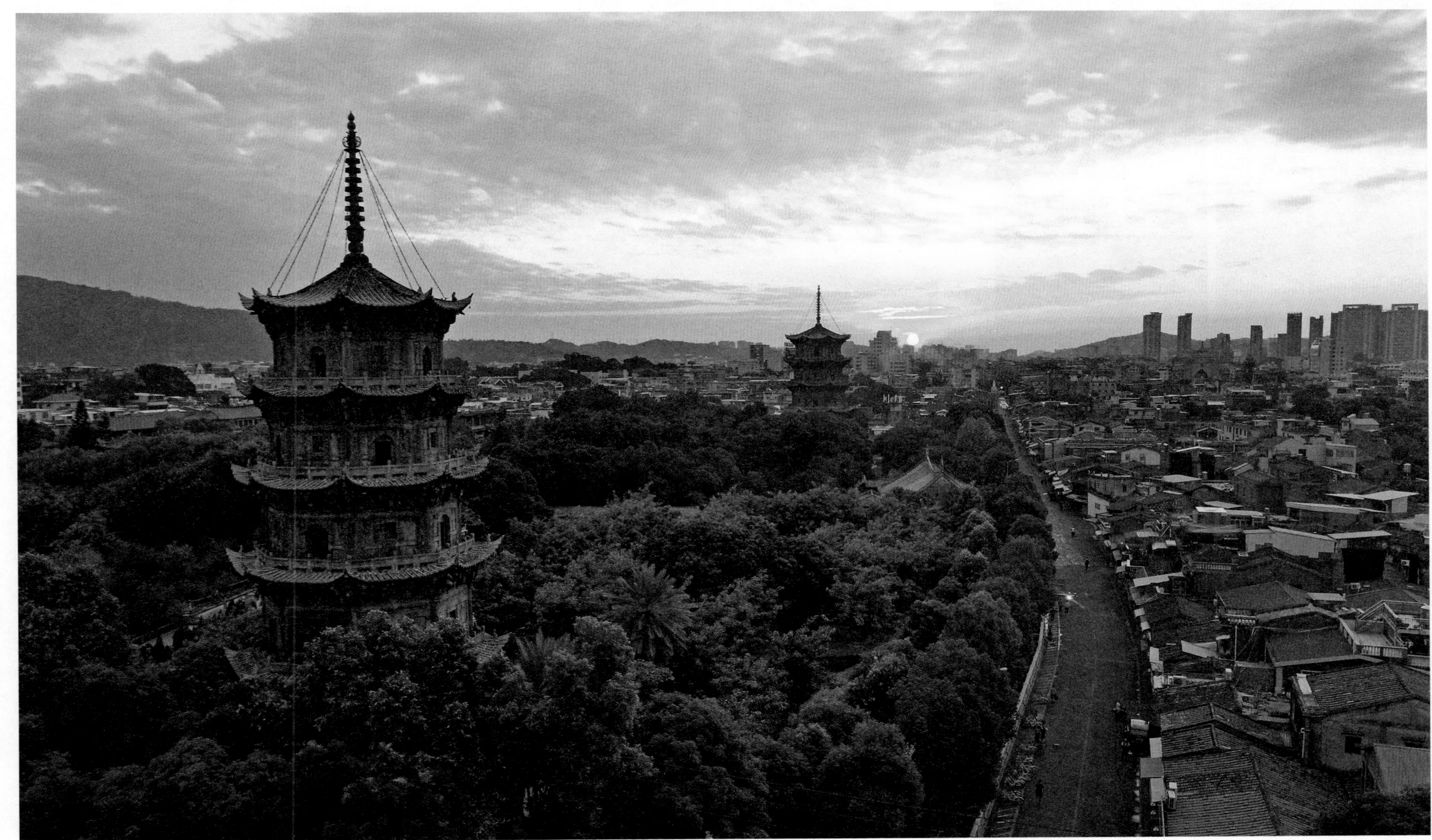

开元寺内的镇国、仁寿二塔。（陈英杰 摄）
Zhenguo Pagoda and Renshou Pagoda in Kaiyuan Temple. (Photo by Chen Yingjie)

泉州天后宫

年代：明、清

地址：泉州市鲤城区天后路 1 号

祀海神妈祖的官庙。始建于南宋庆元二年（1196），明清均有重修和扩建。天后宫坐北朝南，由山门、戏台、东西阙、正殿、东西廊、寝殿等组成。正殿供奉天后圣像，重檐歇山顶，面阔五间，进深五间，殿前设廊，屋脊施灰雕及动物花卉剪瓷片装饰，殿内后照壁保存一幅《敕封天上圣母图》清代壁画。寝殿为明代建筑，硬山顶，七开间，前廊有一对元代印度教寺庙移来的八角形石柱。

Quanzhou Tianhou Temple

Period: Ming and Qing dynasties

Address: No. 1 Tianhou Road, Licheng District, Quanzhou City

This temple that worships the sea goddess Mazu was built in 1196 during the Southern Song Dynasty, rebuilt and expanded during the Ming and Qing dynasties. It sits north and faces south, and is composed of an arch gate, a stage, east and west towers, a main hall, east and west corridors, and a bedchammber hall. The main hall enshrines the icon of Mazu (the Queen of Heaven). It has a double-eave gable and hip roof, and is five rooms wide and five rooms deep. There is a colonnade in front of the hall. The ridge is decorated with lime carvings and animals and flowers made of pieces of colorful porcelain; the back wall of the hall preserves a Qing Dynasty fresco "Picture of Heavenly Mother". The bedchammber hall is a Ming Dynasty building with a flush gable roof and is seven rooms wide. In the front colonnade a pair of octagonal stone pillars was moved from a Hindu temple during the Yuan Dynasty.

天后宫寝殿。（罗春日 摄）
The bedchammber hall of Tianhou Temple. (Photo by Luo Chunri)

寝殿前廊的八角形石柱。（罗春日 摄）
The octagonal stone pillars in the front colonnade of the resting hall. (Photo by Luo Chunri)

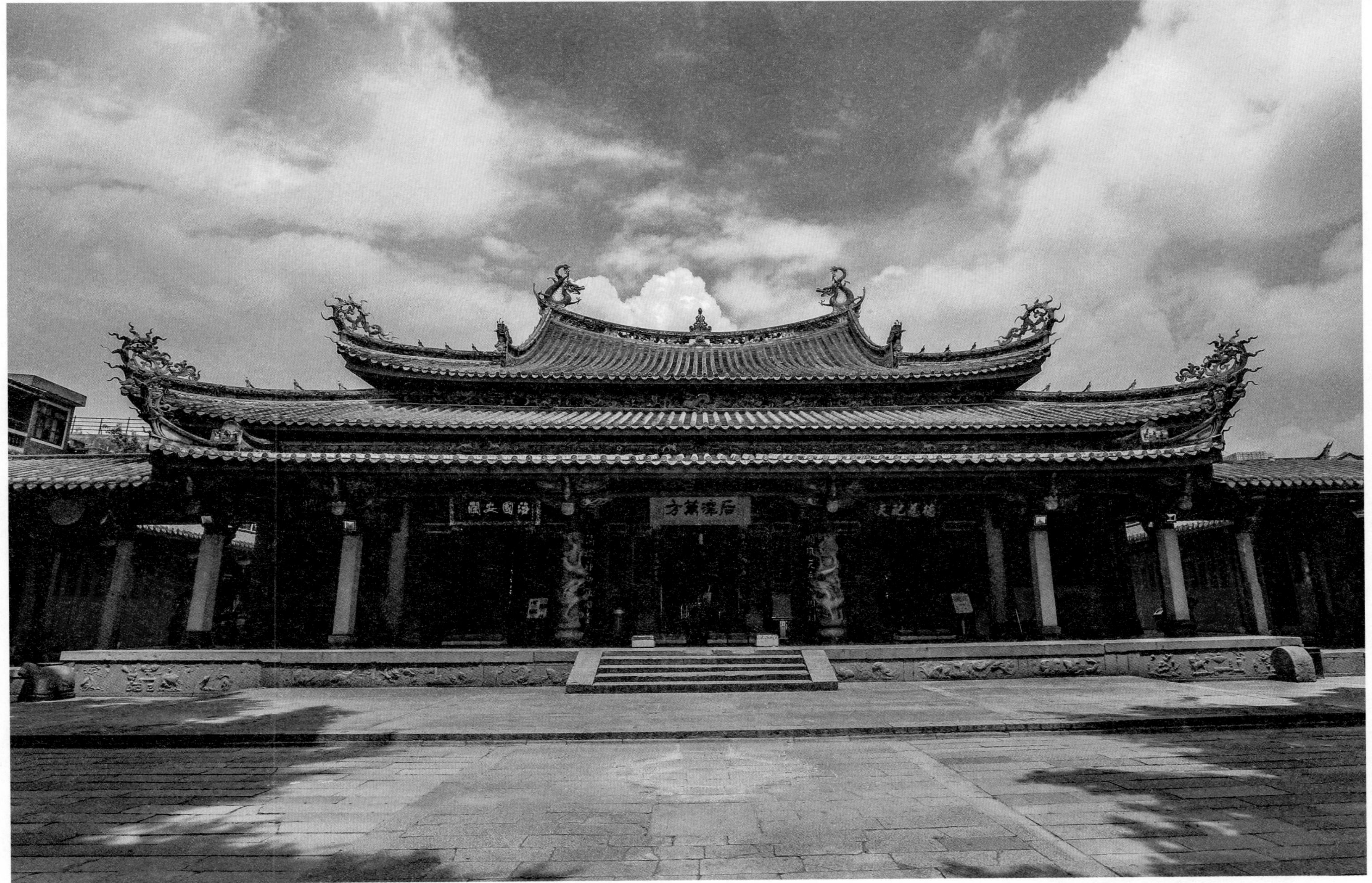

天后宫正殿。（陈英杰 摄）
The main hall of Tianhou Temple. (Photo by Chen Yingjie)

蔡氏古民居建筑群

年代：清

地址：泉州市南安市官桥镇漳里村

建于 1867 年至 1911 年，主要由旅居菲律宾著名侨商、清资政大夫蔡资深所建，是闽南红砖建筑的典型代表。建筑群规模宏大，现存宅第 20 座，书房 1 座，当铺 1 座，宗祠遗址 1 处，总占地面积 3 万多平方米。各宅第自成院落，多由硬山式燕尾脊五开间大厝和左、右卷棚式护厝组成。建筑群布局规整，前后座之间以宽 10 米左右的石埕相连，左右纵列以 1 米—2 米宽的防火通道相间。建筑内石雕、木雕、砖雕、泥塑等雕饰精美、内涵丰富，部分融合了西方、南洋的文化元素。

Cai Family's Ancient Residential Complex

Period: Qing Dynasty

Address: Zhangli Village, Guanqiao Town, Nan'an City, Quanzhou City

It was mainly built between 1867 and 1911 by Cai Zishen, a well-known overseas Chinese businessman living in the Philippines, who was also a Qing Dynasty official with non-substantive appointment. It is typical of red brick buildings of Southern Fujian. The scale of the building complex is huge, with 20 extant building groups, a study house, a pawnshop, and the ruin of an ancestral hall, covering a total area of more than 30,000 square meters. Each group has its own courtyard, surrounded by the main house which is five rooms wide with flush gable roof-style swallow-tailed ridges, and by two rows of wing rooms on both sides, with roll-up sheds. The layout of the complex is symmetrical, and the front and rear parts are connected by stone courtyards with a width of about 10 meters; the left and right rows are separated by fire escape passages as wide as 1 to 2 meters. The buildings are exquisitely decorated with stone carvings, wood carvings, brick carvings, clay sculptures and other carvings that are rich in local meaning, incorporating cultural elements from Western and Southeast Asian countries.

丰富而精美的雕饰。(南安市委宣传部 供图)
Diverse and exquisite carvings. (Courtesy of the Publicity Department of Nan'an Municipal Committee of the CPC)

俯瞰蔡氏古民居建筑群。（卓天然 摄）
Overlooking Cai family's ancient residential complex. (Photo by Zhuo Tianran)

泉州府文庙

年代：宋至清

地址：泉州市鲤城区中山中路 34 号

始建于唐开元年间（713—741），北宋太平兴国初年移建于今址，历代有重修。左学右庙，规制完整。庙由棂星门遗址、大成门、泮池、东西庑、大成殿等组成。大成殿，重檐庑殿顶，抬梁式木构架，面阔七间，进深五间，内檐以五铺作单杪双下昂斗拱承托屋檐，殿身皆石柱，共 48 根，其中石雕盘龙檐柱 8 根。殿内保存有明清成套祭孔器物。学由育英门、学池、明伦堂组成。

Quanzhou Confucius Temple

Period: Song to Qing dynasties

Address: No. 34 Zhongshan Middle Road, Licheng District, Quanzhou City

Built from 713 to 741 and later relocated and rebuilt on this site in the early years of the Northern Song Dynasty, Quanzhou Confucius Temple has been rebuilt throughout the dynasties. The left building is a school and the right one is a temple, with symmetrical planning and design. The temple consists of the ruins of the arch gate Lingxingmen, the arch gate Dachengmen, Pan Pool, east and west wing rooms and Dacheng Hall. Dacheng Hall has a double-eave hip roof, of post-and-lintel wood construction. It is seven rooms wide and five rooms deep, and the inner brackets include single-gong-double-ang and five intermediate sets to support the projecting eaves. There are 48 stone columns in the hall, including 8 carved-dragon stone columns. The hall has preserved the complete set of wares for offering sacrifices to Confucius from the Ming and Qing dynasties. The school consists of the arch gate Yuyingmen, Xue Pool and Minglun Hall.

大成殿内景。（陈英杰 摄）
The interior view of Dacheng Hall. (Photo by Chen Yingjie)

泮桥和泮池。（陈晓东 摄）
Pan Bridge and Pan Pool. (Photo by Chen Xiaodong)

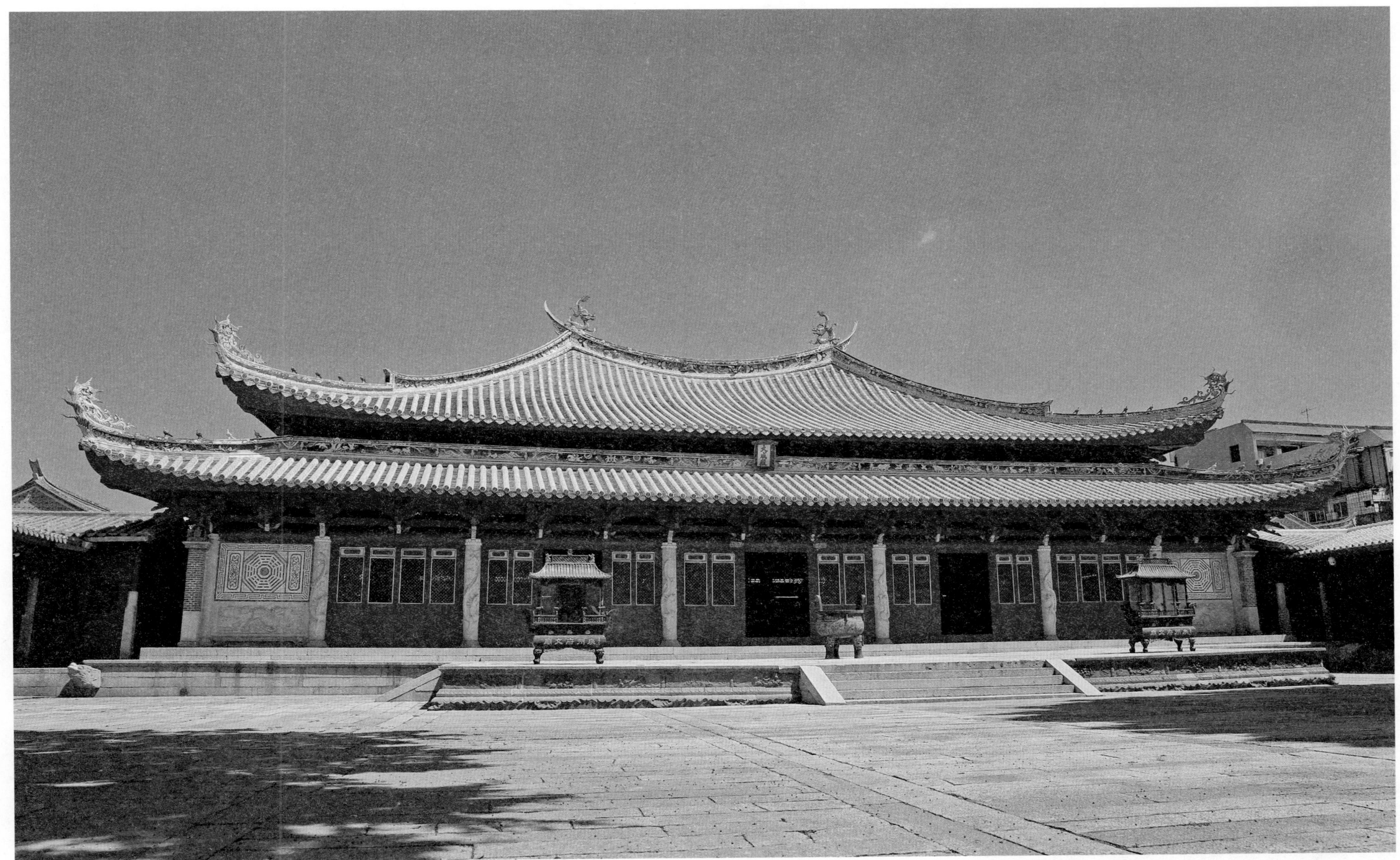

大成殿。（陈英杰 摄）
Dacheng Hall. (Photo by Chen Yingjie)

泉州港古建筑之真武庙

年代：清

地址：泉州市丰泽区通港西街 339 号

始建于宋代，现存建筑为清代重建。祭祀海神真武大帝的庙宇，“宋时为泉郡守望祭海神之所”。庙坐北朝南，依山而筑，由山门、凉亭、真武殿等组成。占地面积约 3,000 平方米，建筑面积 400 平方米。山门为砖木结构牌楼式，重檐歇山顶，檐下施如意斗拱。山门后有 24 级石阶，其顶有一大磐石，立明嘉靖刻“吞海”石碑。凉亭重檐八角攒尖顶。真武殿为歇山顶，面阔五间，进深五间。每年农历正月二十九日当地村民在此举行祭海祈福仪式。

Zhenwu Temple of Quanzhou Port's Ancient Buildings

Period: Qing Dynasty

Address: No. 339 Tonggang West Street, Fengze District, Quanzhou City

The temple was built during the Song Dynasty and the extant building was rebuilt during the Qing Dynasty. The temple was dedicated to the sea god Zhenwu Dadi, at the place where the governor of Quanzhou watched a "sacrifice to the sea god" during the Song Dynasty. The temple sits north and faces south and was built on a hill. It consists of the arch gate, a pavilion, Zhenwu Hall and others. It covers an area of about 3,000 square meters with a building area of 400 square meters. The arch gate is a brick and wood structure, with a double-eave gable, hip roof and Ruyi-shaped bracket sets under the eaves. There are 24 stone steps behind the arch gate, and there is a large rock at the top, and a stele engraved with the words "Swallowing the Sea" from the Ming Dynasty. The pavilion has a double-eave octagonal pyramidal roof. Zhenwu Hall has a gable and hip roof, and is five rooms wide and five rooms deep. Every year on the 29th day of the first lunar month, local villagers hold a sea-worshiping ceremony in the temple.

山门。（陈英杰 摄）
The arch gate. (Photo by Chen Yingjie)

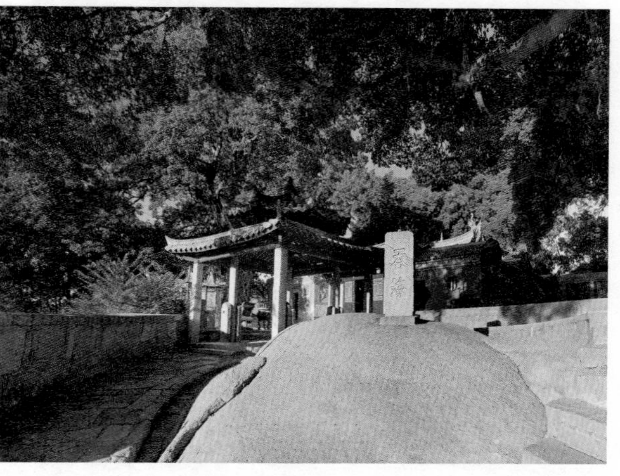

明刻“吞海”石碑。（陈英杰 摄）
The "Swallowing the Sea" stele engraved in the Ming Dynasty. (Photo by Chen Yingjie)

真武殿。（罗春日 摄）
Zhenwu Hall. (Photo by Luo Chunri)

陈埭丁氏宗祠

年代：明

地址：泉州市晋江市陈埭镇岸兜村

阿拉伯穆斯林后裔的宗祠。始建于明代永乐年间（1403—1424），坐北朝南，历经修葺、扩筑，由门厅、中堂、后厅及东西廊组成，平面布局呈“回”字形。采用闽南传统民居的建筑技术，以砖、石、木构造，部分木雕、石雕构件使用阿拉伯文字装饰或用阿拉伯文字绘成“吉祥鸟”装饰。整座建筑既承袭汉族的传统建筑风格，又显现伊斯兰文化特征，是中外文化交流融合的实物见证。

Chendai Ding Family's Ancestral Hall

Period: Ming Dynasty

Address: Andou Village, Chendai Town, Jinjiang City, Quanzhou City

Ding Family's Ancestral Hall was built by Arabic Muslim descendants during the reign of Emperor Yongle in the Ming Dynasty (1403—1424). It sits north and faces south, and has undergone many repairs and expansions. It consists of an entrance hall, a central hall, a rear hall and east and west corridors. The layout is in the shape of a Chinese character " 回 ". It adopts the construction technology of traditional residential houses of Southern Fujian, with brick, stone and wood elements; also, some wood and stone carving components are decorated with Arabic script such as "Auspicious Bird". The whole building inherits the traditional architectural style of the Han people, along with the characteristics of Islamic culture, which is a physical testimony of the integration of Chinese and foreign cultures.

丁氏宗祠内景。（施清凉 摄）

The interior view of Ding Family's Ancestral Hall. (Photo by Shi Qingliang)

丁氏宗祠大门。（泉州市委宣传部 供图）
The arch gate of Ding Family's Ancestral Hall. (Courtesy of the Publicity Department of Quanzhou Municipal Committee of the CPC)

安溪文庙

年代：清

地址：泉州市安溪县凤城镇大同路 141 号

　　始建于宋咸平四年(1001)，现存建筑为清康熙二十五年（1686）重建。左学右庙，规制完整。庙坐北朝南，由泮池、万仞宫墙、棂星门、戟门、前两庑、大成殿、后两庑、崇圣殿、教谕衙等组成，东建明伦堂。大成殿为重檐歇山顶，面阔、进深各三间，明间设精美八卦形藻井。屋脊采用了大量闽南特色的剪瓷堆塑。露台须弥座中间陛石嵌有辉绿岩云龙浮雕。整个建筑内石雕、木雕、砖雕、彩绘种类繁多、工艺精美。

Anxi Confucius Temple

Period: Qing Dynasty

Address: No. 141 Datong Road, Fengcheng Town, Anxi County, Quanzhou City

The temple was originally built in 1001 during the Northern Song Dynasty and the extant building was rebuilt in 1686 of the Qing Dynasty. On the left is a school and on the right is a temple, with symmetrical planning and design. The temple sits north and faces south, and is composed of Pan Pool, Wanrengong Wall, the arch gate Lingxingmen, the arch gate Jimen, two front rooms, Dacheng Hall, two rear rooms, Chongsheng Hall, Jiaoyu Hall, and Minglun Hall on the east. Dacheng Hall has a double-eave gable and hip roof. It is three rooms wide and three rooms deep. There is an amazing Bagua-shaped caisson ceiling in the center. The roof ridge has a large number of figures made up of pieces of colorful porcelain with characteristic features of Southern Fujian. In the middle of the sumeru pedestal on the terrace, there is an imperial path stone slab embedded with relief sculptures of flying dragons made of diabase. There are many other kinds of stone carvings, wood carvings, brick carvings and various paintings in the whole building, and the craftsmanship is exquisite.

大成殿内景。（刘伯怡 摄）
The interior view of Dacheng Hall. (Photo by Liu Boyi)

戟门。（刘伯怡 摄）
The arch gate Jimen. (Photo by Liu Boyi)

大成殿。（刘伯怡 摄）
Dacheng Hall. (Photo by Liu Boyi)

靖海侯府。（张清杰、苏保金 摄）
Jinghai Marquis' Mansion. (Photo by Zhang Qingjie and Su Baojin)

施琅宅、祠和墓之靖海侯府

年代：清

地址：泉州市晋江市龙湖镇衙口村

建于清康熙二十六年（1687），是清代著名军事家、政治家施琅平定台湾荣归故里后所建。系硬山顶建筑，有门厅、中厅、后厅三进，五开间，带双护厝。侯府的面墙、隔墙装饰青砖，外围墙用具有泉州地方特色的“出砖入石”砌法。

Jinghai Marquis’ Mansion of “Shilang’s House, Ancestral Hall and Tomb”

Period: Qing Dynasty

Address: Yakou Village, Longhu Town, Jinjiang City, Quanzhou City

Built in 1687 during the Qing Dynasty, in honor of the famous Qing strategist and politician, Shi Lang, who recovered Taiwan and returned in glory to his hometown. The mansion is five rooms wide, with a flush gable roof, comprising the entrance hall, the middle hall and the rear hall with bilateral guardhouses. The front walls and vertical partition walls of the mansion are decorated with grey bricks, and the outer walls are made in a special “brick-in and stone-out” local construction style of Quanzhou.

靖海侯府面墙以青砖装饰。（张清杰、苏保金 摄）

The front walls of Jinghai Marquis’ Mansion are decorated with grey bricks. (Photo by Zhang Qingjie and Su Baojin)

惠安青山宫

年代：明、清
地址：泉州市惠安县山霞镇青山村

始建于北宋太平兴国六年（981），历代有修葺。奉祀惠安当地特有的历史人物神青山王。南宋初年，青山王信仰得到官方承认，青山王被封为“灵惠侯”，由此赐额“敕封青山灵安王庙”。由灵安王庙、文昌阁、英烈祠等组成。主庙灵安王庙为清代重建，坐北朝南，建筑面积656平方米，由山门、两廊、天井、前殿、拱亭和后殿组成。宫内石雕、木雕、砖雕及泥塑、彩绘、壁画工艺精美。青山王信仰已逾千年，随移民流播台湾地区及东南亚一带。

Hui'an Qingshan Temple

Period: Ming and Qing dynasties
Address: Qingshan Village, Shanxia Town, Hui'an County, Quanzhou City

Originally built in 981 during the Northern Song Dynasty, this temple has been rebuilt throughout the dynasties. The temple is dedicated to the god Qingshanwang, a unique historical figure in Hui'an. In the early years of the Southern Song Dynasty, the faith of Qingshanwang was officially recognized, and Qingshanwang was titled “Linghuihou”, hence the name of “Ling'anwang Temple”. Qingshan Temple is composed of Ling'anwang Temple, Wenchang Pavilion, and Memorial Hall. Ling'anwang Temple was rebuilt in the Qing Dynasty. Sitting north and facing south and covering a construction area of 656 square meters, the temple consists of an arch gate, east and west corridors, a patio, the front hall, Gong Pavilion and the rear hall. The stone carvings, wood carvings, brick carvings, clay sculptures, paintings, and mural paintings in the temple are exquisite. The faith of the god Qingshanwang has spread for a thousand years and has been introduced to Taiwan and Southeast Asia by Fujian migrants.

青山宫。（陈峻峰 摄）
Qingshan Temple. (Photo by Chen Junfeng)

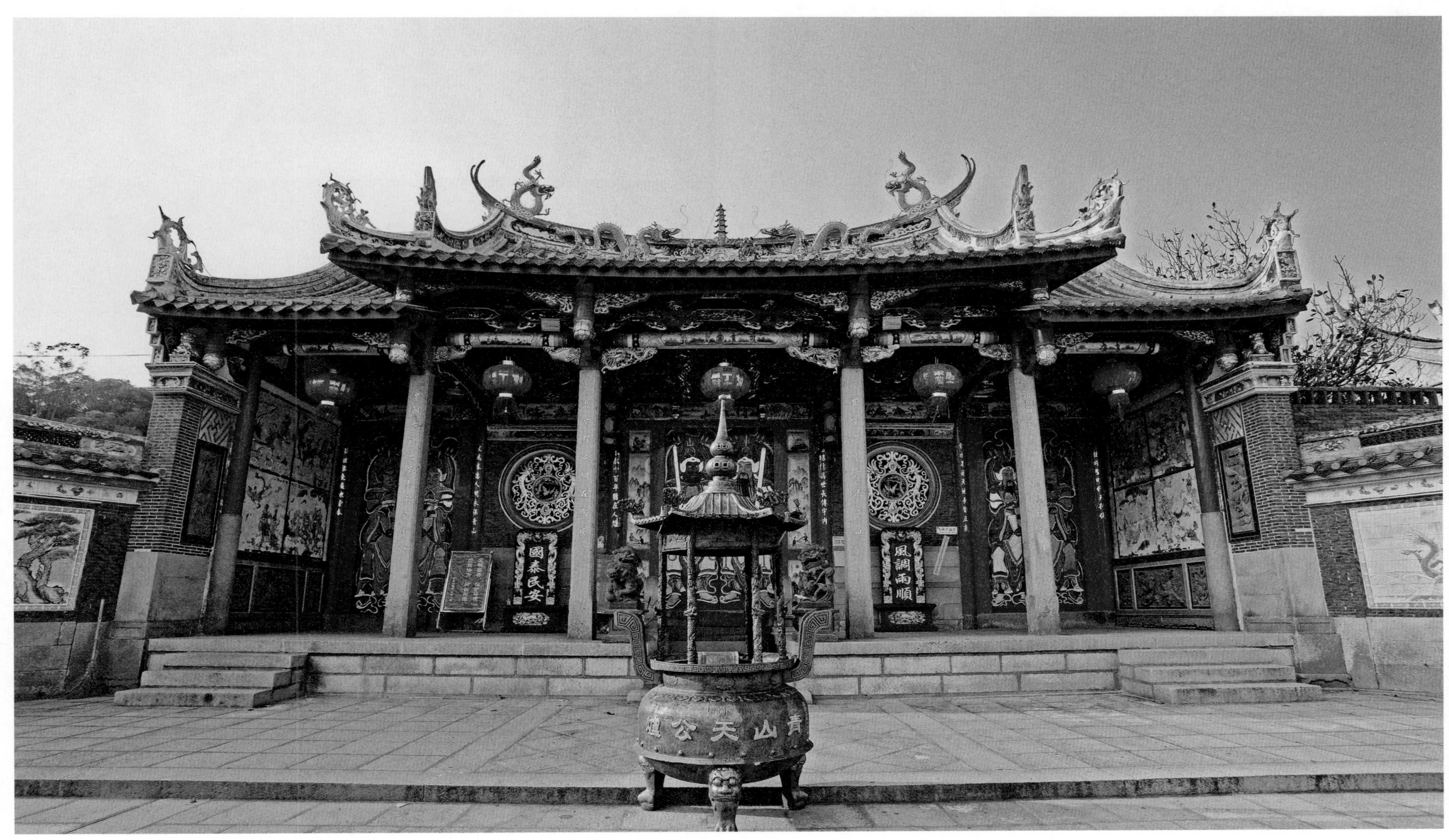

灵安王庙。（张清杰、苏保金 摄）
Ling'anwang Temple. (Photo by Zhang Qingjie and Su Baojin)

安海龙山寺

年代：明、清

地址：泉州市晋江市安海镇型厝村

始建于隋末，现存庙宇为清同治十二年（1873）至光绪五年（1879）所建。寺坐北朝南，从南向北依次为前埕、钟鼓楼、前殿、天井、两庑、拜亭、正殿、后殿，建筑面积达 4,250 平方米。寺内木雕、石雕等装饰精美。寺中主供通高 4.2 米、宽 2.5 米的明代木雕千手千眼观音立像，是稀世珍品。该寺香火自清代闽南百姓大批移台而传入台湾，成为台湾 400 多座龙山寺的祖庙，是海峡两岸密不可分的历史见证。

Anhai Longshan Temple

Period: Ming and Qing dynasties

Address: Xingcuo Village, Anhai Town, Jinjiang City, Quanzhou City

This temple was originally built in the late Sui Dynasty, and the extant temple was rebuilt from 1873 to 1879 during the Qing Dynasty. The temple sits north and faces south. From south to north, there is the front courtyard, bell and drum towers, the front hall, the patio, east and west rooms, the Worship Pavilion, the main hall, and the rear hall, with a building area of 4,250 square meters. The temple is beautifully decorated with wood carvings and stone carvings. The precious statue in the temple is a wooden statue of Guanyin with a thousand hands and eyes, which is 4.2 meters high and 2.5 meters wide—truly a rare treasure. The practice of the temple was transferred to Taiwan during the Qing Dynasty when people from Southern Fujian moved to Taiwan and it became the ancestral hall of more than 400 Longshan Temples in Taiwan. It is a prominent witness for the shared cultures of both sides of the Taiwan Strait.

天王殿。（陈钧 摄）
The Hall of Heavenly King. (Photo by Chen Jun)

千手千眼观音立像。（陈钧 摄）
Statue of Guanyin with a thousand hands and eyes. (Photo by Chen Jun)

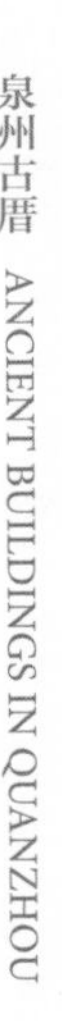

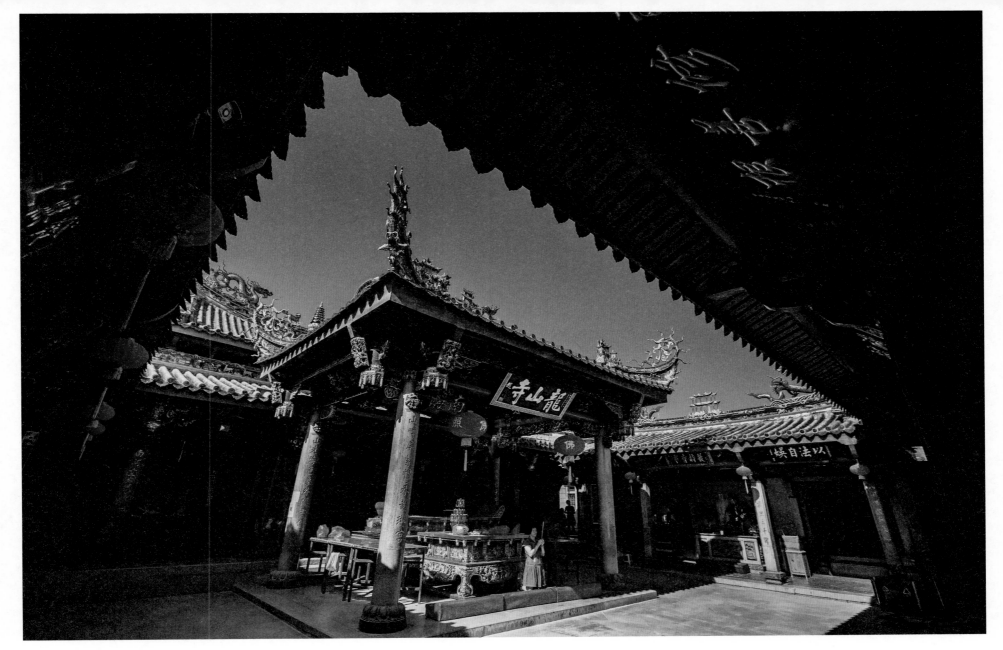

拜亭。（吴宝烨 摄）
The Worship Pavilion. (Photo by Wu Baoye)

清水岩寺

年代：清

地址：泉州市安溪县蓬莱镇鹤前村

包括清水祖师殿、清水法门、三忠庙、蓬莱坊、觉亭等，以及若干宋元以来摩崖题刻、碑刻、墓塔。清水祖师殿，始建于北宋元丰六年（1083），现存建筑依寺中《岩图》碑所记载建筑的规模、尺寸、度数等，于清乾隆二十六年（1761 年）重建，历代均有修葺。殿宇坐东北朝西南，依山面壑就势而建，殿宇三层，呈“帝”字形，总建筑面积约为 3,200 平方米。大殿内部木雕、石雕装饰精美。清水祖师信俗随移民传入台湾，成为两岸同胞寻根认祖的重要见证。

Qingshuiyan Temple

Period: Qing Dynasty

Address: Heqian Village, Penglai Town, Anxi County, Quanzhou City

The temple consists of Qingshui Patriarch Hall, Qingshui Famen (Arch Gate), Sanzhong Temple, Penglaifang, Jue Pavilion, as well as several cliff and stone inscriptions and tomb towers from the Song and Yuan dynasties. Qingshui Patriarch Hall was built in 1083 of the Northern Song Dynasty. The extant building was rebuilt in 1761 during the Qing Dynasty according to the exact scale, size, and directions as recorded in the *Yantu* (Stone Blueprint) monument in the temple, and has been repaired throughout the dynasties. The hall sits northeast and faces southwest and was built according to the mountain terrain with mountains at its back and a gully in front. The three floors of the hall are in the shape of the Chinese character " 帝 " and the total building area is about 3,200 square meters. The interior is beautifully decorated with wood and stone carvings. The faith of Qingshui Patriarch was introduced to Taiwan by Fujian migrants and became an important testimony to the shared histories of compatriots of both sides of the Taiwan Strait honoring their hometowns and ancestors.

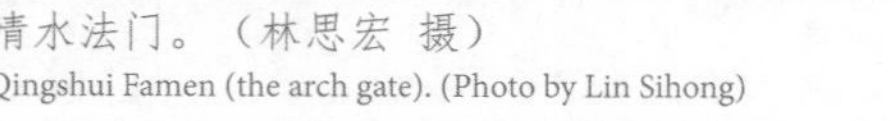

清水法门。（林思宏 摄）
Qingshui Famen (the arch gate). (Photo by Lin Sihong)

摩崖题刻。（刘伯怡 摄）
Cliff inscriptions. (Photo by Liu Boyi)

清水祖师殿。（刘伯怡 摄）
Qingshui Patriarch Hall. (Photo by Liu Boyi)

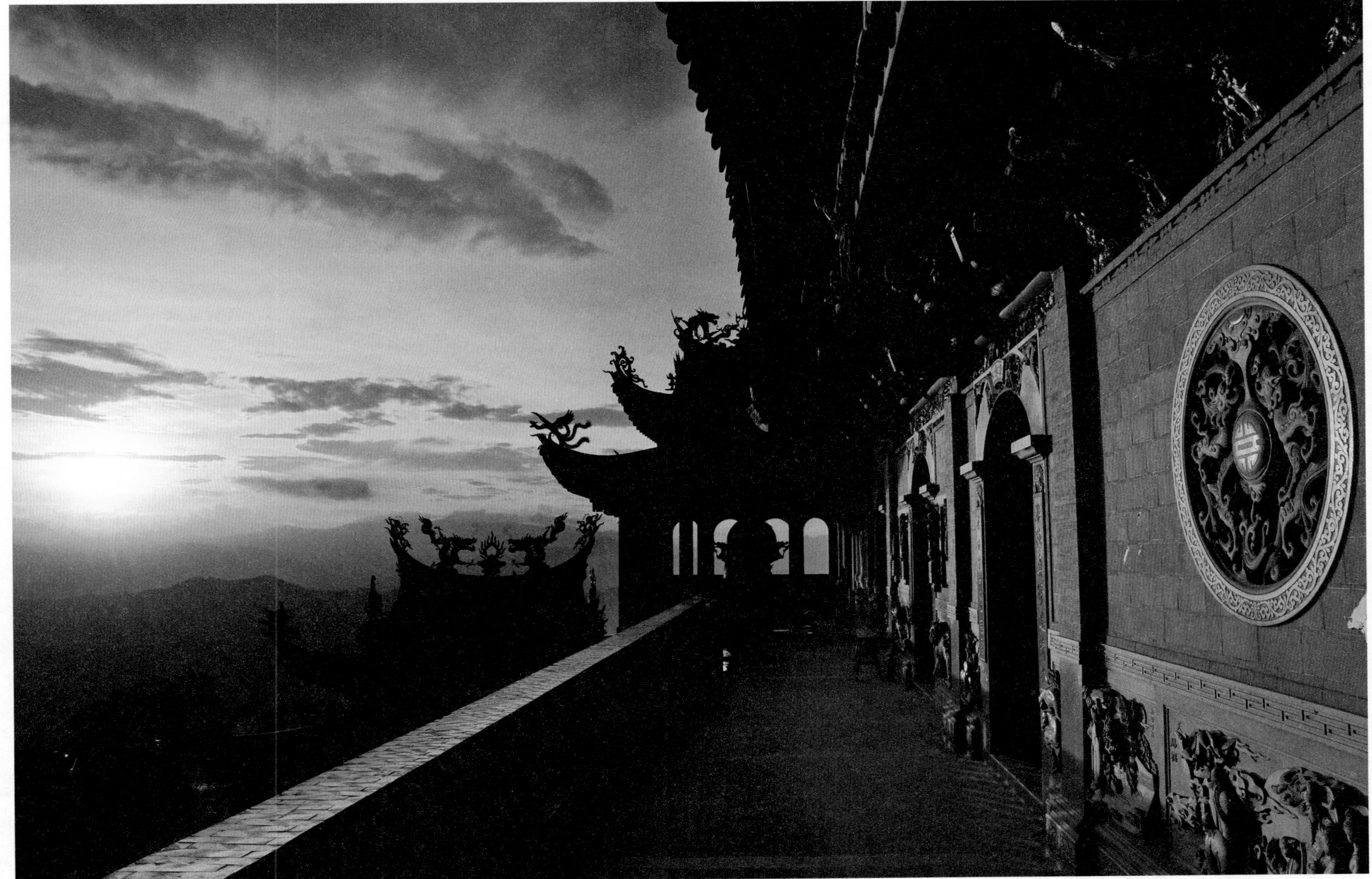

夕阳下的清水岩寺。（林思宏 摄）
Qingshuiyan Temple basking under the sunset. (Photo by Lin Sihong)

亭店杨氏民居

年代：清

地址：泉州市鲤城区凌霄路 12 号

建于清光绪二十年至三十年（1894—1904），系当地著名华侨杨阿苗先生的故居。建筑坐北向南，平面呈方形，为两进五开间带双边护厝建筑。精美绝妙的木雕、砖雕、竹雕、石雕、剪瓷雕、灰雕、彩绘装饰于民居内外。地面铺进口的鲜艳花砖，正面墙身即“镜面墙”用红砖拼贴并镶嵌图案和文字，屋内装饰所用钉子是当时进口的洋铁钉，亦体现了中西建筑文化的结合。

杨氏民居前落。（耿路明 摄）
The front courtyard of Yang family's house. (Photo by Geng Luming)

杨氏民居精美的雕刻。（耿路明 摄）
Fine carvings in Yang family's house. (Photo by Geng Luming)

杨氏民居后厅。（耿路明 摄）
The rear hall of Yang family's house. (Photo by Geng Luming)

Tingdian Yang Family's House

Period: Qing Dynasty

Address: No. 12 Lingxiao Road, Licheng District, Quanzhou City

This building was built from 1894 to 1904 during the Qing Dynasty. It was the former residence of Mr Yang A'miao, a famous local overseas Chinese. The building sits north and faces south, and has a square layout. It is five rooms wide, with two courtyards and bilateral guardhouses. There are exquisite wood carvings, brick carvings, bamboo carvings, stone carvings, porcelain carvings, lime carvings and color paintings decorating the inside and outside of the houses. The floor is covered with bright imported tiles, and the front partition wall is a "mirror wall" made of red brick tiles with inlaid patterns and texts. Even the iron nails used in the interior decoration were imported, which further reflected the combination of Chinese and Western architectural culture.

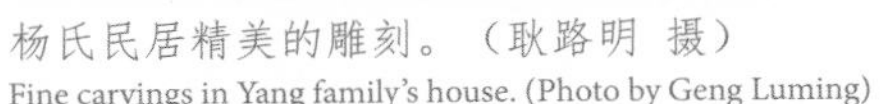

杨氏民居精美的雕刻。（耿路明 摄）
Fine carvings in Yang family's house. (Photo by Geng Luming)

南安林氏民居

年代：清

地址：泉州市南安市省新镇满山红村

建于清光绪晚期，系当地著名华侨建筑家林路先生所建。建筑群坐北朝南，宗祠、正屋、叠楼、书房等由西向东联袂并排而立，通长110多米，占地面积约6,000平方米。建筑材料以闽南传统的砖、石、木为主，随处可见精美的石雕、木雕。建筑墙壁、地板装饰精美的进口水泥花砖，巧妙地将南洋建筑装饰风格融入，是清代闽南地区华侨建筑的经典代表作之一。

Nan'an Lin Family's Residence

Period: Qing Dynasty

Address: Manshanhong Village, Shengxin Town, Nan'an City, Quanzhou City

This building group was built during the late Qing Dynasty by Mr Lin Lu, a well-known overseas Chinese architect. The complex sits north and faces south, with the ancestral hall, main buildings, side buildings, study rooms, etc. standing side by side from west to east. The total length of the building is more than 110 meters with a land area of about 6,000 square meters. The building materials were mainly brick, stone and wood constructed in a traditional Southern Fujian style, with exquisite stone and wood carvings which can be seen throughout the buildings. The imported cement tiles form exquisite decoration on the walls and floors of the buildings and cleverly integrates the decorative style of Southeast Asian architecture. It is one of the classic masterpieces of overseas Chinese architecture in Southern Fujian from the Qing Dynasty.

南安林氏民居。（李长志 摄）
Nan'an Lin family's residence. (Photo by Li Changzhi)

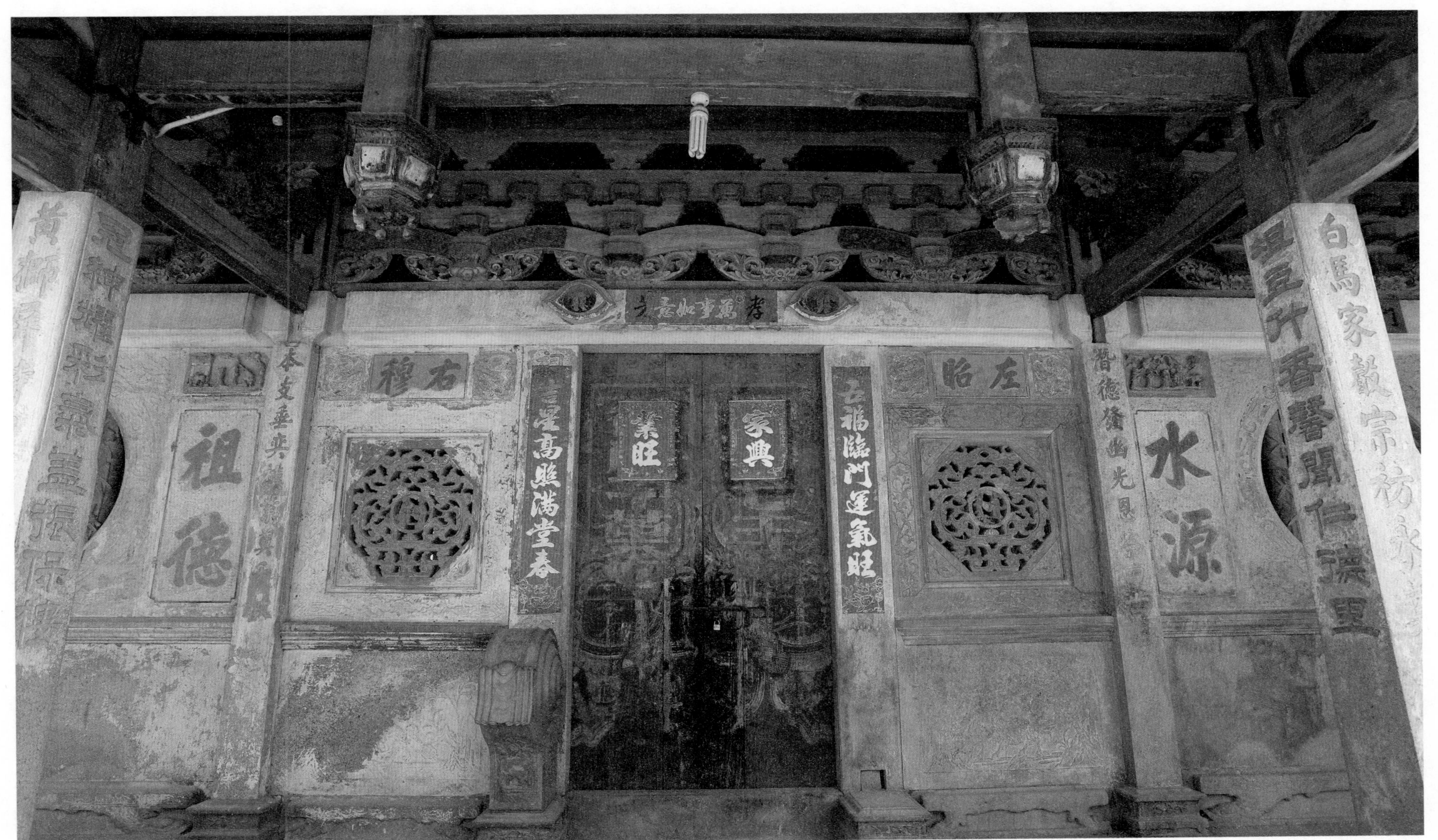

宗祠。（苏保金 摄）
The ancestral hall. (Photo by Su Baojin)

俯瞰中宪第。（张清杰、苏保金 摄）
Overlooking Zhongxian Mansion. (Photo by Zhang Qingjie and Su Baojin)

南安中宪第

年代：清

地址：泉州市南安市石井镇延平街

清雍正六年 (1728) 始建，系南安石井人郑运锦往台湾经商致富后所建，因其长子郑汝成授州司马并诰封中宪大夫，故称“中宪第”。坐南朝北，占地面积 7,780 平方米。平面构筑为围合式，主体建筑由主厝、后落、东护厝、西护厝、西重护厝组成，再间以水榭、曲桥、梳妆楼、演武厅、书轩、亭阁、假山等组合建筑群，规模宏大，布局井然有序。建筑木作及雕饰形式多样，内涵丰富，部分融合了西方、南洋的文化元素。

Nan' an Zhongxian Mansion

Period: Qing Dynasty

Address: Yanping Street, Shijing Town, Nan'an City, Quanzhou City

Zhongxian Mansion was built in 1728 during the Qing Dynasty by Zheng Yunjin, a businessman from Shijing Town, Nan'an City, who went to Taiwan and became successful in business. His eldest son Zheng Rucheng was granted the state official name, Zhongxian Dafu (grand master exemplar), so the mansion was called “Zhongxian Mansion”. Sitting south and facing north, it covers an area of 7,780 square meters. The layout is an enclosed quadrangle style, and the main buildings consists of the main quadrangle, the rear building, east guardhouse, two west guardhouses, the water pavilion, winding bridges, dressing house, Yanwu Hall, windowed veranda, other pavilions, rockeries and so on. The combined building group is large in scale and well-organized. The woodwork and carvings are diverse in style and rich in meaning incorporating many cultural elements of the West and Southeast Asia.

中宪第内景。（张清杰、苏保金 摄）

The interior view of Zhongxian Mansion. (Photo by Zhang Qingjie and Su Baojin)

李光地宅和祠之新衙、贤良祠

年代：清

地址：泉州市安溪县湖头镇湖二村、湖四村

清康熙文渊阁大学士、吏部尚书李光地的宅第及祠堂。新衙，又称“昌佑堂”，建于康熙三十七年（1698），坐北朝南，占地面积3,120平方米。自南向北依次为门厅、接官厅、大厅、后厅，东西侧各有一护厝。贤良祠（李光地祠），原名榕村书屋，建于康熙二十四年（1685），李光地曾在此讲学。雍正十一年（1733），雍正帝以李光地为“卓然一代之完人”谕祭于京城贤良祠，因此榕村书屋改名“贤良祠”，作为李光地之专祠。祠坐西向东，分为门厅、正堂、藏书阁。祠南面设御碑亭，竖一方雍正帝颁下的《谕祭文》石碑，追恤李光地生平之风概节操。

Xinya Official Residence and Xianliang Ancestral Hall of Li Guangdi's Mansion and Ancestral Hall

Period: Qing Dynasty

Address: Hu'er Village and Husi Village, Hutou Town, Anxi County, Quanzhou City

Xinya Official Residence and Xianliang Ancestral Hall are the mansion and ancestral hall of Li Guangdi's, a scholar and high rank official of Emperor Kangxi of the Qing Dynasty. Xinya Official Residence, also known as "Changyou Hall", was built in 1698 of the Qing Dynasty. It sits north and faces south, covering an area of 3,120 square meters. From south to north, there is the entrance hall, the reception hall, the main hall, and the rear hall, and also guardhouses on the east and west sides. Xianliang Ancestral Hall (Li Guangdi's Ancestral Hall), formerly known as Rongcun Study, was built in 1685, and was where Li Guangdi once lectured. In 1733, Emperor Yongzheng commended Li Guangdi as an example of the "Perfect Person of the Generation" and urged people to honor him in the Xianliang Hall in Beijing. Thereafter, Rongcun Study was renamed "Xianliang Ancestral Hall" as a special hall to honor Li Guangdi. The hall sits west and faces east and is divided into the entrance hall, the main hall and the library. On the south side of the hall is the Imperial Stele Pavilion and a stone monument with a "Funeral Oration" issued by Emperor Yongzheng set up to honor Li Guangdi's moral integrity.

贤良祠。（刘伯怡 摄）
Xianliang Ancestral Hall. (Photo by Liu Boyi)

御碑亭。（刘伯怡 摄）
Imperial Stele Pavilion. (Photo by Liu Boyi)

新衙。（刘伯怡 摄）
Xinya Official Residence. (Photo by Liu Boyi)

安溪土楼

年代：明、清

地址：泉州市安溪县西坪镇平原村、赤石村和南岩村

包括映宝楼、聚斯楼、南岩梅记泰山楼，均为方形土楼。三座土楼平面布局规整，屋面层叠错落，结构、外观、装饰均有一定的闽南建筑特色。映宝楼，建于清雍正八年（1730），坐西向东，楼高3层，占地面积792平方米。该楼三层有100多个用来烘干制作茶叶的土灶，见证了当时制茶业的兴旺。聚斯楼，始建于明代，清重修，是安溪县境内最早建造的土楼，坐北朝南，占地面积919平方米。南岩梅记泰山楼，建于清光绪十八年（1892），占地面积488平方米，是梅记茶行的发祥地。

映宝楼。（刘伯怡 摄）
Yingbaolou. (Photo by Liu Boyi)

Anxi Tulou

Period: Ming and Qing Dynasties

Address: Pingyuan Village, Chishi Village and Nanyan Village, Xiping Town, Anxi County, Quanzhou City

Yingbaolou, Jusilou and Taishanlou (Nanyan Meiji) are all square earthen buildings. The three Tulou all have a symmetrical layout, with overlapping roofs. The structure, appearance, and decorations all show the unique characteristics of Southern Fujian architecture. The 3-story Yingbaolou, built in 1730 of the Qing Dynasty, sits west and faces east, covering an area of 792 square meters. On the third floor of the building, there are more than 100 earthen stoves for drying tea, which is a witness to the prosperity of the tea-making industry at that time. Jusilou, originally built in the Ming Dynasty and rebuilt in the Qing Dynasty, is the earliest Tulou built in Anxi County. It sits north and faces south and covers an area of 919 square meters. Taishanlou (Nanyan Meiji), built in 1892 of the Qing Dynasty, covers an area of 488 square meters and is the birthplace of Meiji Tea Shop.

聚斯楼。（刘伯怡 摄）
Jusilou. (Photo by Liu Boyi)

泰山楼。（刘伯怡 摄）
Taishanlou. (Photo by Liu Boyi)

泉港土坑村古建筑群之百万大厝

年代：清
地址：泉州市泉港区后龙镇土坑村

泉港土坑村古建筑群由当地海商刘氏家族兴建，后刘氏族人不断建造新屋，逐渐形成以家族为纽带、各类商业功能齐全、一港三街一码头的古厝街区布局。百万大厝，建于清乾隆十二年（1747），其主人刘端弘从事海上运输和贸易而成远近闻名的富商，被称“刘百万”，故其宅称百万大厝。大厝坐西北朝东南，平面呈规整的矩形，占地面积 1,402.12 平方米。中轴线上由门埕、门厅、正厅、后厅等组成，西侧两列护厝，东侧一列护厝，是闽南红砖建筑的典型代表。

Grand Millionaire Mansion of Ancient Building Complex in Tukeng Village, Quangang District

Period: Qing Dynasty
Address: Tukeng Village, Houlong Town, Quangang District, Quanzhou City

The ancient building complex of Tukeng Village in Quangang was built by the Liu family of local sea merchants. Later, the Liu family continued to build new houses, and the layout of the ancient block of buildings gradually formed with the extended family as the link, plus various commercial functions, including a port, three streets and one wharf. Grand Millionaire Mansion, one of the most important building, was built in 1747 of the Qing Dynasty. Its owner, Liu Duanhong, was engaged in marine transportation and trade and became a well-known successful businessman, and also became known as "Millionaire Liu", hence the name of the mansion. It sits northwest and faces southeast, with a square layout, covering an area of 1,402.12 square meters. Along the central axis there is the front courtyard, the arch gate, the main hall, the rear hall, etc. With two rows of guardhouses on the west side and one row on the east side, it is typical of red brick buildings of Southern Fujian.

百万大厝门埕。（张清杰、苏保金　摄）
The front courtyard of Grand Millionaire Mansion. (Photo by Zhang Qingjie and Su Baojin)

百万大厝俯瞰。（陈晓龙　摄）
Overlooking Grand Millionaire Mansion. (Photo by Chen Xiaolong)

坂埔古厝

年代：清

地址：泉州市南安市英都镇良山村

始建于清乾隆年间，为良山洪氏家族所建造，由顶点金、棋盘厝、在中堂、若莲居、思源居、康美居、存善堂、顺兴居、含章堂、封君祠、近贤堂、德美居、箭楼居共 13 座大厝组成，总占地面积 6,000 余平方米。古厝多为一进或二进，带有单边或双边护厝，立面以闽南传统“出砖入石”营造技法砌筑，白石墙裙，红砖砌壁，地域特点鲜明，是典型的闽南传统建筑。

Banpu Ancient Building Complex

Period: Qing Dynasty

Address: Liangshan Village, Yingdu Town, Nan'an City, Quanzhou City

This complex was built during the reign of Emperor Qianlong in the Qing Dynasty by the Hong family at Liangshan. There are a total of 13 large houses, including Dingdianjin House, Qipan House, Zaizhong Hall, Ruolian House, Siyuan House, Kangmei House, Cunshan Hall, Shunxing House, Hanzhang Hall, Fengjun Hall, Jinxian Hall, Demei House and Jianlou House, covering a total area of more than 6,000 square meters. These ancient houses have mostly one courtyard or two courtyards, with one row or two rows of guardhouses, and the facade is built with the traditional Southern Fujian “brick-in and stone-out” construction techniques, with white stone wainscot and red brick upper walls, displaying distinctive regional features. They are all typical buildings of traditional Southern Fujian architecture.

坂埔古厝全景。（洪炳焕 摄）
The panoramic view of Banpu Ancient Building Complex. (Photo by Hong Binghuan)

顶点金。（洪炳焕 摄）
Dingdianjin House. (Photo by Hong Binghuan)

俯瞰永春文庙。（康庆平 摄）
Overlooking Yongchun Confucius Temple. (Photo by Kang Qingping)

永春文庙

年代：清

地址：泉州市永春县桃城镇桃城路 40 号

现存建筑为清代乾隆五十年（1785）重建。坐北朝南，总体格局保存基本完整，占地面积 3,000 余平方米。左学右庙。庙由万仞宫墙、棂星门、泮池和状元桥、戟门、大成殿、东西廊庑、崇圣祠组成。大成殿为重檐歇山顶，面阔三间，进深四间。永春文庙规格、等级均按州府文庙建制修建。

Yongchun Confucius Temple

Period: Qing Dynasty

Address: No. 40, Taocheng Road, Taocheng Town, Yongchun County, Quanzhou City

The extant building of Yongchun Confucius Temple was rebuilt in 1785 during the Qing Dynasty. Sitting north and facing south, the overall layout is basically intact, covering an area of more than 3,000 square meters. On the left side is a school and on the right side is a temple. The temple is composed of the Wanrengong Wall, the arch gate Lingxingmen, Pan Pool and Zhuangyuan Bridge, the arch gate Jimen, Dacheng Hall, east and west galleries, and Chongsheng Hall. Dacheng Hall has a double-eave gable and hip roof, and is three rooms wide and four rooms deep. Yongchun Confucius Temple was built according to the specifications of a state Confucius temple.

大成殿。（康庆平 摄）
The Dacheng Hall. (Photo by Kang Qingping)

观山李氏民居

年代：1890 年—1936 年

地址：泉州市南安市眉山乡观山村

爱国华侨李功藏及其长子李成器于清末至民国所建，包括番仔楼、功藏厝、成器厝。番仔楼，建于 1899 年，坐西北朝东南，上下两层四面均设外廊，带单边护厝，地面铺设南洋特色瓷砖，形成中西合璧的风格。功藏厝建于 1890 年，坐西北朝东南，建筑面积 530 平方米。成器厝建于 1936 年，坐北朝南，建筑面积 487 平方米。功藏厝、成器厝均为两进带双边护厝的传统闽南红砖大厝，在装饰等方面融入了南洋元素。

Guanshan Li Family's Residence

Period: 1890-1936

Address: Guanshan Village, Meishan Town, Nan'an City, Quanzhou City

Built by the patriotic overseas Chinese, Li Gongcang, and his eldest son Li Chengqi, from the late Qing Dynasty through to the Republic of China, including Fanzai Building, Gongcang House and Chengqi House. Fanzai Building, built in 1899, sits northwest and faces southeast, with verandas on each side of the two floors, and guardhouses on one side. The floors are covered with tiles of Southeast Asian characteristic, forming a Chinese-Western style. Gongcang House, built in 1890, sits northwest and faces southeast, with a construction area of 530 square meters. Chengqi House was built in 1936 and sits north and faces south, with a construction area of 487 square meters. Gongcang House and Chengqi House are traditional Southern Fujian red-brick houses with two courtyards and two rows of guardhouses on both sides. The buildings incorporate Southeast Asian characteristic elements in decoration and other design aspects.

番仔楼和功藏厝。（南安市委宣传部 供图）
Fanzai Building (left) and Gongcang House (right). (Courtesy of the Publicity Department of Nan'an Municipal Committee of the CPC)

番仔楼。（张梓昌 摄）
Fanzai Building. (Photo by Zhang Zichang)

成器厝。（南安市委宣传部 供图）
Chengqi House. (Courtesy of the Publicity Department of Nan'an Municipal Committee of the CPC)

安礼逊图书楼

年代：1927 年
地址：泉州市鲤城区新华北路 345 号培元中学内

建于 1927 年，系泉州培元中学校友为祝贺创始人安礼逊五十大寿、表彰其贡献而集资建造的一座图书楼。坐西南向东北，十字形平面，占地面积 1,246 平方米。楼由民国闽南建筑大师傅维早主持设计，外墙立面采用简化的西洋柱式，楼顶凌云台建闽南地方传统建筑形式，将西式墙身与闽南传统屋顶完美结合，是典型的中西合璧建筑风格，也是近代泉州城标志性建筑之一。

Anderson Library Building

Period: 1927
Address: Peiyuan Middle School, No. 345 Xinhua North Road, Licheng District, Quanzhou City

Built in 1927, it was a library building funded by Quanzhou Peiyuan Middle School alumni to commemorate its founder A. S. Mooye Anderson's 50th birthday and to honor his great contribution. Sitting southwest and facing northeast, the cross-shaped layout covers an area of 1,246 square meters. The building was designed by Fu Weizao, an architecture master of Southern Fujian during the Republic of China. The external facade adopts simplified Western-style columns. Lingyuntai Pavilion on the top of the building displays the traditional local architectural form of Southern Fujian. The pavilion's Western-style wall and traditional style roof of Southern Fujian are perfectly integrated, making it a wonderful combination of Chinese and Western architectural styles. This building is also one of the landmarks of modern Quanzhou City.

安礼逊图书楼。（魏朝全 摄）
Anderson Library Building. (Photo by Wei Chaoquan)

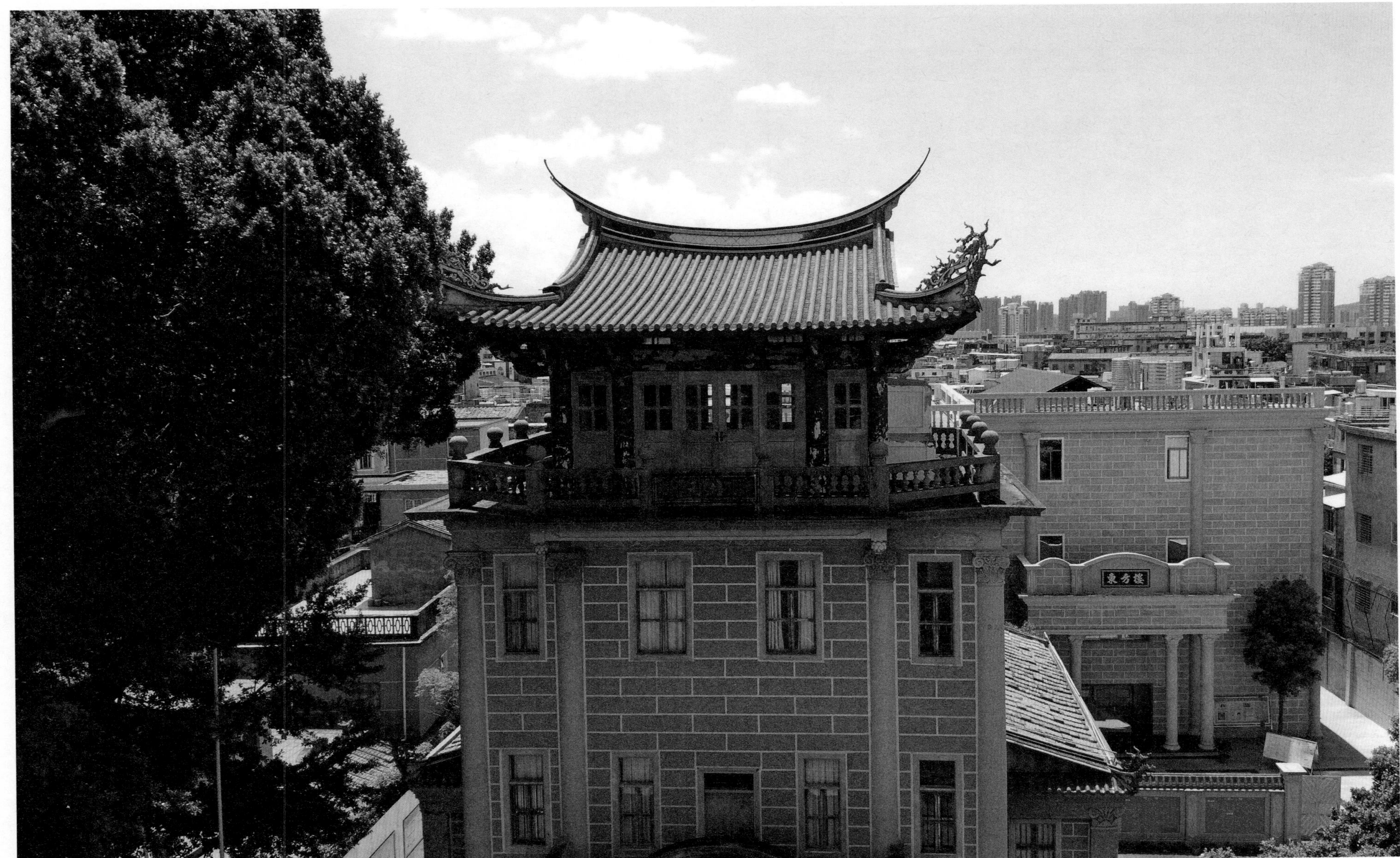

凌云台。（苏保金 摄）
Lingyuntai Pavilion. (Photo by Su Baojin)

永春福兴堂

年代：1943 年—1947 年

地址：泉州市永春县岵山镇塘溪村

建于 1943 年至 1947 年，为爱国商人李武庸、李武宗兄弟所建。坐西朝东，平面呈长方形，占地面积 2,100 平方米，红墙灰瓦，两进五开间，带双边护厝建筑。石雕、木雕、砖雕、灰塑、剪瓷雕和彩画等装饰题材广泛、雕刻细腻，局部融有西方建筑装饰元素，形成闽南侨乡中西合璧的建筑特色。

Yongchun Fuxingtang House

Period: 1943-1947

Address: Tangxi Village, Hushan Town, Yongchun County, Quanzhou City

This house was built from 1943 to 1947, by the patriotic business brothers Li Wuyong and Li Wuzong. It sits west and faces east, with a layout of a rectangle, covering an area of 2,100 square meters. The house is five rooms wide, with two courtyards and two rows of guardhouses on both sides. The walls are made of red brick and the roof is of grey tile. Stone carvings, wood carvings, brick carvings, lime sculptures, porcelain carvings, and color paintings display a wide range of decorative styles and traditional themes. Also some Western architectural decoration elements are blended to form a combination of Chinese and Western architectural styles of Southern Fujian, the hometown of many overseas Chinese.

俯瞰福兴堂。（康庆平 摄）
Overlooking Fuxingtang House. (Photo by Kang Qingping)

丰富的装饰元素。（康庆平 摄）
Diverse decoration elements. (Photo by Kang Qingping)

景胜别墅

年代：1946 年—1949 年
地址：泉州市石狮市宝盖镇龙穴村

建于 1946 年至 1949 年，为华侨高祖景所建。坐西向东，占地面积 1,565 平方米。建筑一、二层四周设外廊，内部为闽南传统民居的单进院落格局。层顶平台中轴线上建两座镇楼亭，均为钢筋混凝土仿木构形式。建筑内外泥塑、石雕、砖雕、木雕、剪瓷堆砌等技艺精湛。别墅在构造、材料、装饰等方面融合南洋建筑文化特色，成为闽南红砖建筑与南洋建筑文化结合的典范。

Jingsheng Villa

Period: 1946-1949
Address: Longxue Village, Baogai Town, Shishi City, Quanzhou City

This large villa was built from 1946 to 1949, by the overseas Chinese, Gao Zujing. Sitting west and facing east, it covers an area of 1,565 square meters. There are verandas around the first and second floors of the building, and the interior is a traditional Southern Fujian folk house of single courtyard. Two pavilions were built along the central axis of the rooftop, both of which are in the form of reinforced concrete in an imitation wood style. There is exquisite craftsmanship in clay sculptures, stone carvings, brick carvings, wood carvings, and pieces of colorful porcelain on display in and around the villa. The villa integrates Southern Fujian red brick buildings with Southeast Asian architectural cultural characteristics in terms of structure, materials, and decoration, and has become an outstanding example of the culture integration of Southern Fujian red brick buildings with Southeast Asian architecture.

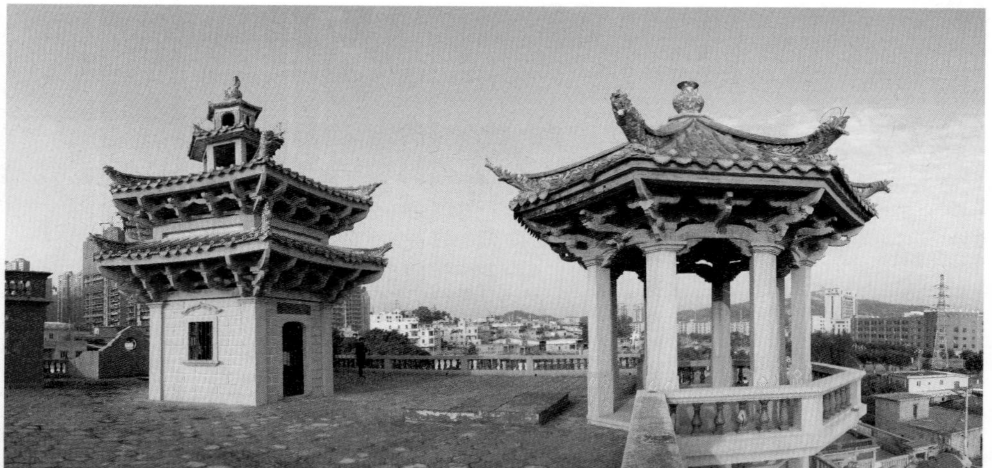

镇楼亭。（茅罗平 摄）
Zhenlou Pavilions. (Photo by Mao Luoping)

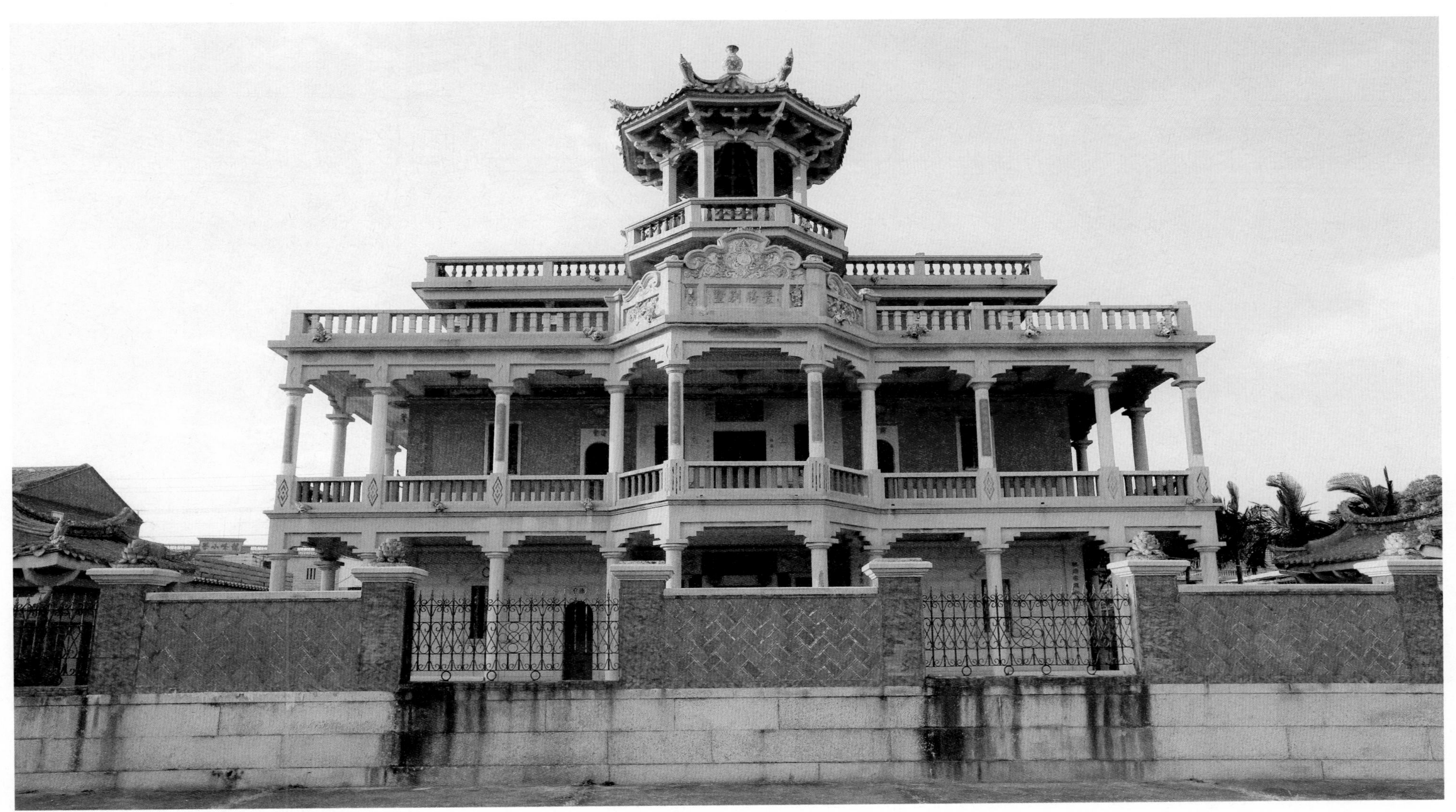

景胜别墅。（茅罗平 摄）
Jingsheng Villa. (Photo by Mao Luoping)

三明

Sanming

張氏家廟
石壁张氏家庙

泰宁尚书第

年代：明

地址：三明市泰宁县城关尚书街

亦称“五福堂”，始建于明天启元年（1621），系明万历四十四年（1616）进士、天启年间协理京营戎政兵部尚书、少保兼太子太师李春烨的府第。整座府第占地5,520平方米，分5幢沿南北方向一字排开，前门设甬道相通，各幢之间又以封火山墙间隔。每幢皆三进，结构大致相同。尚书第内的石雕、木雕、砖雕做工精细，花样繁多。

Taining Shangshu Mansion

Period: Ming Dynasty

Address: Shangshu Street, Taining County Town, Sanming City

Also known as the “Wufu Hall”, it was built in 1621 during the Ming Dynasty. It was the mansion of Li Chunye, who succeeded in the highest imperial examination in 1616, and became the coordinator of the Military Department during the Tianqi period and was honored as the teacher of the prince. The whole mansion covers an area of 5,520 square meters and is divided into 5 buildings lined up in a north-south direction. The front doors are connected with corridors, and each building is separated from another by a firewall. Each building has three quadrangles and the structure of each is roughly the same. The stone carvings, wood carvings and brick carvings in Shangshu Mansion show fine workmanship with various patterns.

规模宏大的尚书第。（刘贤健 摄）

The grand Shangshu Mansion. (Photo by Liu Xianjian)

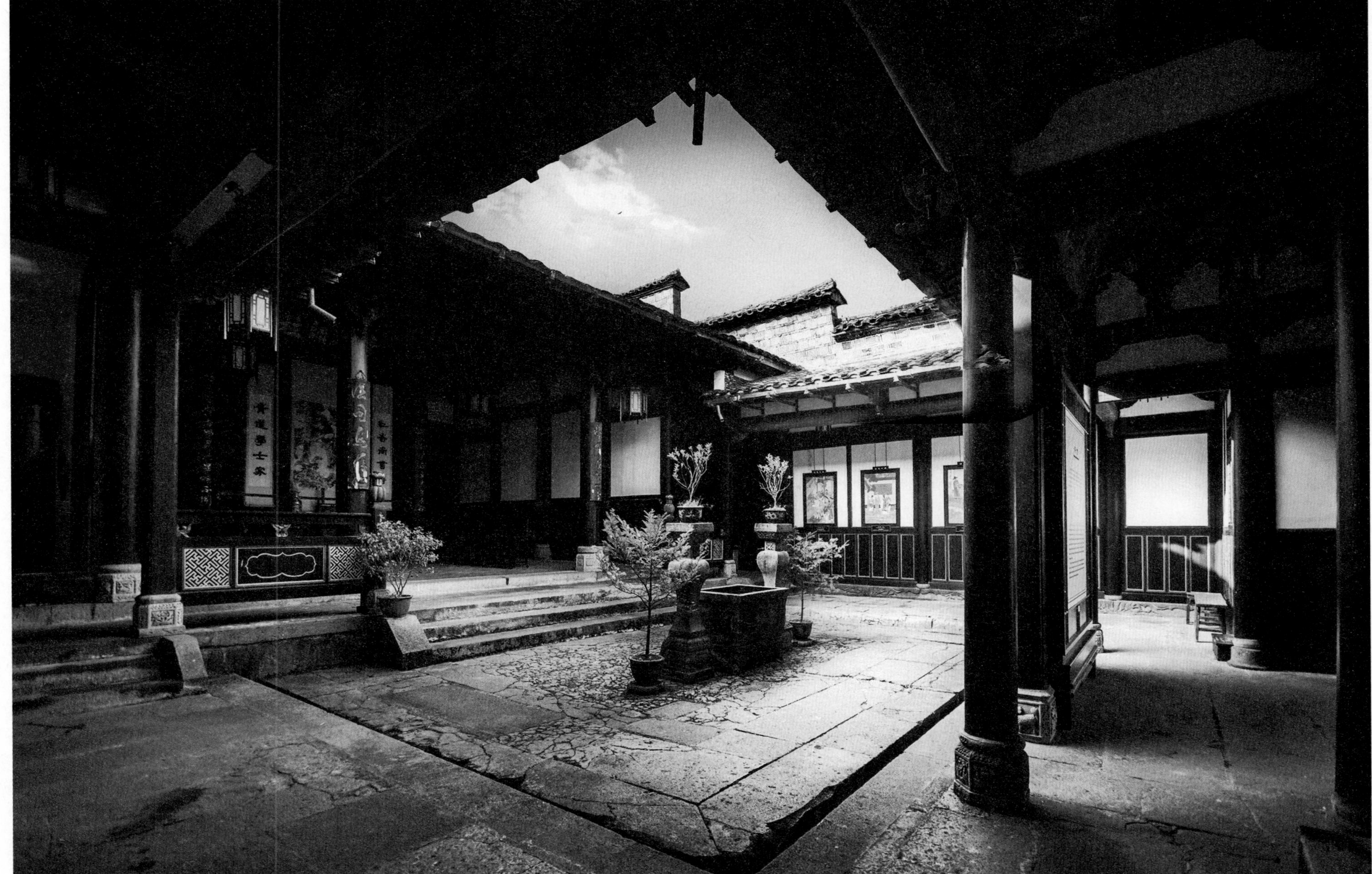

尚书第第二幢天井。（刘贤健 摄）
The patio in the 2nd main building of Shangshu Mansion. (Photo by Liu Xianjian)

安贞堡

年代：清

地址：三明市永安市槐南乡洋头村

又名“池贯城”，建于清光绪十一年至光绪二十四年（1885 – 1898），为大型防御性城堡民居建筑，也是福建土堡之精品。坐西朝东，占地 9,797 平方米，平面前方后圆，呈中轴对称布局。外墙高 9 米，墙基厚约 4 米，向上逐渐收分，墙体下部用毛石垒砌、上部用生土夯筑。堡墙布有射击孔 198 个，瞭望窗 96 个，正门两侧的转角各设一角楼，墙上设一圈跑马道。院内为一组两层两进院落式建筑，四周是以依堡墙而建的两层护楼。

Anzhen Fortress

Period: Qing Dynasty

Address: Yangtou Village, Huainan Township, Yongan City, Sanming City

Also known as “Chiguan City”, it was built between 1885 and 1898 during the late Qing Dynasty. It is a large-scale defensive castle-style residential building, and is also a fine example of Fujian earthen fortresses. Sitting west and facing east, it occupies an area of 9,797 square meters; the front is square and the back is round; the layout is symmetrically arranged along the central axis. The outer wall is 9 meters high and the wall base is about 4 meters thick, which gradually converges upward. The lower part of the wall is made of rough stone and the upper part is of rammed earth. The fortress wall is set up with 198 window holes for shooting, 96 lookout windows, a corner tower on each side of the main entrance, and a bridleway along the top of the wall. Inside the courtyard is a group of two-story buildings and two courtyards, surrounded by two-story guard buildings adjacent to the fortress wall.

安贞堡内景。（郑承水 摄）
The interior of Anzhen Fortress. (Photo by Zheng Chengshui)

防御性城堡安贞堡。（罗联勇 摄）
Defensive Anzhen Fortress. (Photo by Luo Lianyong)

正顺庙

年代：明

地址：三明市梅列区列西街 1 号

宋绍定六年（1233）始建，明代重建，清、民国有修葺。是祭祀“护国卫民”有功的当地名人谢祐的庙宇。坐北朝南，占地面积 535 平方米，由门楼、正殿组成。正殿为歇山顶，抬梁穿斗混合木结构，面阔七间，进深五间，先后维修 14 次，木构件上保存了各个时代的历史信息，殿内四根大型梭柱和覆盆式柱础保留有宋代建筑特点，16 个瑞兽图案童柱为闽西北古代建筑中所独有，具有浓厚的地方特色。

Zhengshun Temple

Period: Ming Dynasty

Address: No. 1 Liexi Street, Meilie District, Sanming City

Founded in 1233 during the Southern Song Dynasty, rebuilt in the Ming Dynasty, and repaired during the Qing Dynasty and the Republic of China, it is a temple dedicated to Xie You, a local patriot who was famous for protecting the country and the people. Sitting north and facing south, it covers an area of 535 square meters and consists of an arched gatehouse and a main hall. The main hall has a gable hip roof. It is a post-and-lintel construction combined with column and tie-beam wooden structure. It is seven rooms wide and five rooms deep and has been repaired 14 times. The historical information of each era has been preserved on the wooden components. The four large columns and foundations in the main hall retain the architectural characteristics of the Song Dynasty, and the 16 pillars with the pattern of folk beasts are unique to ancient buildings of Northwestern Fujian and have important historical local meanings.

正顺庙大门。（黄舒祥 摄）
The arch gate of Zhengshun Temple. (Photo by Huang Shuxiang)

清幽的正顺庙。（黄舒祥 摄）
The quiet Zhengshun Temple. (Photo by Huang Shuxiang)

大田土堡群之琵琶堡

年代：明至清

地址：三明市大田县建设镇建国村

明洪武七年（1374）始建，明清均有修葺。由游氏族人修建，以防御和家族祭祀为其主要功能。依地势而筑，平面状如琵琶，故称琵琶堡。堡墙高 7 米，毛石砌基，生土夯墙，墙上设宽 1.7 米的跑马道，四周布满瞭望窗和射击孔，西向设门。内院由前楼、后楼和三圣祠等组成，前楼和后楼均为二层，分别为祭祀祖先和观音菩萨场所。是大田土堡群的精品之作。

Pipa Fortress of Datian Earthen Fortress Group

Period: Ming to Qing dynasties

Address: Jianguo Village, Jianshe Town, Datian County, Sanming City

This building was first built in 1374 during the Ming Dynasty and was repaired during the Ming and Qing dynasties. Built by the people of the You clan, its main functions were defense and family worship. Built according to the terrain, the layout is shaped like a "pipa" (a stringed instrument), so it is called "Pipa Fortress". The fortress wall is 7 meters high, with a masonry foundation, a rammed earth wall, and a 1.7-meter-wide bridleway on the top of the wall, surrounded by lookout windows and shooting holes, with a door set in the west wall. The inner courtyard is composed of the front building, the back building, and the Three Sages Temple. The front building and the back building are two-story buildings which were places for worshiping ancestors and the Guanyin Bodhisattva. It is a fine work of the earthen fortresses group in Datian area.

秋日琵琶堡。（林建伟 摄）

Pipa Fortress in autumn. (Photo by Lin Jianwei)

青山环绕琵琶堡。（林跃 摄）
Green hills surround Pipa Fortress. (Photo by Lin Yue)

玉井坊郑氏大厝

年代：清

地址：三明市尤溪县西滨镇厚丰村

清乾隆五十五年（1790）始建，为典型的闽中特色的大型乡土民居建筑。坐北向南，占地面积约 3,800 平方米。平面呈方形圆角，由中路主厝、东路两层横厝、两侧单层壁舍及后花台组成。主厝依次为门厅、正堂和三层的后楼。横厝内设钱库、粮库和小姐书斋等设施。建筑规模宏大，居住、生产经营、学习（书斋）、库房（钱库、粮库）、防御（碉式角楼）等各种功能用房布局合理。厝内木雕、石雕等装饰工艺做工精细、题材丰富。

Yujingfang Zheng Family's Mansion

Period: Qing Dynasty

Address: Houfeng Village, Xibin Town, Youxi County, Sanming City

This mansion was built in 1790 during the Qing Dynasty and is a large-scale rural residential building with typical characteristics of Central Fujian. Sitting north and facing south, it covers an area of about 3,800 square meters. The layout is square with round corners, and is composed of the main middle house, the two-story wing rooms on the east side, the single-story buildings on both sides and the rear flower platform. The main mansion is entered through a foyer into the main hall and then through to the three-story back building. It is equipped with facilities such as a bank, grain storages, and a study room for girls. The scale of the mansion is huge, and the layout of the various functional uses such as residence, production and operation, study room (library), storerooms (money store, grain storehouse) and defense (turrets) is well planned. The decorations such as wood carvings and stone carvings in the interior are fine in workmanship and rich in themes.

大厝的局部。（黄春霖 摄）
Part of the mansion. (Photo by Huang Chunlin)

郑氏大厝全景。（黄春霖 摄）
Panoramic view of Zheng Family's Mansion. (Photo by Huang Chunlin)

水美土堡群之双元堡

年代：清

地址：三明市沙县水美村

水美土堡群是闽南迁来的张氏族人为防御土匪，先后于清同治、咸丰年间所建造，由平面呈“品”字形的双吉、双兴、双元三座防御性土堡组成。双元堡，清道光年间始建，同治元年（1862）完工。坐西向东，平面呈前方后弧，占地面积 6,500 平方米。堡墙在块石基础上夯筑生土而成，设有枪眼、瞭望窗，墙上设跑马道，南北角设角楼。堡内建“慎修堂”，由前堂、中堂、后堂和两侧横屋组成。木雕装修装饰遍布建筑之公共空间，雕刻技艺精美、题材丰富多样。

Shuangyuan Fortress in the Shuimei Earthen Fortress Group

Period: Qing Dynasty

Address: Shuimei Village, Shaxian County, Sanming City

The Shuimei Earthen Fortress Group is a defensive work of the Zhang clan who moved there from Southern Fujian. It was built in the reigns of Tongzhi and Xianfeng during the Qing Dynasty and consists of three defensive fortresses in the shape of “品” layout — Shuangji, Shuangxing and Shuangyuan. Shuangyuan Fortress was first built during 1821—1850 and completed in 1862. Sitting west and facing east, the layout follows the front arc and covers an area of 6,500 square meters. The fortress wall is made of a mixture of rammed raw soil on a foundation of stone, with gun holes and lookout windows, a bridleway on the top wall, and a turret on the north and south corners. The “Shenxiu Hall” was built inside the fortress and consists of the front hall, the middle hall, the back hall and wing rooms on both sides. There are woodcarving decorations all over the public spaces of the buildings, with exquisite carvings of rich and diverse themes.

双元堡全景图。（邓毅坚 摄）
Panoramic view of Shuangyuan Fortress. (Photo by Deng Yijian)

俯瞰水美土堡群。（陈成才 摄）
Overlooking the Shuimei Earthen Fortress Group. (Photo by Chen Chengcai)

吉山抗战旧址群之萃园

年代：清

地址：三明市永安市燕西街道吉山村 302 号

清顺治四年（1647）建，雍正年间（1723—1735）重修。坐西朝东，占地面积 1,529 平方米。是由门楼、半月池、下堂、上堂、护厝组成的园林式书院建筑。大门正面门楣刻有“萃园”二字。梁枋、雀替、柁墩、窗棂等木构件雕刻精细，彩绘精美。抗日战争时期，福建省卫生处、福建省卫生防疫大队、省卫生处制药厂在此办公。

Cui Garden in Jishan

Period: Qing Dynasty

Address: No. 302 Jishan Village, Yanxi Street, Yongan City, Sanming City

This complex was built in 1647 during the Qing Dynasty and rebuilt between 1723 and 1735. Sitting west and facing east, it covers an area of 1,529 square meters. It is a garden-style academy building composed of an arch gatehouse, a half-moon pool, a lower hall, an upper hall, and a guard house. On the front door lintel is engraved with the name “Cui Yuan”. The wooden components such as timber beams, tie-beams, sparrow braces, wooden piers, and window lattices are finely carved and beautifully painted. During the War of Resistance Against Japanese Aggression, the Fujian Provincial Health Department, Fujian Provincial Health and Anti-Epidemic Brigade, and Provincial Health Department Pharmaceutical Factory all worked here.

萃园内景。（罗健 摄）

萃园全景。（罗健 摄）
Panoramic view of the Cui Garden. (Photo by Luo Jian)

石壁张氏家庙

年代：清

地址：三明市宁化县石壁镇石碧村

建于清康熙五十三年（1714），占地约1330平方米，由前埕、门楼、下堂、正堂等组成。门楼八字开，重檐歇山顶，檐下四层如意斗拱出跳。正堂为抬梁穿斗混合木构架，面阔五间，进深五柱，供奉张氏肇基以来各世祖神牌位。下堂、正堂各大小梁枋上陈列历代牌匾，匾联数方。是客家宗祠的典型代表，也是宁化石壁作为客家祖地的实物见证。

Shibi Zhang Family's Ancestral Hall

Period: Qing Dynasty

Address: Shibi Village, Shibi Town, Ninghua County, Sanming City

The hall was built in 1714 during the Qing Dynasty and covers an area of about 1,330 square meters. It is composed of a front open ground, the arch gate, the lower hall and the main hall. The double-eave gable and hip roof of the arch gate is shaped like "八", with four layers of projecting, overhanging brackets under the eaves. The main hall is featured with both post-and-lintel construction and column and tie-beam construction. It is five rooms wide and five columns deep and is dedicated to the ancestral tablets of all generations of the Zhang family. On beams of all sizes in the lower hall and the main hall are plaques and couplets from the past dynasties. It is a typical example of the Hakka ancestral hall and a physical testimony of Shibi as the Hakka ancestral land.

家庙里的牌匾。（陈端 摄）
The plaques in the ancestral hall. (Photo by Chen Duan)

张氏家庙大门。（吴立银 摄）
The arch gate of the Zhang Family's Ancestral Temple. (Photo by Wu Liyin)

陈塘修齐堂

年代：清

地址：三明市宁化县石壁镇陈塘村

又名“上新屋”，清咸丰五年（1855）始建。坐东北朝西南，平面呈“L”形，占地面积约 4,330 平方米，由正落及左、右各两列横屋组成，前有池塘、院坪，后置化胎。前院坪以墙围合，西侧设八字形青砖风水门楼，石质门额上刻墨书“爽挹西门”。正落由门厅、上堂和两廊构成合院。上堂为悬山顶，面阔三间，进深五柱，太师壁上方正中悬挂“修齐堂”牌匾。左右各两列横屋，与正落间由回廊雨廊相连。

Chentang Xiuqi Hall

Period: Qing Dynasty

Address: Chentang Village, Shibi Town, Ninghua County, Sanming City

Also known as “Shangxin House”, it was built in 1855 of the Qing Dynasty. Sitting northeast and facing southwest, the layout is “L” shaped and covers an area of about 4,330 square meters. It is composed of the main quadrangle with two rows of wing houses on the left and right. There is a pond and courtyard in the front, and the Huatai (a symbol of peace and safety) is placed in the rear. The front yard is surrounded by walls, with an “八”-shaped grey brick Fengshui arch gate set on the west side. The stone board over the door is engraved with the words “Shuangyi West Arch Gate”. The main quadrangle is composed of the entrance hall, the upper hall and two corridors. The upper hall has an overhanging gable roof and is three rooms wide and five columns deep. The “Xiuqi Hall” plaque is hung in the middle of the Taishi (central decorated) wall. The wing houses on the left and right are connected to the main quadrangle by a covered corridor.

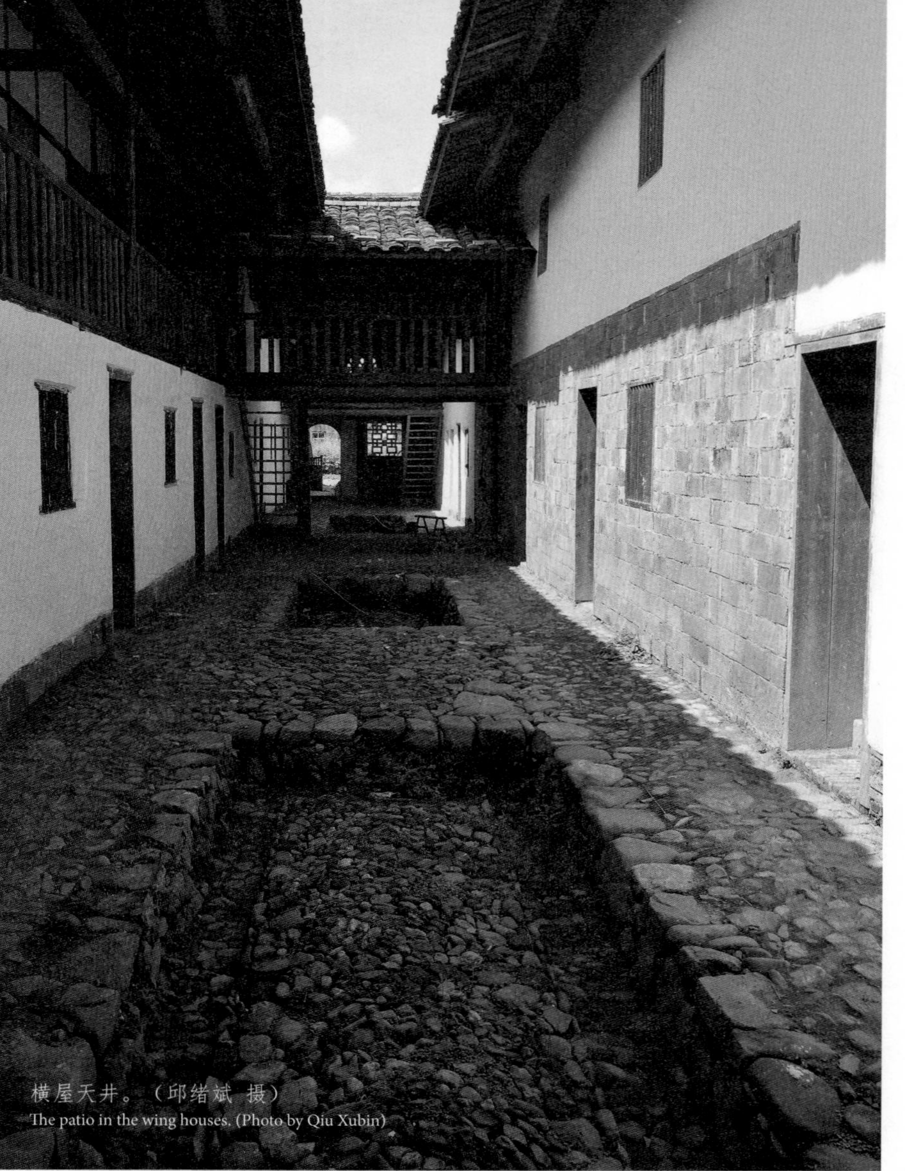

横屋天井。（邱绪斌 摄）
The patio in the wing houses. (Photo by Qiu Xubin)

修齐堂大门。（吴立银 摄）
The arch gate of Xiuqi Hall. (Photo by Wu Liyin)

沧海畲族建筑群之龙德堂

年代：清

地址：三明市永安市青水畲族乡沧海畲族村

以化龙桥、龙长坊、龙昌坊、龙德堂为代表的沧海畲族建筑群是闽中地区畲族风格建筑的典型代表。龙德堂，畲族钟姓始建于清乾隆十七年（1752），坐东朝西，由正落和左右横屋及化胎组成。正落依次为门楼、下堂、上堂，通过姑亭与左右横屋相连。上堂、下堂建筑均为悬山顶，穿斗式木构架，青砖墙体，青瓦屋面。梁、枋、驼峰等部位雕有精美图案，特别是木构件和三合土地面上有大量体现畲族文化的凤凰图案。

Longde House of the *She* Building Group in Canghai

Period: Qing Dynasty

Address: Canghai *She* (Ethnic Group) Village, Qingshui *She* Township, Yongan City, Sanming City

These buildings of the *She* ethnicity include Hualong Bridge, Longchang House, Longchang House and Longde House which are typical examples of the *She*-style architecture of Central Fujian. Longde House was built by the Zhong clan of the *She* ethnicity in 1752 during the Qing Dynasty. Sitting east and facing west, it consists of the main quadrangle and wing houses on the right and left, and also a Huatai. The main quadrangle includes the arch gate building, the lower hall and the upper hall, which are connected to the wing houses through the pavilion. The upper and lower halls all have overhanging gable roofs, of wooden column and tie-beam construction, covered with black tiles. The walls are made of grey bricks. Exquisite patterns are carved on the timber-beams, tie-beams, then camel-hump shaped supports and other parts, especially on the wooden components and even on the floor. Among them there are a large number of phoenix patterns reflecting the *She* culture.

龙德堂里的畲族姑娘。（罗联永 摄）
Girls of *She* ethnicity in Longde House. (Photo by Luo Yonglian)

沧海畲族建筑群。（罗联永 摄）
The building group of the *She* ethnicity in Canghai Village. (Photo by Luo Lianyong)

莆田

Putian

師泉

元妙观三清殿

年代：宋

地址：莆田市荔城区梅园东路 391 号

元妙观建于唐贞观二年（628），宋大中祥符八年（1015）重修，初名天庆观，元改名玄妙观，清初更今名。建筑群现存山门、三清殿及东岳殿、西岳殿、五帝庙、五显庙等。三清殿坐北向南，重檐歇山顶，面阔五间，进深五间，前檐及两侧设廊。历代虽有修葺，但明间、次间仍为宋代建筑。殿内斗拱用材硕大，柱头施双杪双下昂重拱偷心造七铺作。拱、枋、昂存有云纹、卷草等彩绘。

元妙观三清殿内景。（许金珊 摄）
An interior view of Sanqing Hall. (Photo by Xu Jinshan)

Sanqing Hall of Yuanmiao Temple

Period: Song Dynasty

Address: No. 391 East Meiyuan Road, Licheng District, Putian City

Yuanmiao Temple was built during the Tang Dynasty in 628 and repaired during the Song Dynasty in 1015. The first name of the temple was Tianqing, then changed to Xuanmiao during the Yuan Dynasty and later got the name Yuanmiao in the early Qing Dynasty. The existing buildings are the archway, the Sanqing Hall, the East Yue Hall, the West Yue Hall, the Five Emperors Hall, and the Wuxian Hall. Sanqing Hall sits north and faces south, with a double-eave gable and hip roof, and is five rooms wide and five rooms deep. There is a corridor under the front eaves and on the two sides of the hall. Although it had been repaired during later dynasties, the main hall and the side halls retain the architectural style of the Song Dynasty. The bracket sets in this hall are made of large sized wood, and the seven intermediate sets on columns are of a very special style—stolen-heart double-gong-double-ang combination, with a cloud pattern and also curly grass, and other decorative color paintings.

大殿梁架。（陈飞新 摄）
The main timber beams in Sanqing Hall. (Photo by Chen Feixin)

大殿斗拱。（陈飞新 摄）
The bracket sets in Sanqing Hall. (Photo by Chen Feixin)

湄洲妈祖庙

年代：清

地址：莆田市湄洲镇宫下村

奉祀海上守护神妈祖的庙宇。始建于宋，经历代不断扩建重修，主要建筑有寝殿、正殿和圣父母祠。寝殿原为正殿，始建于宋雍熙四年（987），是世界上第一座妈祖庙，故被后人尊称为“祖庙”，占地面积238平方米，由门殿、主殿和两庑组成，保存部分明、清石柱和柱础及宋代天井。清代闽浙总督姚启圣重修奉天阁并将之改为正殿，原正殿后更名为寝殿，殿内供奉宋代妈祖金身及陪神，还保存有元代石雕妈祖神像及清代御赐宝玺。

Mazu Temple in Meizhou

Period: Qing Dynasty

Address: Gongxia Village, Meizhou Town, Putian City

This temple honors Mazu, the patron goddess of the sea. Founded in the Song Dynasty, it has experienced continuous expansion and renovation through the years. The main buildings are the Bedchamber Hall, the Main Hall and the Holy Parents' Hall. The Bedchamber Hall was originally the main hall, built in 987 during the Song Dynasty. It was the world's first Mazu Temple, so later generations call it "Ancestral Temple", and it covers an area of 238 square meters, consisting of the entrance hall, the main hall, two side rooms. One can view the preservation of some stone columns and bases from the Ming and Qing dynasties and the courtyard from the Song Dynasty. Yao Qisheng, governor of Fujian and Zhejiang provinces during the Qing Dynasty, rebuilt the Fengtian Temple and changed it to the main hall, later it was renamed the Bedchamber Hall. The Ancestral Temple has the Song Dynasty Mazu golden body and accompanying gods, and also a stone statue of Mazu preserved from the Yuan Dynasty as well as a Qing Dynasty royal treasure.

祖庙侧影。（庄清贵 摄）
The side view of the Ancestral Temple. (Photo by Zhuang Qinggui)

祖庙寝殿内景。（庄清贵 摄）
The view inside the Bedchamber Hall. (Photo by Zhuang Qinggui)

湄洲妈祖祖庙建筑群。（庄清贵 摄）
The Meizhou Mazu Temple complex. (Photo by Zhuang Qinggui)

平海天后宫

年代：清

地址：莆田市秀屿区平海镇平海村

主祀妈祖，始建于北宋咸平二年（999），清康熙二十二年（1683）收复台湾后，施琅奏请朝廷重建此宫，并分灵至台湾。天后宫坐东北朝东南，占地面积 1,064 平方米。因宫内有 108 根木柱，又称“百柱宫”。主要建筑有山门、拜亭、东西两庑及正殿。正殿为悬山顶，面阔五间，进深五间。宫内保存有《师泉井记》《平海天后庙重修碑记》等碑刻。

Pinghai Tianhou Temple

Period: Qing Dynasty

Address: Pinghai Village,Pinghai Town, Xiuyu District, Putian City

This temple was mainly used for worship services to the Goddess Mazu, founded in 999 during the Northern Song Dynasty. After the recovery of sovereignty over Taiwan in 1683, Shi Lang pleaded the court to rebuild the temple and bring the worship traditions to Taiwan. Tianhou Temple is located northeast and faces southeast, and covers an area of 1,064 square meters. There are 108 wooden columns in the temple, also known as the “Hundred Columns Temple”. The main buildings consist of the archway, worship pavilion, east and west wing rooms and the main hall. The main hall has an overhanging gable roof, and is five rooms wide and five rooms deep. “*The Record of Shiquan Well*” and “*The Record of Renovation of Pinghai Tianhou Temple*” and other inscriptions are well preserved here.

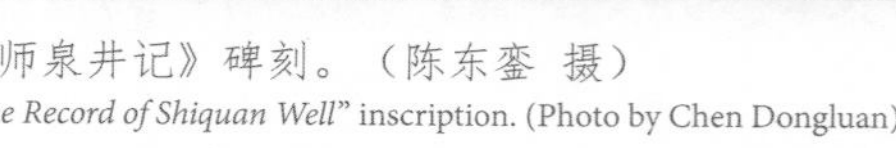

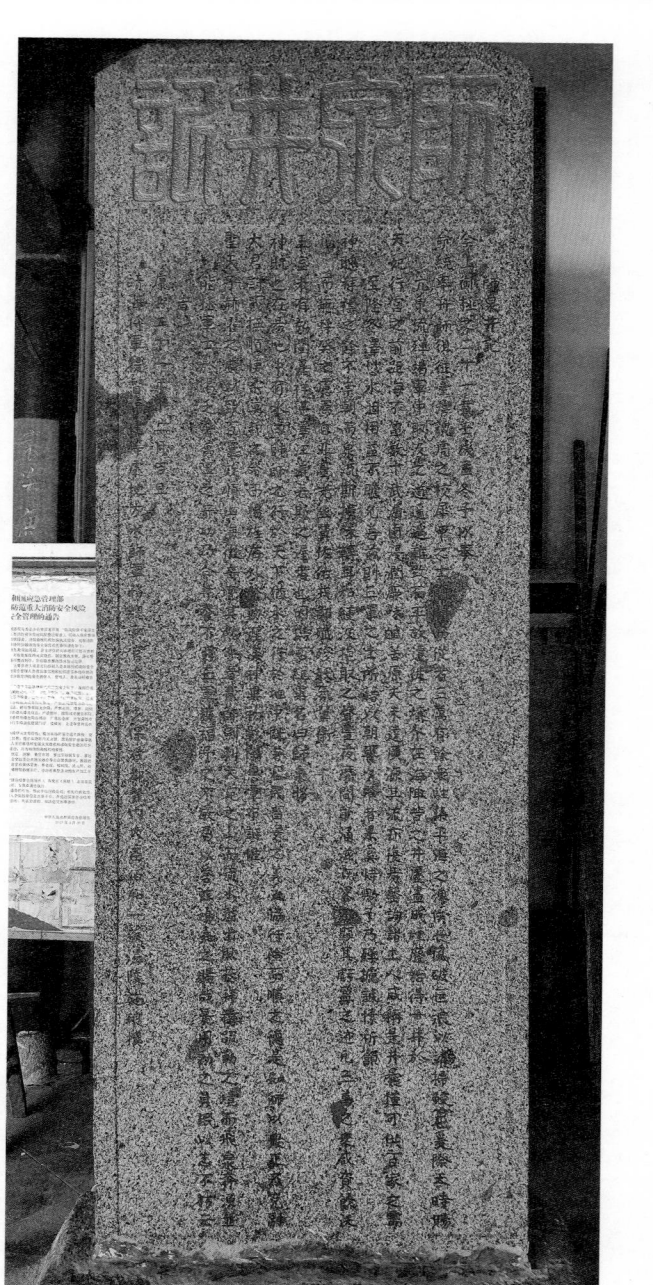

《师泉井记》碑刻。（陈东銮 摄）
“*The Record of Shiquan Well*” inscription. (Photo by Chen Dongluan)

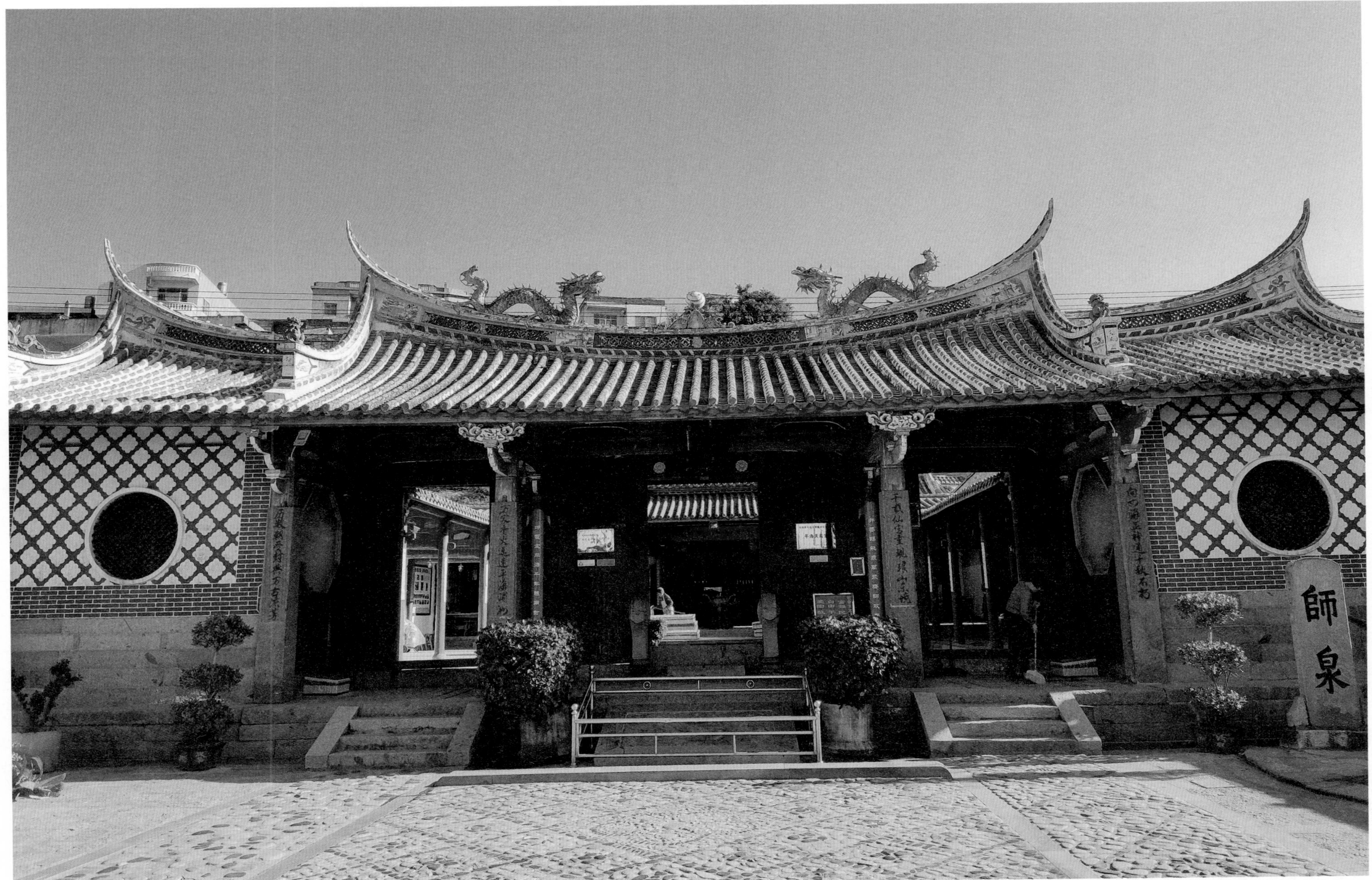

平海天后宫大门。（陈东銮 摄）
The arch gate of Pinghai Tianhou Temple. (Photo by Chen Dongluan)

仙游文庙

年代：清

地址：莆田市仙游县师范路 1 号

宋初建于城西，宋咸平五年（1002）迁至今址，历经兴替，清乾隆四十五年（1780）重建。坐北向南，左学右庙，完整规制，规模宏大，占地 7,600 多平方米。庙由戟门、泮池、大成殿、殿前两庑、崇圣祠组成。大成殿为重檐歇山顶，面阔五间，进深四间，殿内明间上置八方形重拱藻井，内外梁架和构件遍布彩绘雕饰。大成殿和戟门前各有两对青石透雕龙柱，为清乾隆仙游石雕名匠郭怀师徒之佳作。

梁架遍布彩绘雕饰。（茅玉香 摄）
Beam racks are covered with painted carvings and paintings. (Photo by Mao Yuxiang)

Xianyou Confucius Temple

Period: Qing Dynasty

Address: No. 1 Shifan Road, Xianyou County, Putian City

This temple was built at the beginning of the Song Dynasty on the west side of the city and was later moved to the present site in 1002; then after many years, it was reconstructed in 1780 during the Qing Dynasty. Sitting north and facing south, it covers an area of 7,600 square meters. The left side is a school and the right side is a temple, with symmetrical planning and design. The temple is composed of the arch gate, the pool, Dacheng Hall and its two wing rooms, and the sacred shrine. Dacheng Hall has a double-eave gable and hip roof, and is five rooms wide and four rooms deep. It is decorated with an octagonal caisson ceiling, and the inner and outer beam frames and components are full of painted carvings and paintings. In front of Dacheng Hall and the arch gate, there are two pairs of stone pillars with openwork dragons, which are among the best works of the stone carving master Guo Huai and his apprentices of the Qing Dynasty.

青石透雕龙柱。（游心华 摄）
Stone pillars with openwork dragons; (Photo by You Xinhua)

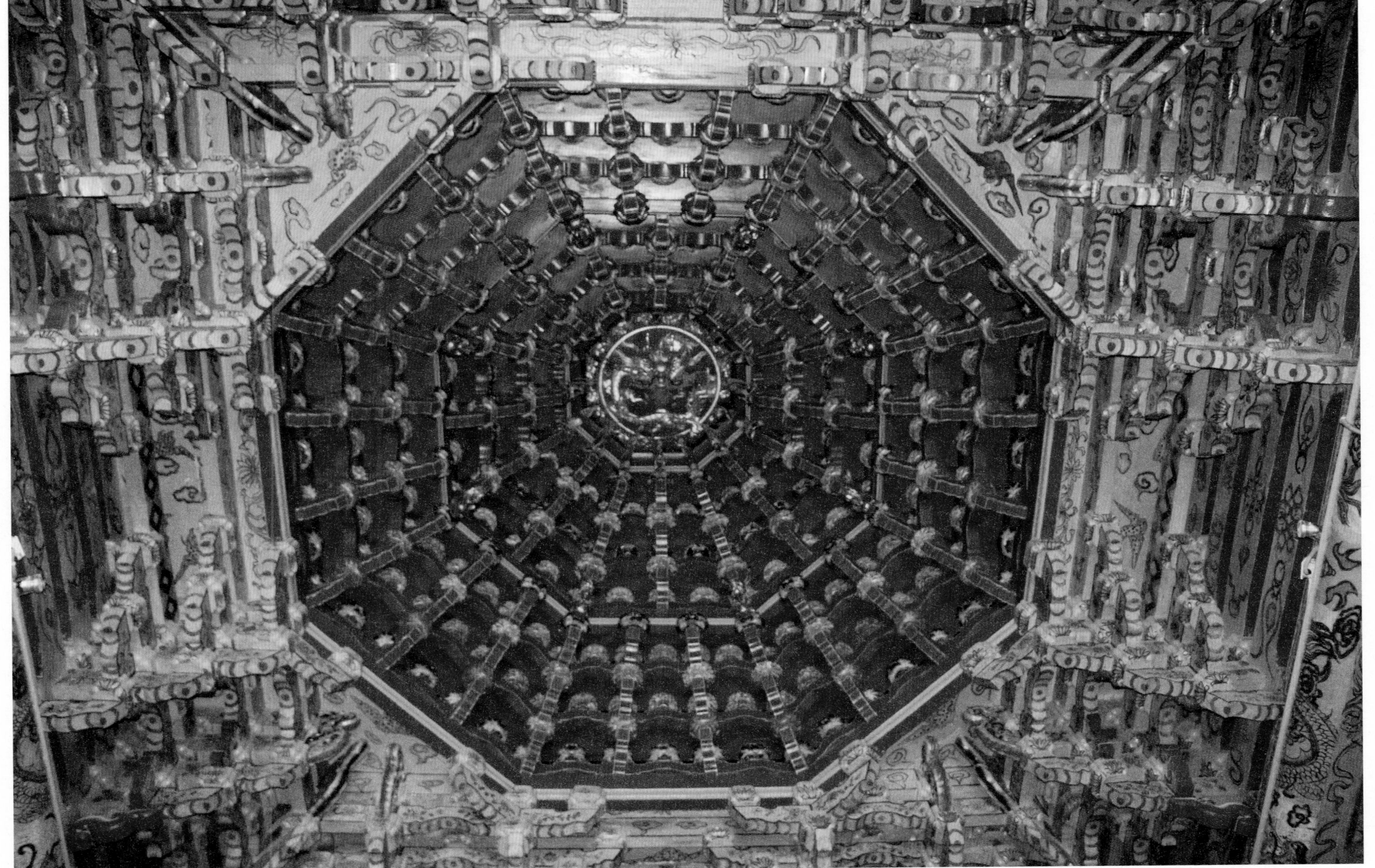

八方形重拱藻井。（茅玉香 摄）
Octagonal caisson ceiling. (Photo by Mao Yuxiang)

大宗伯第

年代：明

地址：莆田市荔城区庙前路

始建于明万历二十年（1592），明代礼部尚书陈经邦府第。按明制一品官府第规格建造，坐西向东，占地面积 1,724 平方米。整座府第由正落和南、北侧落以及 3 个院坪、9 个天井组成，平面呈长方形。正落由倒朝厅、门厅、前厅、中厅、后厅组成，以院坪或天井为间隔。各厅均为悬山顶，抬梁穿斗混合木构架。外大门的门额“大宗伯第”是明隆庆二年（1568）状元罗万化所书。

Minister of Etiquette's Mansion

Period: Ming Dynasty

Address: Miaoqian Road, Licheng District, Putian City

Founded during the Ming Dynasty in 1592, it was the mansion of the Minister of Etiquette, Chen Jingbang. Built according to the specifications for the first class officals' mansions, sitting west and facing east, it covers an area of 1,724 square meters. The whole mansion consists of the middle main quadrangle, south and north side quadrangles, as well as 3 courtyards and 9 patios, forming a rectangular layout. The main quadrangle is composed of the Daochao Hall, the foyer, the front hall, the central hall, and the back hall, with a courtyard or patio connecting them. Each hall has an overhanging gable roof, of post-and-lintel construction combined with column and tie-beam wooden structure. The name of the mansion on the outer arch gate was written by the number one scholar, Luo Wanhua, who won the first in the imperial examination in 1568.

大宗伯第梁架。（刘鹏志 摄）
Timber beams and purlins in the mansion. (Photo by Liu Pengzhi)

俯瞰大宗伯第。（陈晓 摄）
Overlooking the mansion. (Photo by Chen Xiao)

南平古厝

Ancient Buildings in Nanping

宝山寺大殿

年代：元

地址：南平市顺昌县大干镇上湖村

元至正二十三年（1363）建，明万历四十二年（1614）局部维修。大殿为悬山顶，面阔五间，进深四间。除实榻大门是木作外，柱、梁、斗拱、檩、屋面瓦件、脊饰、鸱吻等构件均由仿木构砂岩制成。殿身梁架按木构形制作出梭柱、月梁、弯曲的劄牵及两端收分的檩条。柱础有素面、覆盆、覆莲三种形式，并与柱顶石连为一体。随脊檩下皮刻有元代修建纪年。宝山寺大殿是全国罕见的、有明确修建纪年的古代仿木石构建筑，乃精品之作，也为研究中国南方宋元建筑形式及技术发展提供了实物例证。

Baoshan Temple Hall

Period: Yuan Dynasty

Address: Shanghu Village, Dagan Town, Shunchang County, Nanping City

This hall was built in 1363 during the Yuan Dynasty and partially repaired in 1614 during the Ming Dynasty. The main hall has an overhanging gable roof, and is five rooms wide and four rooms deep. Aside from the solid door, which is made of wood, the pillars, beams, brackets, purlins, roof tiles, and ridge ornaments are all made of imitation-wood sandstone. According to the structural pattern, the beamed frame of the hall is made of shuttle-shaped columns, crescent beams, curved pullers, and purlins that are soaring at both ends. The pillar bases show three patterns: plain, basin and lotus, and are connected to the rising pillars and capitals. The construction date in the Yuan Dynasty is carved at the bottom of the ridge purlin. Baoshan Temple Hall is a rare ancient wood-like stone building with clearly inscribed construction date. It is an outstanding workpiece, and provides a good example for the study of architectural form and technical development of the Song and Yuan dynasties in southern China.

宝山寺大殿石梁。（余少雄 摄）
The stone beams of Baoshan Temple Hall. (Photo by Yu Shaoxiong)

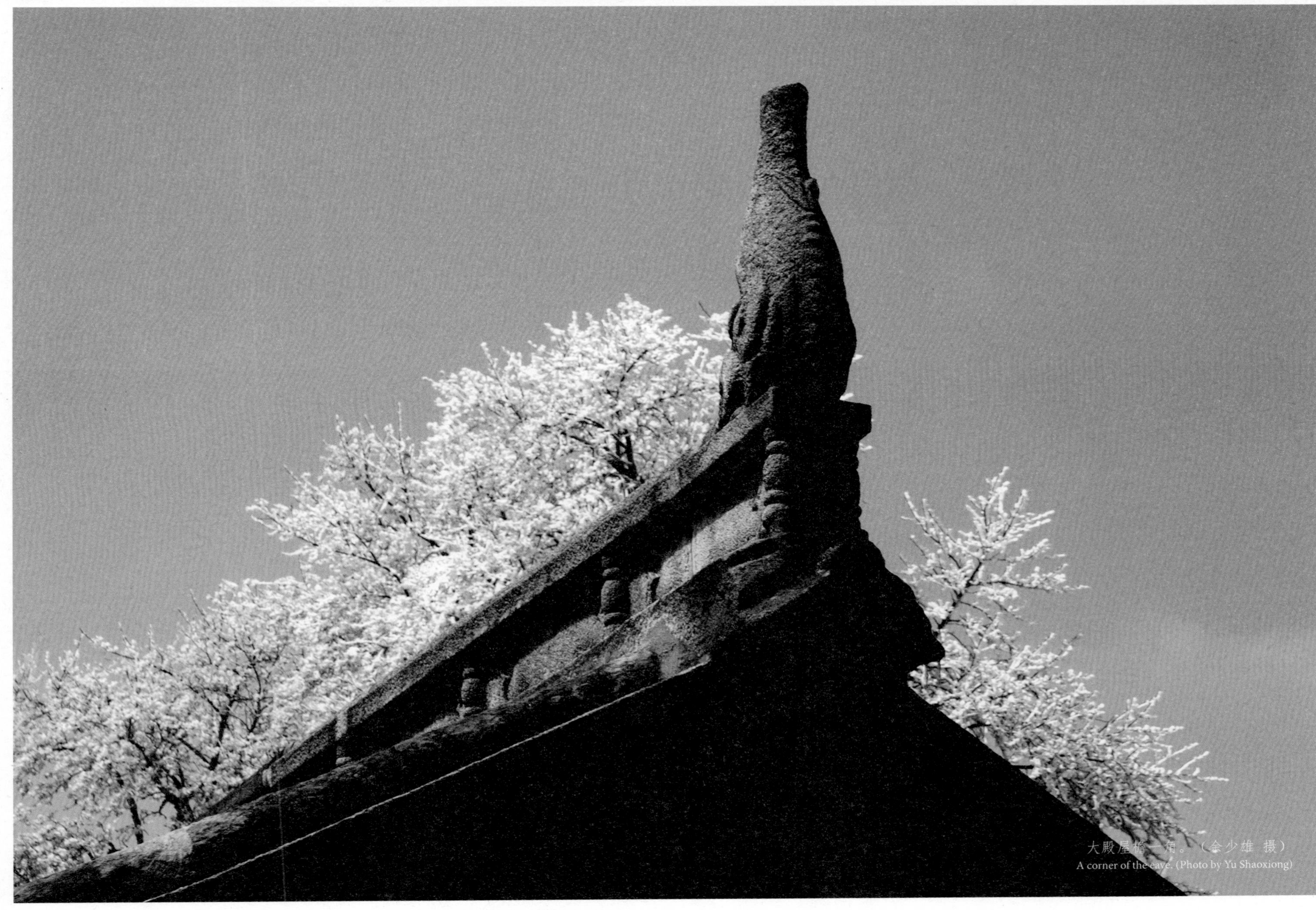

大殿屋檐一角。（余少雄 摄）
A corner of the eave. (Photo by Yu Shaoxiong)

宝严寺大殿内部斗拱、梁栿及彩绘。（余晓勤 摄）
Beams, bracket sets and coloured patterns in Baoyan Temple Hall. (Photo by Yu Xiaoqin)

宝严寺大殿

年代：明

地址：南平市邵武市新建路 6 号

唐大顺元年（890）始建，现存大殿为明嘉靖十二年（1533）重建。大殿坐北朝南，平面呈正方形，占地面积约 400 平方米。重檐歇山顶，抬梁穿斗混合木构架，面阔与进深均为五间。明间为五铺作昂形斜拱，普柏枋与阑额呈“T”字形断面，檐柱上为象鼻斗拱，均体现明代建筑特色。明间四椽袱下皮存明代重建纪年墨书。梁栿、斗拱均彩绘佛像、花卉鸟兽及几何图案，是明代著名画家严宗儒、上官伯达手迹。

Baoyan Temple Hall

Period: Ming Dynasty

Address: No. 6 Xinjian Road, Shaowu City, Nanping City

Baoyan Temple was built in 890 during the Tang Dynasty, and the extant hall was rebuilt in 1533 during the Ming Dynasty. The main hall sits north and faces south; the layout is a quadrangle, covering an area of about 400 square meters. It has a double-eave gable and hip roof, along with post-and-lintel construction combined with a column and tie-beam wooden structure. The width and depth are five rooms each. The five bracket sets in the middle were made into an angled oblique arch. The tie-beam and the architrave (the main support beam on top of the columns) with a T-shaped cross-section, and the elephant-trunk shaped brackets on the eave columns all embody the architectural features of the Ming Dynasty. The handwriting of the reconstruction date in the Ming Dynasty has been preserved on the original four rafters. The beams and bracket sets have paintings of Buddha, flowers, birds, beasts and geometric patterns, painted by the famous Ming Dynasty painters, Yan Zongru and Shangguan Boda.

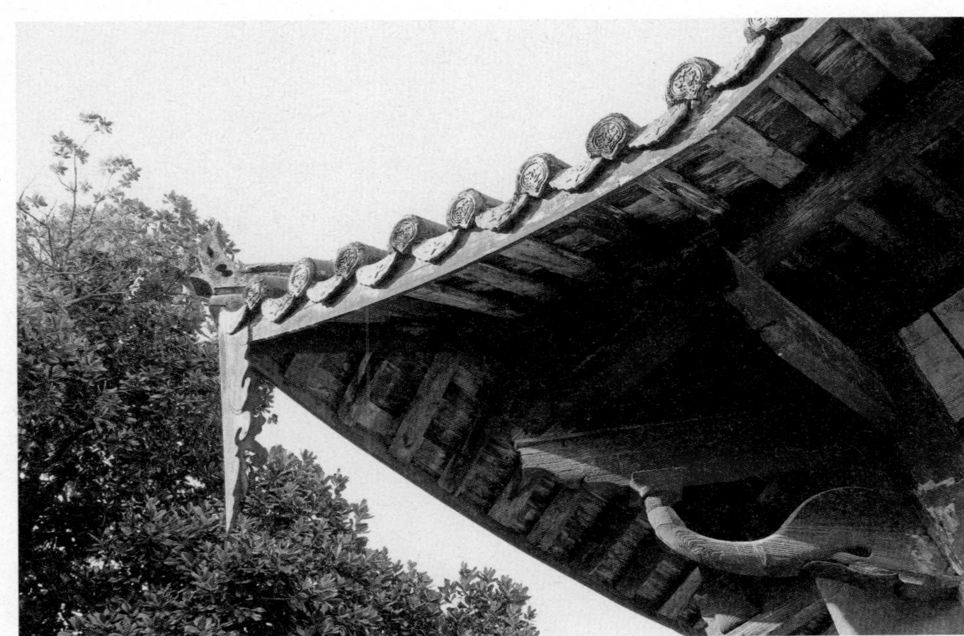

具有浓烈南平邵武地方特色的象鼻斗拱。（余晓勤 摄）
The elephant-trunk shaped bracket with a strong local style. (Photo by Yu Xiaoqin)

覆莲盆石柱础。（余晓勤 摄）
The lotus pattern base. (Photo by Yu Xiaoqin)

建瓯东岳庙

时代：清

地址：南平市建瓯市建安街道白鹤山南麓

始建年代不详，清康熙十一年（1672）重建。建筑群坐北朝南，依山而建，自南向北依次为金刚殿（山门）、阎罗殿、戏台、圣帝殿。圣帝殿为重檐歇山顶，抬梁穿斗混合木构架，面阔五间，两侧带边廊，进深七柱带前廊。屋面坡度倾斜达 50 度，具有典型的闽北山区风格。殿内金柱直径粗大，达 75—78 厘米；覆盆式柱础为明代风格。

Jian'ou Dongyue Temple

Period: Qing Dynasty

Address: South foot of Baihe Mountain, Jian'an Street, Jian'ou City, Nanping City

The original date of this temple's construction is unknown, but it was rebuilt in 1672 during the Qing Dynasty. The architectural complex sits north and faces south and was built on the mountain. From south to north, there is Jingang Hall (archway), Yanluo Hall, the stage and Shengdi Hall. Shengdi Hall has a double-eave gable and hip roof, with both post-and-lintel construction and column-and-tie-beam construction. It is five rooms wide with side porches on both sides, and seven-pillars deep with a front porch. The roof slope is almost 50 degrees, and it shows the typical style of northern Fujian mountain areas. The diameter of the columns in the hall is large, reaching 75—78cm; the basin-pattern column bases are in the style of the Ming Dynasty.

阳光下的东岳庙圣帝殿。（魏永青 摄）

Shengdi Hall of Dongyue Temple in the sunshine. (Photo by Wei Yongqing)

俯瞰东岳庙。（魏永青 摄）
Overlooking Dongyue Temple. (Photo by Wei Yongqing)

云峰寺大殿

年代：明

地址：南平市浦城县水北街镇曹村村

始建于唐，大殿重建于明成化十八年（1482）。殿身坐西朝东，占地面积 172 平方米，重檐歇山顶，面阔三间，进深四间。大殿的大木构架为殿阁式抬梁造，属“前后七檩、殿身分心槽加副阶周匝”类型，沿袭了宋代《营造法式》制度。大殿里普柏枋与阑额呈“T”字形断面、“插柱造”、梭柱与覆盆式柱础等，均为早期建筑手法。覆莲式石柱础上刻“成化拾捌”等字。寺内存成化十四年（1478）《云峰禅寺碑记》及弘治二年（1489）《上原里云峰寺记》等碑刻。

Yunfeng Temple Hall

Period: Ming Dynasty

Address: Caocun Village, Shuibeijie Town, Pucheng County, Nanping City

The temple was founded in the Tang Dynasty, and the main hall was rebuilt in 1482 during the Ming Dynasty. The temple, siting west and facing east, covers an area of 172 square meters. It has a double-eave gable and hip roof and is three rooms wide and four rooms deep. The large wooden structure of the main hall is made of pavilion-style post-and-lintel construction, following the Song Dynasty “Building Style” system. The “T” shaped cross-sections of tie-beam and the architrave in the main hall, the “pillar-making” style, shuttle-shaped columns and basin-pattern column foundations are all early architectural techniques. The construction date is engraved on the base of the lotus-pattern stone column. The stone inscriptions—“Inscriptions on Yunfeng Temple” (made in 1478) and “Inscriptions on Yunfeng Temple in Shangyuanli” (made in 1489)—attest to its history.

云峰寺大殿檐角。（徐强 摄）
The double eaves of Yunfeng Temple Hall. (Photo by Xu Qiang)

云峰寺大殿。（张万春 摄）
Yunfeng Temple Hall. (Photo by Zhang Wanchun)

建瓯文庙

年代：清

地址：南平市建瓯市仓长路 163 号

北宋宝元年间（1038—1040）始建于建州建溪门内之东，南宋建炎年间（1127—1130）毁于战乱，后重建文庙于建州州学，绍兴年间（1131—1162）建州州学改为建宁府府学，始称建宁府文庙，绍兴十四年（1144）毁于水，之后屡有兴废，明永乐初年为避水患，府学及文庙迁移新建至现今地址。现存有棂星门、步云桥、泮池、戟门、大成殿，为清代重建，其中大成殿重建于同治八年至光绪五年（1869—1879）间，重檐歇山顶，面阔五间，进深四间。明、次间施天花，全殿有楠木柱 34 根，内柱间横额和普柏枋呈 T 字形。殿内存明代孔子画像碑 1 方。

Jian'ou Confucius Temple

Period: Qing Dynasty

Address: No. 163 Cangchang Road, Jian'ou City, Nanping City

Originally built from 1038 to 1040 during the Northern Song Dynasty, this temple was situated on the east side of Jianximen in Jianzhou. During the period of Jianyan in the Southern Song Dynasty (1127—1130), it was destroyed by war. The Confucius Temple was rebuilt inside Jianzhou's official school, and later changed to Jianning's official school and named Jianning Confucius Temple during 1131—1162. But it was again destroyed by water in 1144. After that, it prospered but was destroyed repeatedly. In the early years of the Yongle period during the Ming Dynasty, in order to avoid floods, the school and the Confucius Temple were relocated to the present site. Rebuilt during the Qing Dynasty, there is Lingxingmen (an arch gate), Buyun Bridge, the Pan Pool, the arch gate Jimen and Dacheng Hall left. Dacheng Hall was rebuilt from 1869 to 1879, with a double-eave gable and hip roof, and is five rooms wide and four rooms deep. There are ceilings for the main and side halls and altogether 34 nanmu (wooden) pillars stand there, and the inner pillars are connected by beams and architraves in a T-shape. There is also a monument tablet of Confucius set up during the Ming Dynasty.

殿内孔子画像碑。（魏永青 摄）
The Confucius Tablet Monument in the hall. (Photo by Wei Yongqing)

在建瓯文庙研学的孩子。（魏永青 摄）
Children at a field study in Jian'ou Confucius Temple. (Photo by Wei Yongqing)

建瓯文庙大成殿。（魏永青 摄）
Dacheng Hall in Jian'ou Confucius Temple. (Photo by Wei Yongqing)

下梅大夫第

年代：清

地址：南平市武夷山市武夷街道下梅村

清乾隆年间（1736—1795）建。户主邹英章为下梅著名茶商，建筑因其诰封奉直大夫而得名。坐北朝南，由主落、东厅和后花园组成。主落为三进合院式建筑，包括前厅、中厅、后厅、过厅，门面砖雕呈现精美的人物故事、花卉、祥禽瑞兽等图案。过厅左侧开边门，通东厅。东厅后墙两侧开边门通往名为“小樊川”的后花园。建筑四面砖砌封火墙围护。前坪两侧有拴马石和旗杆石。

Xiamei Dafu Mansion

Period: Qing Dynasty

Address: Xiamei Village, Wuyi Street, Wuyishan City, Nanping City

This mansion was built during the Qianlong period (1736—1795) of the Qing Dynasty. The owner of the house, Zou Yingzhang, was a famous tea merchant in Xiamei. The building was named after his imperial honorary position. Sitting north and facing south, it is composed of the main building, the east hall and the back garden. The main building is a three-entry courtyard-style building, which includes the front hall, the middle hall, the back hall, and the corridor hall. The brick carvings on the facade display exquisite patterns of characters, flowers, birds and animals. The side door on the left side of the corridor hall opens to the east hall. On the sides of the back wall of the east hall, there are side doors opening to the back garden named “Little Fanchuan”. The four sides of the mansion are enclosed by fire walls. There are stone horse ties and pedestals for flagpoles on both sides of the front yard.

下梅大夫第的精美砖雕和石雕。（郑友裕 / 宋春 摄）
The exquisite brick and stone carvings in Xiamei Dafu Mansion. (Photo by Zheng Youyu & Song Chun)

下梅大夫第砖雕门楼。（郑友裕 摄）
The arch gate with brick carvings of Dafu Mansion. (Photo by Zheng Youyu)

龙岩古厝

~~~

Ancient Buildings in Longyan

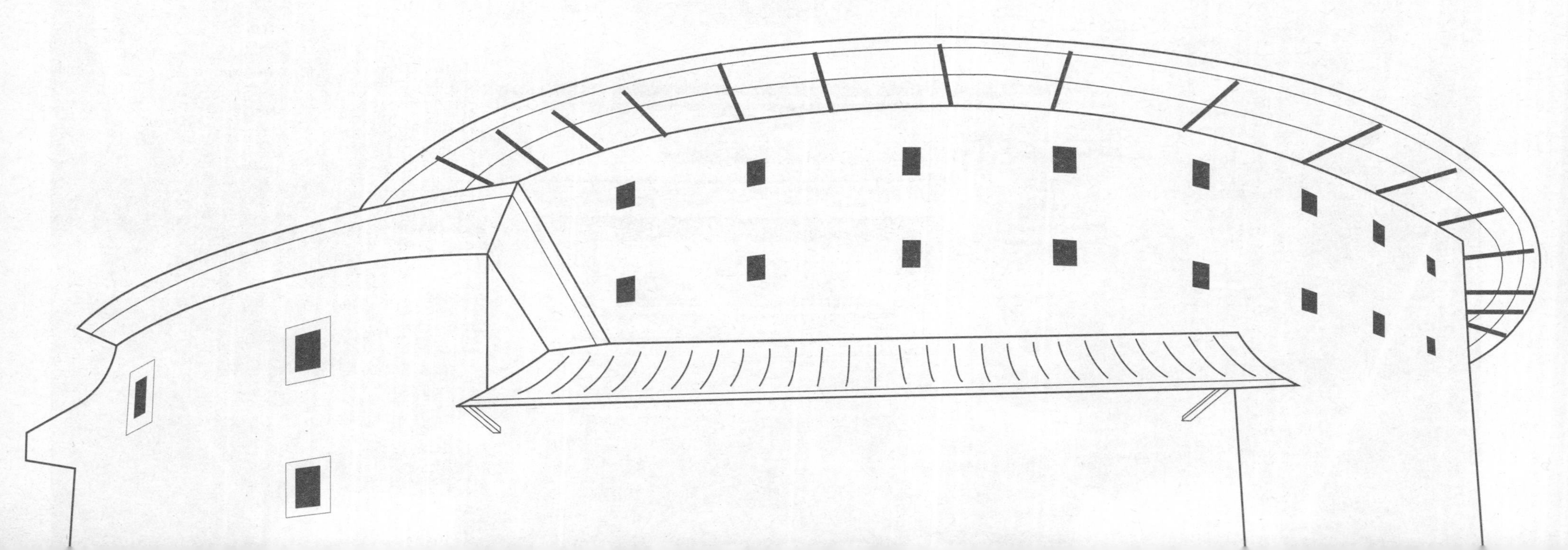
~~~

洪坑土楼群之福裕楼

年代：清

地址：龙岩市永定区湖坑镇洪坑村

洪坑土楼群错落分布于洪川溪两岸，由方形的光裕楼、福兴楼、奎聚楼、庆城楼和府第式（又称五凤楼）的福裕楼及圆形的如升楼、振成楼等组成。

福裕楼建于清光绪六年（1880），坐西朝东，占地4,000平方米。由中轴线的门楼、厅堂、正楼（后堂）和两侧横楼组成三横两纵的府第式土楼，以内通廊相接。建筑内二层以上木地板均以青砖铺面，既防火又隔音。厅堂雕梁画栋，装饰精美。整座建筑呈中轴对称，屋顶错落，气势轩昂，是府第式土楼的杰出代表。

Fuyulou of Hongkeng Tulou Cluster

Period: Qing Dynasty

Address: Hongkeng Village, Hukeng Town, Yongding District, Longyan City

Scattered on both sides of Hongchuan Stream, Hongkeng Tulou Cluster consists of the square-shaped Guangyulou, Fuxinglou, Kuijulou, Qingchenglou, the mansion-style Fuyulou (also known as five-phoenix-style Tulou), and round buildings such as Rushenglou, Zhenchenglou.

Fuyulou, built in 1880 during the Qing Dynasty, sits west and faces east and covers an area of 4,000 square meters. Along the central axis there is the arch gate, the front hall, the main building (rear hall) and rooms on both sides, which form a three-horizontal and two-vertical mansion-style Fujian Tulou, connected by interior corridors. The wooden floors above the second floor in the building are all covered with grey bricks, which are both fireproof and soundproof. The hall is decorated with carved beams and other beautiful decorations. As an outstanding example of the mansion-style Tulou, the whole building is symmetrical around the central axis, with rolling roofs arranged in a magnificent style.

府第式土楼福裕楼。（胡家新 摄）
The mansion-style Fuyulou. (By Hu Jiaxin)

洪坑土楼群。（胡家新 摄）
Hongkeng Tulou Cluster. (Photo by Hu Jiaxin)

高北土楼群之承启楼

年代：明

地址：龙岩市永定区高头乡高北村

高北土楼群由方形的五云楼、世泽楼和圆形的承启楼和侨福楼组成。楼群背靠山，楼与楼之间以青石板小道相连，高头溪自东向西从楼群前穿流而过。

承启楼，外环始建于明崇祯年间（1628—1644），而后从外到内依次建第二、三、四环，清康熙四十八年（1709）落成，占地面积 5,376 平方米。外环为主楼，高四层，一、二层不开窗，分别为厨房和粮仓，三、四层为卧室，设内通廊；二环高两层，楼下为客厅或饭厅，楼上为卧室；三环单层，为子女读书的私塾；四环为主堂，单层，比三环稍低。形成外高内低、逐环递减的四圈同心环建筑格局。

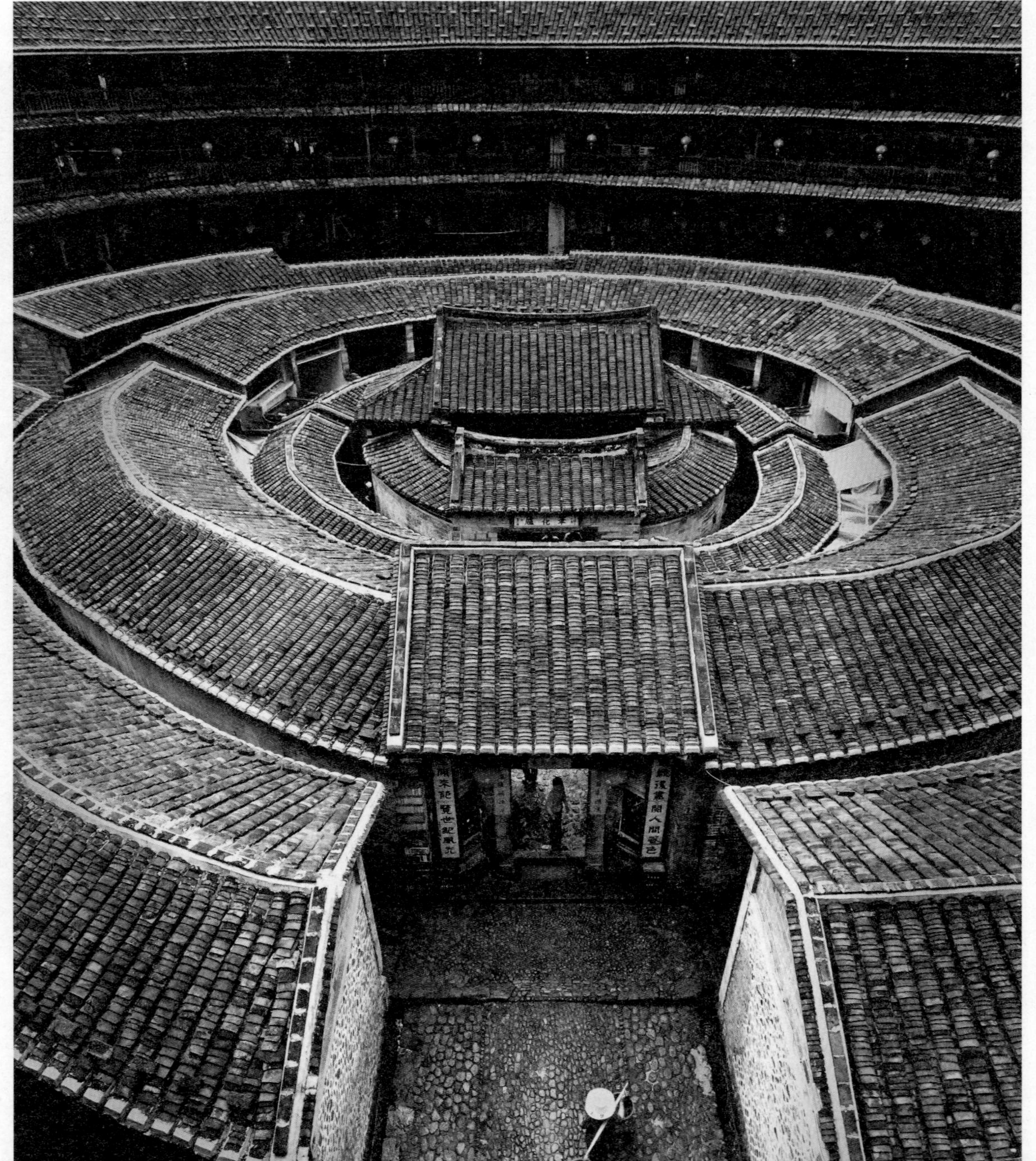

Chengqilou of Gaobei Tulou Cluster

Period: Ming Dynasty

Address: Gaobei Village, Gaotou Township, Yongding District, Longyan City

Gaobei Tulou Cluster consists of the square Wuyunlou, Shizelou and the circular Chengqilou, Qiaofulou. The buildings enjoy a mountain background and are connected by blue slab-stone trails. Gaotou Stream flows in front of the buildings from east to west, bringing fresh water and a cleansing breeze throughout.

Chengqilou's outer ring was built from 1628 to 1644 during the Ming Dynasty . Then the second, third, and fourth rings were built in order from the outside to the inside, and the whole building was completed in 1709 during the Qing Dynasty, covering an area of 5,376 square meters. The four-floor outer ring is the main building, with no windows on the first and second floors, which are for the kitchens and granaries; and the third and fourth floors are for bedrooms with internal corridors. The second ring is two floors high, with the living rooms or dining rooms downstairs, and the bedrooms upstairs. Being single-story, the third ring serves as a private school for children. As the ancestral hall, the single-story fourth ring is slightly lower than the third ring. This layout forms a four-concentric ring building pattern with a decreasing elevation from the outer ring to the lowest inner ring.

承启楼内景。（胡家新 摄）
The interior view of Chengqilou. (Photo by Hu Jiaxin)

高北土楼群。（胡家新 摄）
Gaobei Tulou Cluster. (Photo by Hu Jiaxin)

初溪土楼群之集庆楼

年代：明至清

地址：龙岩市永定区下洋镇初溪村

初溪土楼群由从明永乐年间（1403—1424）至 1978 年建造的十余座土楼组成，包括圆形的集庆楼、余庆楼、庚庆楼、善庆楼，方形的绳庆楼，长方形的华庆楼、锡庆楼、藩庆楼，椭圆形的福庆楼及六角形的共庆楼等。

集庆楼，坐南朝北，两环圆形土楼，占地面积 2,826 平方米。外环一至四层原为内通廊式，清乾九年（1744）维修时，对原来的结构稍作改变，底层仍为内通廊式，二层以上改为单元，每个单元各设一楼梯。单元与单元之间的廊道以杉木板相隔。外环第四层外墙有 9 个瞭望台，楼后侧底层设有一秘密通道，用于紧急疏散。主堂位于内院中心，内环与主堂均为单层。

Jiqinglou of Chuxi Tulou Cluster

Period: Ming to Qing dynasties

Address: Chuxi Village, Xiayang Town, Yongding District, Longyan City

Chuxi Tulou Cluster consists of more than ten Tulou built from 1403 to 1424 during the Ming Dynasty up to 1978, including the round Jiqinglou, Yuqinglou, Gengqinglou, Shanqinglou, the square Shengqinglou, the rectangular Huaqinglou, Xiqinglou, Fanqinglou, the oval Fuqinglou and the hexagonal Gongqinglou, etc.

Jiqinglou, which sits south facing to the north, is a circular Tulou with two rings, and covers an area of 2,826 square meters. The first to fourth floors of the outer ring originally had inner corridors. In a remodeling in 1744 during the Qing Dynasty, the original structure was slightly changed. The bottom floor retains its inner corridor, while the 2nd to 4 floors are divided into units, each with a staircase. The corridors between the units are separated by fir wood boards. There are 9 watchtowers on the outer wall on the fourth floor of the outer ring and a secret passageway on the ground floor at the back of the building, which is used for emergency evacuation. The main hall is located in the center of the inner courtyard. The inner ring and the main hall are both single story.

初溪土楼群。（胡家新 摄）

Chuxi Tulou Cluster. (Photo by Hu Jiaxin)

双环圆形土楼集庆楼。（胡家新 摄）
The double-ring circular Jiqinglou. (Photo by Hu Jiaxin)

衍香楼

年代：清

地址：龙岩市永定区湖坑镇新南村

位于土楼沟景区，建于清道光二十二年（1842），坐东北朝西南，单环圆形土楼，内院中心建祖堂，占地面积 4,300 平方米。楼高 4 层，直径 40 米，内通廊式，外墙厚度自下而上逐层递减。一、二层不开窗，分别为厨房和粮仓，三、四层为卧室。全楼设一大门，门楣上方设防火水槽，以防火攻。

Yanxianglou

Period: Qing Dynasty

Address: Xinnan Village, Hukeng Town, Yongding District, Longyan City

Located in Tulougou Scenic Area, it was built in 1842 during the Qing Dynasty. It sits northeast and faces southwest. It is a single-ring circular Tulou and there is an ancestral hall amidst the inner courtyard. With interior corridors, the building is 4 stories high, 40 meters in diameter, and the outer wall decreasing in width gradually from bottom to top. The first and second floors do not have open windows, and are used for kitchens and granaries, while the third and fourth floors for bedrooms. There is only one entrance for the whole building with a fire-proof water sink above the lintel for fire protection.

美丽如画的衍香楼。（赖永生 摄）
The picturesque Yanxianglou. (Photo by Lai Yongsheng)

土楼沟景区。（胡家新 摄）
Tulougou Scenic Area. (Photo by Hu Jiaxin)

四堡书坊建筑

Sibao Shufang Complex

龙岩连城四堡，是明清时期与北京、汉口、江西浒湾齐名的雕版印刷基地。四堡刻书业始于明代中晚期，至清康熙初年开始兴盛，到了乾隆、嘉庆年间进入全盛时期。在清咸丰、同治年间到民国，四堡刻书业逐渐走向衰落直至终结。目前四堡镇还拥有着保存比较完整的雕版印刷遗存——书坊建筑、刻本书籍印刷工具等。书坊建筑是融居住、制作、销售于一体的家庭作坊式建筑。

Sibao of Liancheng in Longyan City was one of the four major wood engraving printing bases during the Ming and Qing dynasties along with Beijing, Hankou and Huwan in Jiangxi. Sibao engraving industry began during the middle to late Ming Dynasty and prospered in the early 1660s during the Qing Dynasty. It reached its heyday between 1736 and 1796, and then declined. The building retains a relatively complete setup for engraving, such as printing workshops and tools for printing. Shufang was a family-workshop-style building that integrated rooms for residence, production and sales.

古书坊门楼。（陈银池 摄）
The arch gate of an old Shufang where books were printed and sold. (Photo by Chen Yinchi)

四堡书坊建筑群俯瞰。（胡家新 摄）
Overlooking Sibao Shufang Complex. (Photo by Hu Jiaxin)

林兰堂

年代：清

地址：龙岩市连城县四堡镇马屋村

林兰堂建于清嘉庆十一年（1806），是四堡民居建筑与印刷作坊合二为一的典型代表。书坊创办人为马源锡，印刷书籍销往江南各省及东南亚诸国。坐西朝东，临河而建，占地3,200平方米。平面上采用双座堂屋（兆宜、兆广）、双座大门并列而建。每座堂屋建筑的主座均由前厅、中厅、后厅及后楼组成，两座堂屋建筑的两侧及中间各有一列横屋。主座为生活居室，两侧横屋为雕版印刷作坊，布局上充分体现生活和生产功能的有机结合。

Linlan Hall

Period: Qing Dynasty

Address: Mawu Village, Sibao Town, Liancheng County, Longyan City

Linlan Hall was built in 1806 during the Qing Dynasty, and it is a typical example of the combination of Sibao residential architecture and the printing workshop. The founder of Linlan Hall was Ma Yuanxi, and books printed here were sold to provinces south of the Yangtse River, as well as some Southeast Asian countries. Sitting west and facing east, the buildings were near the river and covers an area of 3,200 square meters. The two halls (Zhaoyi and Zhaoguang) and two entrance arch gates were built side by side. The main layout of each building is composed of the front hall, the middle hall, the rear hall and a back building. There is a row of houses on both sides and in the middle of the two main halls. The main halls were residential areas, and the wing rooms on both sides were engraving and printing workshops. The layout fully reflects the organic combination of living and production functions.

林兰堂内部。（马昭泰 摄）

The interior view of Linlan Hall. (Photo by Ma Zhaotai)

林兰堂俯瞰。（胡家新 摄）
Overlooking Linlan Hall. (Photo by Hu Jiaxin)

定敷公祠

年代：清

地址：龙岩市连城县四堡镇雾阁村

清乾隆二十一年（1756）始建，原为邹氏祖祠。坐东朝西，由下堂（门厅）、上堂和左右回廊组成。下堂前廊做四柱三间三楼式门楼，如意斗拱叠涩挑檐。上堂为硬山顶，面阔五间，进深三间。现辟为中国四堡雕版印刷博物馆。

作为雕版印刷博物馆的定敷公祠。（胡家新 摄）
Sir Dingfu Memorial Hall is used as the Sibao Wood Engraving Printing Museum. (Photo by Hu Jiaxin)

Sir Dingfu Memorial Hall

Period: Qing Dynasty

Address: Wuge Village, Sibao Town, Liancheng County, Longyan City

This ancestral hall was built in 1756 during the Qing Dynasty and was originally the Zou Family's Ancestral Hall. Sitting east and facing to the west, it is comprised of the lower entrance hall, the back upper hall and left and right corridors. The front porch of the lower hall is three rooms wide with three arches and four pillars deep, and the bracket arches are stacked high to raise the eaves. The upper hall has a flush gable roof, and is five rooms wide and three rooms deep. It is open daily as the Sibao Wood Engraving Printing Museum of China.

定敷公祠内景。（胡家新 摄）
The interior view of Sir Dingfu Memorial Hall. (Photo by Hu Jiaxin)

培田古民居一隅（王福平 摄）
A corner of Peitian ancient buildings (Photo by Wang Fuping)

培田村古建筑群

培田村位于龙岩市连城县宣和乡，拥有类型丰富和数量众多的古建筑、独特的聚落格局及优美的自然生态景观。培田村古民居建筑群始建于南宋，明中叶初具规模，鼎盛于康乾盛世，占地 71,900 平方米。明清时期先后修建了 50 多座宗祠、书院、民居、寺庙、牌坊等，至今仍保存完好。

Ancient Buildings in Peitian Village

Peitian Village is located in Xuanhe Township, Liancheng County, Longyan City. It has numerous beautifully-styled ancient buildings and a unique settlement pattern all in a fascinating natural ecological setting. The ancient residential building complex of Peitian Village was first built in the Southern Song Dynasty, and it took shape in the middle of the Ming Dynasty. During the Ming and Qing dynasties, more than 50 ancestral halls, academies, residences, temples, archways, etc. were set up successively, covering an area of 71,900 square meters, and all of them remain intact today.

培田村古建筑群俯瞰。（胡家新 摄）
Overlooking the ancient buildings in Peitian Village. (Photo by Hu Jiaxin)

继述堂正门。（胡家新 摄）
The arch gate of Jishu Hall. (Photo by Hu Jiaxin)

继述堂（大夫第）

年代：清

地址：龙岩市连城县宣和乡培田村

清道光九年（1829）始建。坐西向东，占地面积6,900平方米。由主座的前厅、中厅、大厅、后厅及左一列、右三列横屋组成，整个建筑共有18个厅、24个天井、72个房间。闽西客家人通常将这种院落重重、天井众多的合院式建筑称之为“九厅十八井”。

Jishu Mansion (Dafu Mansion)

Period: Qing Dynasty

Address: Peitian Village, Xuanhe Township, Liancheng County, Longyan City

Jishu Mansion was first built in 1829 during the Qing Dynasty. Sitting west and facing east, it covers an area of 6,900 square meters. It consists of the front hall, the middle hall, the central hall, the back hall, one row of wing rooms on the left and three rows on the right. The whole complex has 18 halls, 24 patios and 72 rooms. The Hakka people in Western Fujian usually refer to this kind of courtyard-style building with many courtyards and patios as “nine halls and eighteen wells”.

继述堂一瞥。（胡家新 摄）
A glance at Jishu Mansion. (Photo by Hu Jiaxin)

规模宏大的继述堂。（胡家新 摄）
Grand Jishu Hall. (Photo by Hu Jiaxin)

衡公祠

Sir Henggong Memorial Hall

年代：清

地址：龙岩市连城县宣和乡培田村

又称继德堂。始建于清，坐西朝东，专为祭祀吴氏先祖而建，为吴氏十五世祖祠堂。由门厅、正厅和两廊组成合院式建筑，占地面积 148 平方米。门楼为四柱三间三楼式，如意斗拱叠涩挑檐。正厅为硬山顶，面阔三间，进深四间。众多彩绘、雕花精美细腻。

Period: Qing Dynasty

Address: Peitian Village, Xuanhe Township, Liancheng County, Longyan City

Also known as "Jide Hall", this hall was first built during the Qing Dynasty and sits west, facing to the east. It was built specifically for the veneration of Wu clan ancestors and has been the ancestral hall for fifteen generations of the Wu clan. The entrance hall, the main hall and the two corridors form a courtyard-style building, covering an area of 148 square meters. The arch gatehouse is four columns deep, three rooms wide with three arches, and the bracket arches are stacked high to raise the eaves. The main hall has a flush gable roof and is three rooms wide and four rooms deep. Many paintings and carved flowers add to the exquisite decoration.

衡公祠内景。（马碧锋 摄）
The interior view of Sir Henggong Memorial Hall. (Photo by Ma Bifeng)

衡公祠门楼。（马碧锋 摄）
The arch gate of Sir Henggong Memorial Hall. (Photo by Ma Bifeng)

西陂天后宫

年代：明至清

地址：龙岩市永定区高陂镇西陂村

明嘉靖二十一年（1542）始建，清康熙元年（1662）落成。天后宫坐东南朝西北，分为前、中、后三部分。前部为大门、戏台及两边的看楼；中部为大宝殿及厢房；后部为七层楼阁、孔庙以及科举时代用于会文讲学的登云馆。楼阁的一层至三层为四方形，土木结构；四至七层转为八角形，五层为砖木结构，六、七层为纯木结构。一层至四层分别供奉天后圣母、关帝君、文昌帝君、魁星尊神雕像，五层供奉仓颉先师柱牌。

Xibi Tianhou Temple

Period: Ming to Qing dynasties

Address: Xibei Village, Gaobi Town, Yongding District, Longyan City

Xibi Tianhou Temple was started in 1542 during the Ming Dynasty and completed in 1662 during the Qing Dynasty. Sitting southeast and facing to the northwest, the temple is divided into three parts: front, middle and back. The front part has the entrance arch gate, the stage and the two sides of a viewing tower; the middle part consists of Dabao Hall and wing rooms; the rear part is a seven-story pavilion, with a Confucius temple and Dengyun Hall used for lectures during the Imperial Examination period. The first to third floors of the pavilion were built in a square construction; the fourth to seventh floors are octagonal. The fifth floor is of brick and wood structure, while the sixth and seventh floors are of entirely wood structure. The first to fourth floors are dedicated to the statues of Goddess Mazu, God Guandi, God Wenchang and God Kuixing, while the fifth floor is dedicated to the soul tablet of Cangjie.

西陂天后宫内部。（胡家新 摄）
The interior of Xibi Tianhou Temple. (Photo by Hu Jiaxin)

西陂天后宫大门。（胡家新 摄）
The arch gate of Xibi Tianhou Temple. (Photo by Hu Jiaxin)

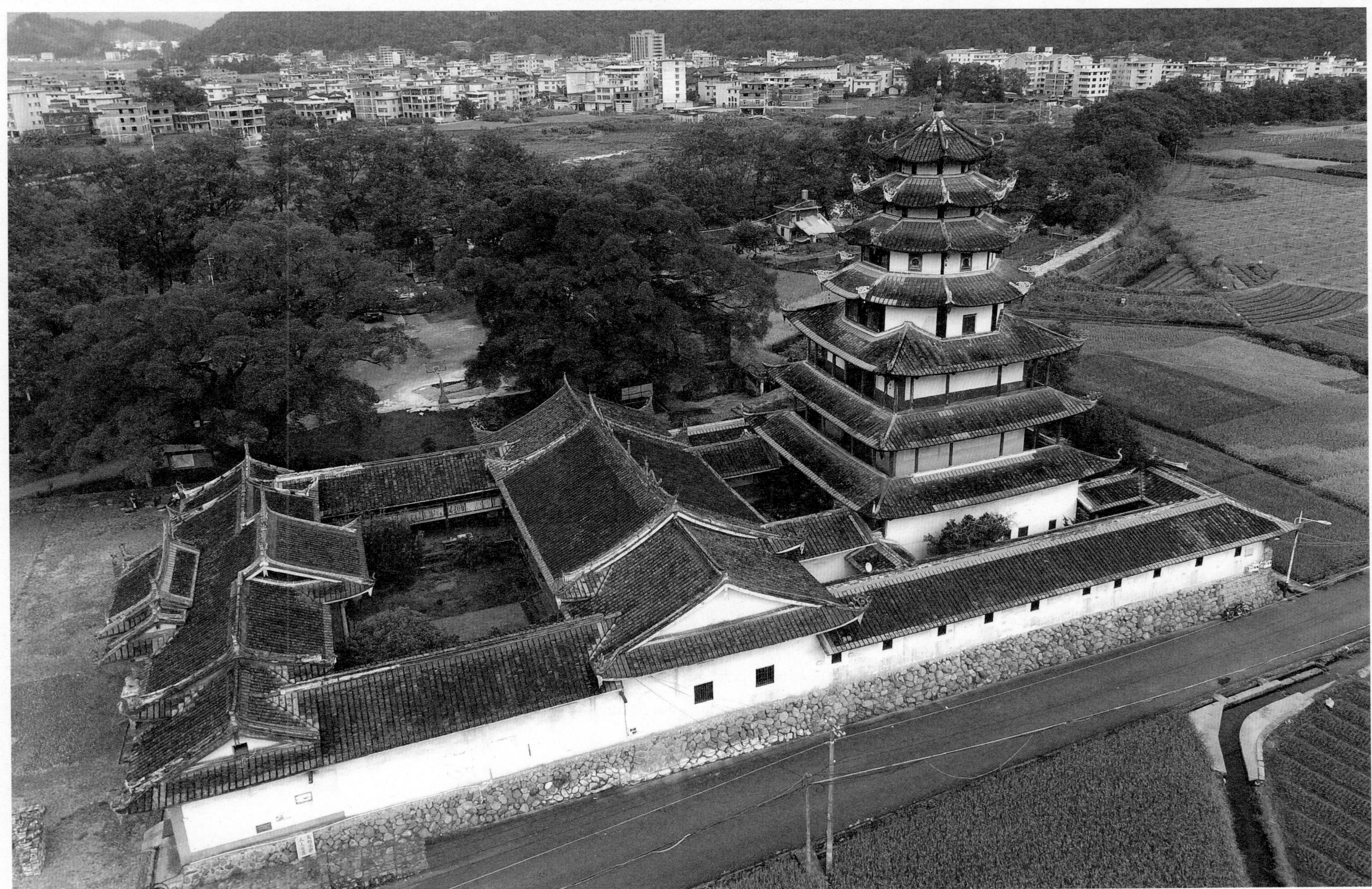

西陂天后宫俯瞰。（胡家新 摄）
Overlooking Xibi Tianhou Temple. (Photo by Hu Jiaxin)

官田李氏大宗祠

年代：清

地址：龙岩市上杭县稔田镇官田村

也称惇叙堂，建于清道光十六至十九年（1836—1839），乃宋代入闽始祖李火德之纪念祠。坐北朝南，占地面积5,600平方米。平面呈“回”字形，前方后圆，前低后高，由中轴线的前坪、门厅、中堂、上堂（惇叙堂），后院和半圆围屋，左右横屋组成。宗祠规模宏大，布局独特，是一座典型的客家围屋与宗祠功能相结合的建筑物。

Guantian Li Family's Ancestral Hall

Period: Qing Dynasty

Address: Guantian Village, Rentian Town, Shanghang County, Longyan City

Also known as "Dunxu Hall", it was built between 1836 and 1839 during the Qing Dynasty, and it was the memorial hall to Li Huode, the Li ancestor who first came to Fujian during the Song Dynasty. Sitting north and facing to the south, it covers an area of 5,600 square meters. The layout is in the shape of the Chinese character "回", with a low square front façade and a high round backside. It is composed of the front courtyard, the entrance hall, the middle hall, the upper hall (Dunxu Hall), as well as a semi-circular enclosure with left and right wing rooms off the central axis. With a large scale and the unique layout, this ancestral hall is a typical combination of Hakka-style circular houses and ancestral hall functions.

李氏大宗祠内景。（李文强 摄）
The interior view of Li Family's Ancestral Hall. (Photo by Li Wenqiang)

李氏大宗祠俯瞰。（胡家新 摄）
A bird's eye view of Li Family's Ancestral Hall. (Photo by Hu Jiaxin)

芷溪宗祠建筑

位于龙岩市连城县庙前镇的芷溪村是一个大型闽西客家古村落，聚居着黄、杨、邱、华等姓客家人，其中以黄、杨两姓居多。芷溪村落格局保存完整，现存集中连片的明清建筑 200 余座，仅宗祠建筑就多达 74 座。芷溪明清建筑均采用了该地域较为典型的宗祠建筑格局，既有祠居合一类型，又有单一家祠类型。

Ancestral Buildings in Zhixi Village

Zhixi Village, located in Miaoqian Town, Liancheng County, Longyan City, is one of the largest ancient Hakka villages in Western Fujian, inhabited by Hakkas with the surnames of Huang, Yang, Qiu, and Hua, of which the majority were Huang and Yang. The original pattern of Zhixi Village has been kept intact. There are more than 200 existing buildings built during the Ming and Qing dynasties, and there are as many as 74 ancestral halls. The buildings in Zhixi built during the Ming and Qing dynasties all adopted the typical Hakka ancestral architecture pattern of the region. However, there are different styles like combinations of residence and worship, and separate ancestral halls.

芷溪古村。（胡家新 摄）
The ancient Zhixi Village. (Photo by Hu Jiaxin)

黄氏家庙

年代：清

地址：龙岩市连城县庙前镇芷溪村

始建于清顺治十三年（1656），康熙三十年（1691）落成，是芷溪黄氏开基祖庚福公纪念祠。坐东向西，占地面积 3,022 平方米，由半月塘、雨坪、门楼、门厅、正厅等组成，以墙围之。家庙设内外两个门楼，进入院坪的外门楼（即大门）为八字石门楼，门厅前的内门楼为木牌楼，为四柱三间三楼式，施斗拱叠涩挑檐，歇山顶。门厅、正厅以回廊相通的。家庙内彩绘、壁画和木雕精美，题材丰富。

Huang Family's Ancestral Hall

Period: Qing Dynasty

Address: Zhixi Village, Miaoqian Town, Liancheng County, Longyan City

This hall was started in 1656 and completed in 1691 during the Qing Dynasty. It is the memorial hall for Sir Gengfu, the founder of Zhixi Huang family. Sitting east and facing west, it covers an area of 3,022 square meters and is composed of Banyue Pool, the courtyard, the arch gatehouse, the entrance hall, the main hall, etc., all surrounded by walls. The family hall has two arch gates inside and outside. The outer arch gate that opens to the courtyard is "八"-shaped and made of stone. The inner one in front of the hall is made of wood. The hall has a gable and hip roof, and is four columns deep and three rooms wide, with three decorated arches. The foyer and main hall are connected by a corridor. The paintings, murals and wood carvings in the family hall are exquisite and rich in various historical themes.

黄氏家庙内景。（杨天鑫 摄）
The interior of Huang Family's Ancestral Hall. (Photo by Yang Tianxin)

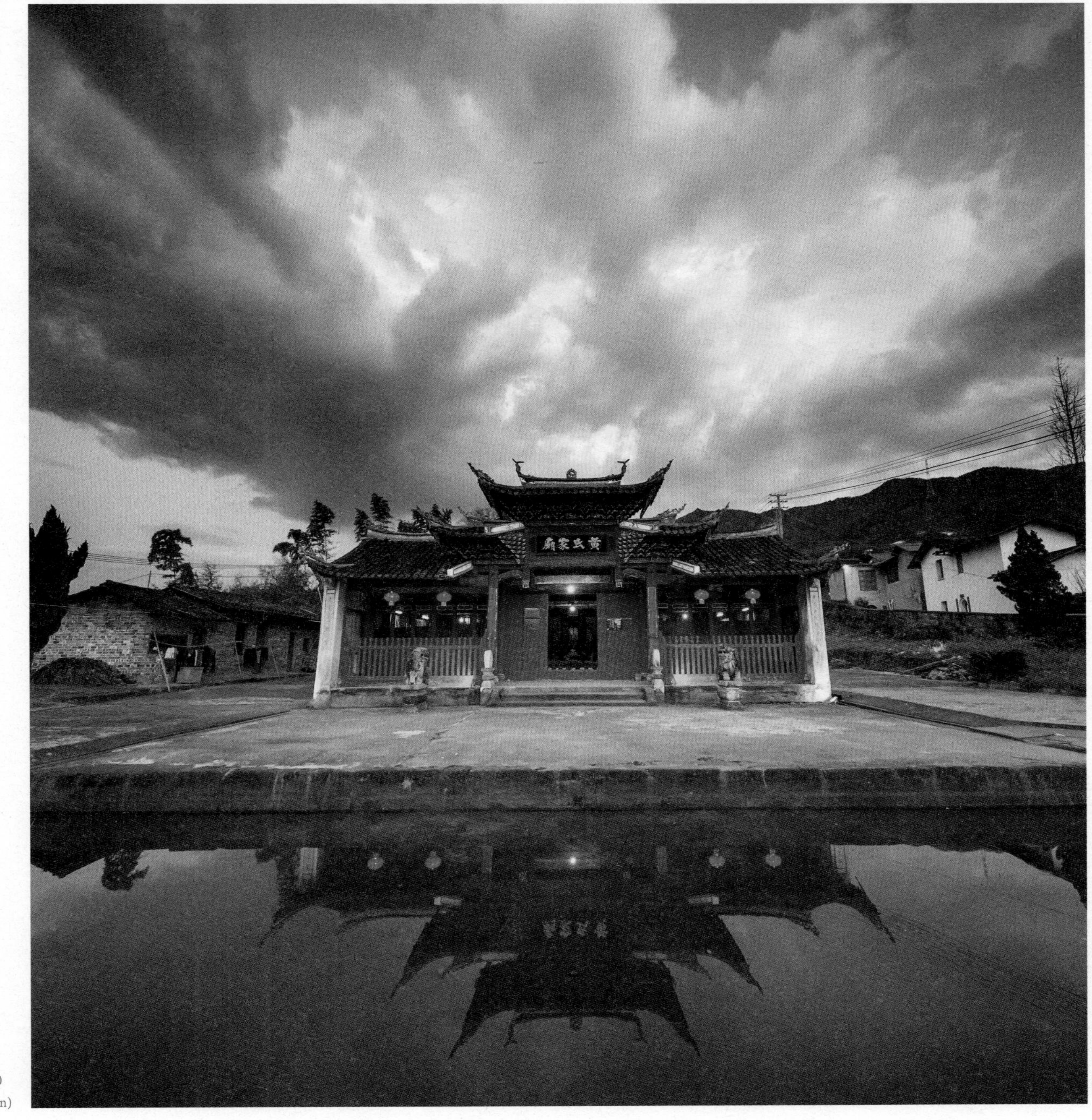

黄氏家庙。（胡家新 摄）
Huang Family's Ancestral Hall. (Photo by Hu Jiaxin)

杨氏家庙

年代：清

地址：龙岩市连城县庙前镇芷溪背园

又名龟山公祠，建于康熙六年（1667），奉祀闽理学大师杨时（号龟山，谥文靖），是广东、江西和福建三省联宗的祠堂。由中轴线的门楼、下厅、上厅和左右各一列横屋组成，以左右回廊连接上、下厅。门楼为木牌楼，为四柱三间三楼式，施斗拱叠涩挑檐，歇山顶，绘有“八仙过海”“三英战吕布”等传统故事彩绘。

Yang Family's Ancestral Hall

Period: Qing Dynasty

Address: Zhixi Bei Garden, Miaoqian Town, Liancheng County, Longyan City

Also known as "Sir Guishan Memorial Hall", it was built in 1667 during the Qing Dynasty and dedicated to the Master of Neo-Confucianism, Yang Shi. It is the Yang clan's ancestral hall for three provinces (Guangdong, Jiangxi and Fujian). It is composed of the arch gate house, the lower hall and the upper hall located along the central axis, and a row of wing rooms on the left and right sides. The upper and lower halls are connected by left and right corridors. The arch gate house has a wooden archway, with the style of four columns deep, three rooms wide with three arches. Bracket sets stacked high raise the soaring eaves with a gable and hip roof, and there are traditional stories painted such as "Eight Immortals Crossing the Sea", "Three Great Heroes Fight with Lyu Bu".

杨氏家庙内景。（杨天鑫 摄）
The interior of Yang Family's Ancestral Hall. (Photo by Yang Tianxin)

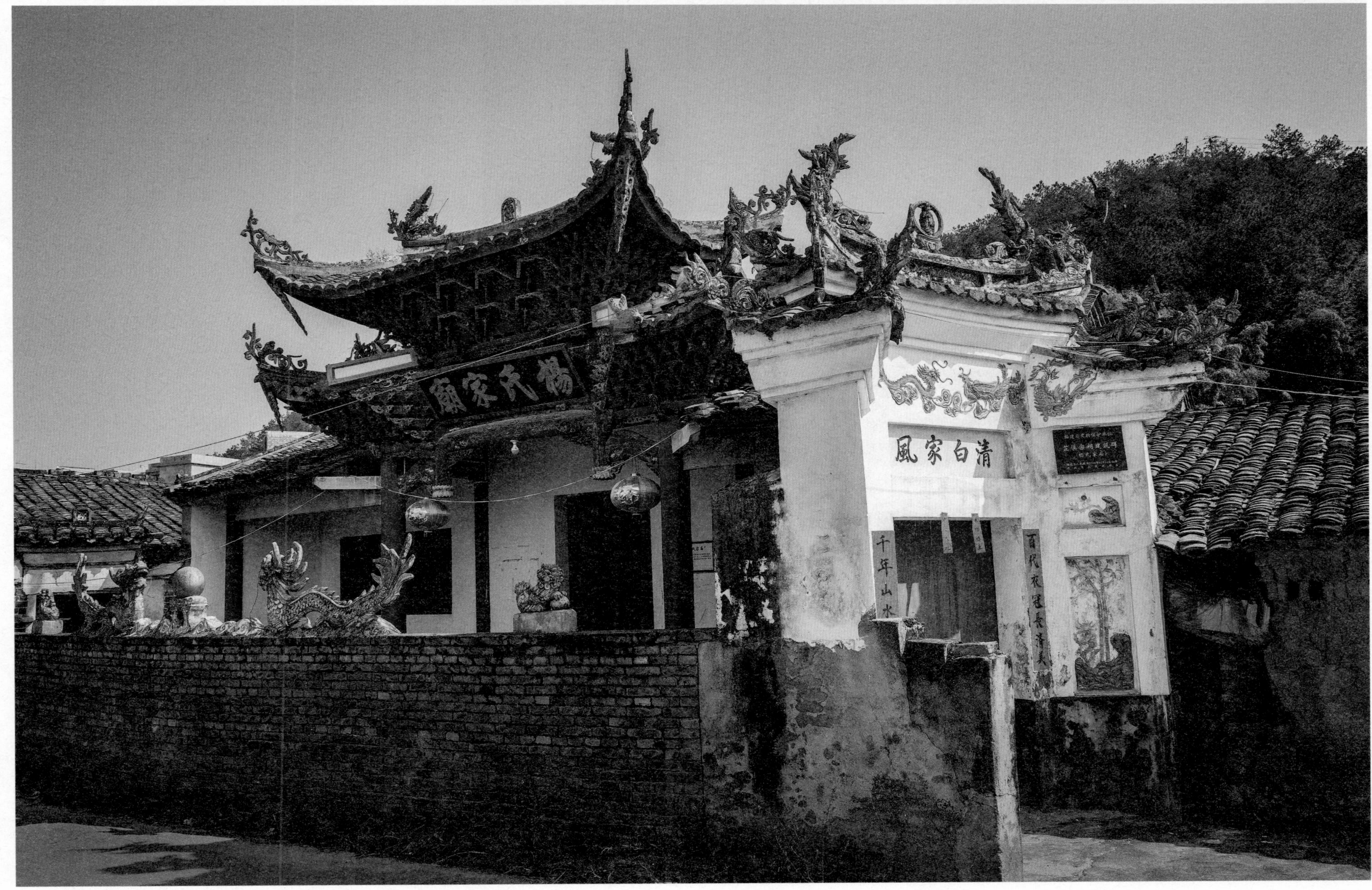

杨氏家庙。（胡家新 摄）
Yang Family's Ancestral Hall. (Photo by Hu Jiaxin)

采陔公祠

年代：清

地址：龙岩市连城县庙前镇庙上村

建于清代晚期，是当地江氏十四世祖采陔公的纪念祠，占地面积 4,865 平方米。祠分为前落斯馨堂和后落聚欢堂两大部分。斯馨堂由门楼、下厅、上厅及南侧二列横屋、东侧三列横屋组成。斯馨堂石门楼为四柱三楼，石构斗拱，做工精细，雕刻图样精美。聚欢堂由下厅、中厅、上厅及南侧三列横屋、东侧四列横屋组成。采陔公祠是闽西客家地区的大型传统祠堂建筑的典型代表。

Sir Caigai Memorial Hall

Period: Qing Dynasty

Address: Miaoshang Village, Miaoqian Town, Liancheng County, Longyan City

Built during the late Qing Dynasty, it is a memorial hall to the local Jiang family's 14th ancestor, Sir Caigai, covering an area of 4,865 square meters. The shrine is divided into two parts: the front Sixin Hall and the back Juhuan Hall. Sixin Hall is composed of the arch gate tower, the lower hall, the upper hall, with two rows of wing rooms on the south side and three rows of wing rooms on the east side. The stone arch gate tower of Sixin Hall is of the style with four pillars; the stone structure and bracket sets are of fine workmanship with exquisite carvings. Juhuan Hall consists of the lower hall, the middle hall, the upper hall, three rows of wing rooms on the south side, and four rows of wing rooms on the east side. Sir Caigai Memorial Hall is a typical example of the large traditional ancestral buildings in the Hakka area of Western Fujian.

采陔公祠大门。（胡家新 摄）
The arch gate of Sir Caigai Memorial Hall. (Photo by Hu Jiaxin)

采陔公祠俯瞰。（胡家新 摄）
A bird's eye view of Sir Caigai Memorial Hall. (Photo by Hu Jiaxin)

廖氏宗祠（古田会议会址）

年代：清

地址：龙岩市上杭县古田镇溪背村

又名万源祠。建于清道光二十八年（1848）。典型的客家宗祠建筑。坐东朝西，由前院、正门、前厅、正厅和左、右各一列横屋组成，后有化胎、风水林。民国初，为推行新学，该祠改为和声小学。1929年5月，红四军第二次入闽，开展土地革命，改名为曙光小学。1929年12月28日至29日，毛泽东、朱德、陈毅等在此主持召开了中国共产党红军第四军第九次代表大会（即著名的古田会议）。

Liao Family's Ancestral Hall (Gutian Conference Site)

Period: Qing Dynasty

Address: Xibei Village, Gutian Town, Shanghang County, Longyan City

Also known as Wanyuan Hall, this ancestral hall was built in 1848 during the Qing Dynasty. It is a typical Hakka ancestral building. Sitting east and facing to the west, it is composed of the front yard, the main entrance, the front hall, the main hall, a row of wing rooms on both the left and right, the Huatai (a symbol of peace and safety), and Fengshui woods in the back. Right after the establishment of the Republic of China, the shrine was changed to Hesheng Elementary School in order to promote new learning. In May 1929, when the Red Army entered Fujian for the second time to carry out the Agrarian Revolution, it was renamed Shuguang Primary School. From December 28 to 29, 1929, Mao Zedong, Zhu De and Chen Yi hosted the Ninth Congress of the Fourth Army of the Chinese Communist Red Army (the famous Gutian Conference).

古田会议召开处。（胡家新 摄）
The site of the famous Gutian Conference. (Photo by Hu Jiaxin)

春日廖氏宗祠。（胡家新 摄）
Liao Family's Ancestral Hall in spring. (Photo by Hu Jiaxin)

宁德古厝

Ancient Buildings in Ningde

廣化禪林
世界三千毫光普照
因緣十二妙悟皆通
南無阿彌陀佛

狮峰寺

年代：明

地址：宁德市福安市溪柄镇楼下村

狮峰寺于唐景福元年（892）始建，明永乐年间（1403—1424）移建今址，历代屡有修葺。大殿建于明万历四十年（1612），重檐歇山顶，殿堂式建筑，抬梁式木构架，草架为穿斗式。殿身面阔一间，进深三间，副阶周匝。殿堂分前、后双槽，正中顶棚为重拱八角藻井。殿内有 24 根抹角石柱。木构架、铺作层存有大面积清晰完整的明代彩绘图案。

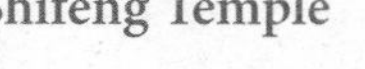

Shifeng Temple

Period: Ming Dynasty

Address: Louxia Village, Xibing Town, Fu'an City, Ningde City

Shifeng Temple was built in 892 during the Tang Dynasty and moved to the present site between 1403 and 1424 during the Ming Dynasty. The main hall was built in 1612 during the Ming Dynasty, with a double-eave gable and hip roof, of typical post-and-lintel construction. It is one room wide and three rooms deep, surrounded by a colonnade. The main hall is divided into the front and back parts, with a beautiful octagonal caissson ceiling in the middle. There are also 24 stone pillars in the temple. There are clear and intact paintings of the Ming Dynasty style at the wooden frame and the intermediate sets.

殿内八角藻井。（薛明瑞 摄）
The octagonal caisson ceiling inside the hall. (Photo by Xue Mingrui)

大殿飞天彩绘。（张玉文 摄）
A fine painting in the main hall. (Photo by Zhang Yuwen)

狮峰寺侧影。（薛明瑞 摄）
A silhouette of Shifeng Temple. (Photo by Xue Mingrui)

观音亭寨之观音亭寺

年代：明至清

地址：宁德市霞浦县水门畲族乡半岭畲族村

半岭畲族观音亭寨由观音亭寺、观音亭寨及古驿道组成，庙因路兴，寨由庙名，所处位置是古代福州通往浙江温州的必经之地。观音亭寺始建于明洪武二年（1369），清康熙年间（1662—1722）重修。寺身依山面向古驿道而建，坐西北朝东南，占地面积 427 平方米，由门楼、前殿、后殿组成，四周围以砖墙。大殿为单檐歇山顶，面阔三间，进深两间，梁底墨书“福宁地方总镇都督府法洪阿图鲁主建，清康熙五年荔月立”字样。

Guanyinting Temple of Guanyinting Fort

Period: Ming to Qing dynasties

Address: Banling *She* (Ethnic Group) Village, Shuimen She Township, Xiapu County, Ningde City

Guanyinting Fort in Banling *She* Village is composed of Guanyinting Temple, Guanyinting Fort and the ancient post road. The temple was prosperous because of the road, and the village is named after the temple. It is located along the only way where people passed by when traveling from ancient Fuzhou to Wenzhou in Zhejiang Province. Guanyinting Temple was built in 1369 during the Ming Dynasty and repaired between 1662 and 1722 during the Qing Dynasty. Built on a mountain facing the ancient post road, the temple sits northwest facing southeast, and covers an area of 427 square meters. It is composed of the arch gatehouse, the front hall, and the rear hall, surrounded by brick walls. The main hall has a single-eave gable and hip roof, and is three rooms wide and two rooms deep. On the bottom of the main beam is an inscription, "Built by Fahong Atulu, the Governor of the town of Funing, in the six lunar month of 1666 during the Qing Dynasty".

观音亭寨寨门。（马立坤 摄）
The arch gate of Guanyinting Fort. (Photo by Ma Likun)

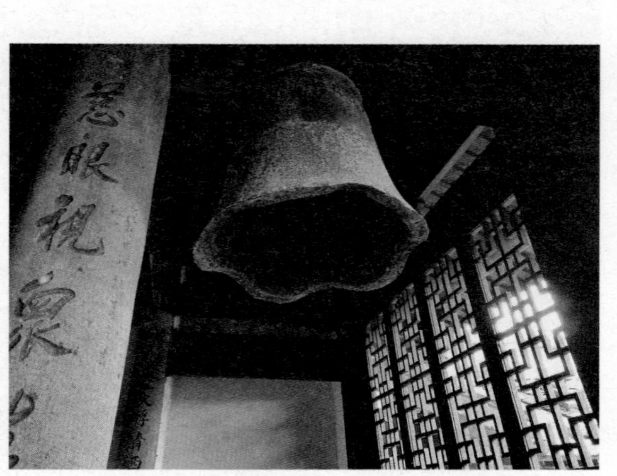

大殿内的石柱及古钟。（马立坤 摄）
The stone column and ancient bell in the main hall. (Photo by Ma Likun)

观音亭寺大门 （马立坤 摄）
The arch gate of Guanyinting Temple. (Photo by Ma Likun)

林公忠平王祖殿

年代：明至清

地址：宁德市周宁县玛坑乡杉洋村

明正德八年（1513）始建，清嘉庆十年（1805）增建太子亭、钟鼓楼、东西配殿等，坐南向北，占地面积1,364 平方米。大殿为单檐歇山顶，面阔五间，进深四间，神龛祭林公泥塑。殿内石雕、木刻、泥塑、彩绘精美，皆保存完好。太子亭上有透雕龙头石匾，竖刻“敕封林公忠平王祖殿”。

Memorial Hall of Sir Lingong, the Zhongping King

Period: Ming to Qing dynasties

Address: Shanyang Village, Makeng Township, Zhouning County, Ningde City

This beautiful building was built in 1513 during the Ming Dynasty, and rebuilt in 1805 during the Qing Dynasty, when they added the Prince Pavilion, the bell and drum tower, the east and west halls and more to cover an area of 1,364 square meters. Five rooms wide and four rooms deep, the main hall has a single-eave gable and hip roof with a shrine offered to the clay sculpture of Sir Lingong. The stone carvings, wood carvings, clay sculptures and paintings in the hall are all delicate artworks and well preserved. On the Prince Pavilion there is an openwork dragon-head stone plaque with a vertical engraving “Ancestral Hall of Faithful and Brave Sir Lingong conferred by the emperor”.

殿内透雕龙头石匾（郑禧春 摄）
The openwork dragon-head stone plaque in the hall. (Photo by Zheng Xichun)

林公忠平王祖殿全貌。（郑禧春 摄）

The overall perspective of the memorial hall. (Photo by Zheng Xichun)

古田临水宫

年代：明至清

地址：宁德市古田县大桥镇洋中村

唐贞元八年（792）始建，历代均有修葺，现存建筑为明、清重建。临水宫为祭祀临水夫人陈靖姑的祖宫，坐北朝南，占地面积8,000多平方米。宫依山而建，自南向北层层高起，依次为戏台、拜亭、正殿、后殿等。拜亭两侧立钟、鼓楼，正殿东侧有太保殿，西侧有婆奶殿，后殿东侧则排列梳妆楼等建筑。宫庙内外装饰精细繁缛，太保殿山墙保留数十幅精美壁画，极具艺术魅力。临水宫作为临水夫人信仰的祖庙，是连接海内外同胞亲情、友情的一座重要桥梁。

Gutian Linshui Temple

Period: Ming to Qing dynasties

Address: Yangzhong Village, Daqiao Town, Gutian County, Ningde City

This temple was built in 792 during the Tang Dynasty and has been repaired often throughout the dynasties. The extant building was rebuilt during the Ming and Qing dynasties. Linshui Temple is an ancestral temple dedicated to Lady Linshui, Chen Jinggu. Sitting north and facing south, it covers an area of more than 8,000 square meters. It was built on a mountain, rising from the south to the north, in proper order there is the stage, the worshiping pavilion, the main hall and the rear hall. There are bell and drum towers on both sides of the worshiping pavilion. On the east side of the main hall lies Taibao Hall. Ponai Hall is on the west side, and a dressing tower and other buildings are on the east side of the rear hall. The decorations inside and outside the temple are fine and detailed, and the gable walls of Taibao Hall retain dozens of exquisite murals, which are extremely attractive. Linshui Temple, as the ancestral temple of Lady Linshui belief, is an important bridge for the friendship of compatriots at home and abroad.

临水宫内的精美木雕。（余新星 摄）
Fine wood carvings in Linshui Temple. (Photo by Yu Xinxing)

临水钟楼。（薛明瑞 摄）
The bell tower in Linshui Temple. (Photo by Xue Mingrui)

临水宫侧影。（黄谷上 摄）
A silhouette of Linshui Temple. (Photo by Huang Gushang)

漈下建筑群精美墙饰。（邱仰左 摄）
Beautiful wall ornaments in Jixia Architectural Complex. (Photo by Qiu Yangzuo)

漈下建筑群

漈下村为甘氏族人聚族而居的传统村落，故亦称甘漈下。建筑群格局可清晰地分为明、清两个时期。宫、庙、祠、宅、亭等古建筑分布于穿村而过的溪流两岸，数量众多，存续时间长，保存完好，是研究闽东地区传统村落形态和古建筑结构特征、历史演变的极好实例。

Jixia Architectural Complex

Jixia Village is a traditional village inhabited by the Gan family, so it is also called Gan Jixia. The structure of the architectural complex can be clearly divided into two periods, Ming Dynasty and Qing Dynasty. Ancient buildings such as temples, shrines, houses and pavilions are distributed on both sides of the stream passing through the village. These ancient buildings are in large number and well preserved. Jixia Architectural Complex is an excellent place to study the traditional village morphology and historical evolution of ancient buildings in eastern Fujian.

漈下建筑群一隅。（邱仰左 摄）
A section of Jixia Architectural Complex. (Photo by Qiu Yangzuo)

龙漈仙宫

年代：明至清

地址：宁德市屏南县甘棠乡漈下村

又名瀛仙宫，祀马氏仙姑。始建年代不详，明隆庆三年（1569）重建，清光绪十七年（1891）重修，坐南向北，是由门头房、天井及两侧厢房、大殿组成的合院式建筑。大殿面阔三间，进深七柱，明间减中柱，上覆藻井。屋面重檐，上檐圆形攒尖顶，下檐四面坡，形成外观独特的圆穹隆顶屋面，取“天圆地方”之意。大殿的平板天花及四壁隔板等处均留有清代彩画。

Longji Fairy Temple

Period: Ming to Qing dynasties

Address: Jixia Village, Gantang Township, Pingnan County, Ningde City

Also known as “Yingxian Temple”, it worships the legendary celestial Fairy Ma. The date of its construction is unknown. It was rebuilt in 1569 during the Ming Dynasty and in 1891 during the Qing Dynasty. It is a courtyard-style building consisting of the arched gatehouse, the patio, wing rooms and the main hall. The main hall is three rooms wide and seven pillars deep, with a beautiful caisson ceiling in the middle. The roof has double eaves. The upper eave is round with a spire, and the lower eave is sloped on all sides, forming a unique dome. It aptly displays the meaning of “round sky and square earth”. The flat ceilings and the four-wall clapboard of the main hall retain beautiful colored paintings from the Qing Dynasty.

俯瞰龙漈仙宫。（邱仰左 摄）
A bird's eye view of Longji Fairy Temple. (Photo by Qiu Yangzuo)

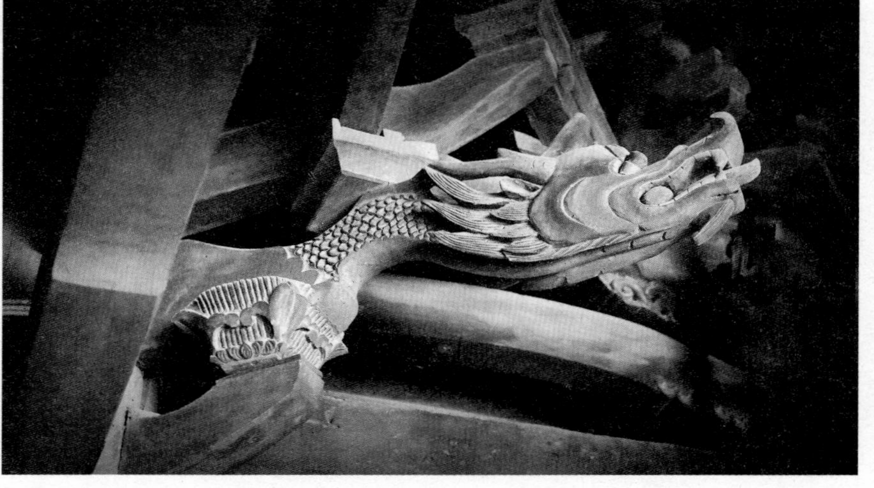

宫内龙头木雕。（邱仰左 摄）
The dragon-head wood carving in the temple. (Photo by Qiu Yangzuo)

宫内藻井。（邱仰左 摄）
The caisson ceiling in the temple. (Photo by Qiu Yangzuo)

甘氏支祠正门。（郑陈丹 摄）
The front door of Gan Family's Ancestral Hall. (Photo by Zheng Chendan)

甘氏支祠

年代：清

地址：宁德市屏南县甘棠乡漈下村

又名“良清公祠”，堂号“善继堂”，是漈下甘氏开基三世祖良清公的祠堂。清嘉庆年间（1796—1820）建。单进合院式，由门厅和厅堂（享堂）组成。厅堂与后墙间设后天井。厅堂为双坡顶，两侧封火墙，面阔三间，进深七柱，穿斗式梁架，两侧次间山墙搁檩，前廊轩顶。

Gan Family's Ancestral Hall

Period: Qing Dynasty

Address: Jixia Village, Gantang Township, Pingnan County, Ningde City

Also known as “Sir Liangqing Memorial Hall” or “Shanji Hall”, it is the ancestral hall dedicated to Sir Liangqing, a third generation ancestor of the Gan family. It was built between 1796 and 1820 during the Qing Dynasty. The single-courtyard-style hall consists of the entrance hall and the main hall. There is a back patio between the main hall and the back wall. The hall has a double-sloped roof of column and tie-beam construction, with fire walls on both sides. It is three rooms wide and seven columns deep, with purlins set on the gable on both sides and has a front gallery.

祠内雀替。（郑陈丹 摄）

The sparrow brace in Gan Family's Ancestral Hall.(Photo by Zheng Chendan)

凤岐吴氏大宅

年代：清

地址：宁德市柘荣县乍洋乡凤里村凤岐村

建于清乾隆、嘉庆年间（1736—1820），是古代凤岐村唯一的民居建筑，形成一村一屋、一屋成村的壮观景象。大宅坐东北向西南，依山而建，层层高起，占地面积达 14,312 平方米。由围墙内的主体建筑、围墙外的书苑类附属建筑、外围的台埕类附属建筑等组成，由内向外依次分布，主从有序，功能分明。主体建筑四面围以青砖匡斗墙，平面呈纵向的长方形，由门楼、下厅、中厅、上厅和后花台组成，左右则以纵向插屏式廊道和横屋分隔整体空间。

一屋成村的吴氏大宅。（林文强 摄）
Wu Family's Mansion, one house forming a village. (Photo by Lin Wenqiang)

Wu Family's Mansion in Fengqi

Period: Qing Dynasty

Address: Fengqi Village, Fengli Village, Zhayang Township, Zherong County, Ningde City

This mansion was built from 1736 to 1820 during the Qing Dynasty. It is the only residential building in the ancient Fengqi Village, forming a spectacular scene of "one house forming a village". Built on a mountain, the mansion sits northeast and faces southwest. Rising level by level and covering an area of 14,312 square meters, it is composed of the main buildings inside the walls, the ancillary academies outside the walls and the outer terrace-like annexes, which are distributed in proper order from the inside to the outside with respectively clear functions. The main buildings are surrounded by grey brick walls on four sides, and the layout is in a quadrangle. It is composed of the arch gatehouse, the lower hall, the middle hall, the upper hall, and the rear flower terrace, with the left and right sides separated by a vertical corridor and rows of wing rooms.

大门背面。（林文强 摄）
The back of the arch gate. (Photo by Lin Wenqiang)

天井过道的原木顶。（林可资 摄）
The log ceiling of the patio corridor. (Photo by Lin Kezi)

福安黄氏祠堂

年代：清

地址：宁德市福安市阳头街道阳下村黄厝上巷 58 号

始建于宋末，清乾隆三十三年（1768）重建，1920年增建戏楼并重修大厅。祠堂坐西南朝东北，占地面积2,516 平方米。由东北至西南依次为仪门、泮池、照壁、大门、戏楼、前座、覆龟亭、后座、后天井和后厢房等建筑。戏楼之上设四柱三间牌楼，并大量采用砖雕彩绘和灰塑装饰，木构件雕刻花鸟、人物、瑞兽图案，工艺精美。黄氏祠堂参照孔庙规制建造，设置仪门、泮池和照壁，体现了“立庙于学”的寓意。

Huang Family’s Ancestral Hall in Fu’an

Period: Qing Dynasty

Address: No. 58, Huangcuo Shang Alley, Yangxia Village, Yangtou Street, Fu’an City, Ningde City

This ancestral hall was built in the late Song Dynasty and was rebuilt in 1768 during the Qing Dynasty. In 1920, an opera building was added, and the hall was rebuilt. It sits southwest and faces northeast, covering an area of 2,516 square meters. From northeast to southwest, there is the etiquette gate, the Pan Pool, the Fengshui wall, the arch gate, the opera building, the front hall, the covered pavilion, the rear hall, the rear patio, rear rooms, etc. There are four pillars and three groups of hall-style archways above the opera building, which are heavily decorated with brick carvings and grey-stone decorations. The wooden components are carved with flowers, birds and various animals with exquisite craftsmanship. The Huang Family’s Ancestral Hall was built in accordance with the Confucius Temple regulations, with the etiquette gate, the Pan Pool and the Fengshui wall that embody the meaning of “the Confucius Temple serving as a school”.

祠堂牌楼。（张玉文 摄）
The soaring roofs of the ancestral hall. (Photo by Zhang Yuwen)

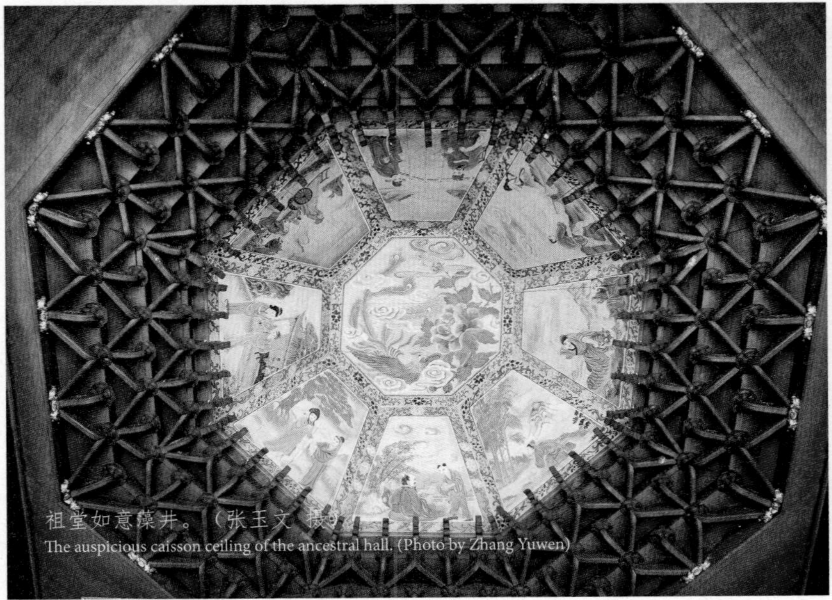

祖堂如意藻井。（张玉文 摄）
The auspicious caisson ceiling of the ancestral hall. (Photo by Zhang Yuwen)

戏台如意藻井。（张玉文 摄）
The auspicious caisson ceiling of the opera building. (Photo by Zhang Yuwen)

平潭古厝

Ancient Buildings in Pingtan

上攀村侧影。（念望舒 摄）
A silhouette of Shangpan Village. (Photo by Nian Wangshu)

上攀古建筑群

Shangpan Ancient Building Group

年代：清至民国
地址：平潭综合实验区平原镇上攀村

Period: Qing Dynasty to the Republic of China
Address: Shangpan Village, Pingyuan Town, Pingtan Comprehensive Pilot Zone

由上攀村七幢古民居和旧村委会石构建筑组成。古建筑群为清代至民国时期的石构建筑，俗称石头厝，是福建沿海石头厝建筑的典型代表。各幢建筑多为合院式，由门墙、天井、两侧护厝和正厝组成。正厝多为两层建筑，双坡顶，石砌外墙，搁檩式结构，一般面阔三间，中为厅堂，两侧次间为卧房。

This group of buildings is composed of seven ancient stone dwellings and the adjacent old site of the Village Committee. This ancient architecture group dates back to the stone architecture style spanning from the Qing Dynasty to the Republic of China, commonly known as the “Stone House”, which is typical of Fujian coastal stone houses. Most of the buildings are courtyard-style houses, which are composed of entrance door walls, courtyards, side guardhouses and main houses. The main houses are mostly two-story buildings, with a double sloping roof, stone walls, generally three rooms wide, one hall in the middle, with bedrooms on both sides.

近看石头厝。（念望舒 摄）
A close look at the stone houses. (Photo by Nian Wangshu)

五福庙

年代：清

地址：平潭综合实验区潭城镇五福街

又称威灵公庙，明代始建，清康熙年间（1662—1722）重建，雍正七年（1729）海坛总镇吕瑞麟续修，乾隆三十八年（1773）续建前座及龙凤戏台，道光二十六年（1846）王三聘父子和翁郁林、纪朝元等主持重修，同治十二年（1873）再次修葺。由戏台、城隍殿、太岁殿等组成。城隍殿坐北朝南，占地面积336平方米，硬山顶，穿斗抬梁混合木构架，面阔三间，进深五柱。明间神龛供奉五福都城隍威灵公和台湾城隍神像，其中台湾城隍神像是清代福建水师官兵换防时自台湾澎湖带回，为闽台两地文化交流源远流长的历史佐证。

五福庙龙凤台。（念望舒 摄）
The Dragon-Phoenix Stage in Wufu Temple. (Photo by Nian Wangshu)

Wufu Temple

Period: Qing Dynasty

Address: Wufu Street, Tancheng Town, Pingtan Comprehensive Pilot Zone

Also called "Sir Weiling Temple", Wufu Temple was built during the Ming Dynasty, rebuilt in the period of Kangxi (1662—1722) during the Qing Dynasty, repaired in 1729 by naval leader Lyu Ruiling, who extended and added the front part and the Dragon-Phoenix Stage in 1773. It was rebuilt yet again by Wang Sanping and his sons, also Weng Yulin and Ji Chaoyuan in 1846, and then repaired in 1873. The temple is composed of the stage, Chenghuang Hall, Taisui Hall and other buildings. Chenghuang Hall sits north and faces south, and covers an area of 336 square meters, with a flush gable roof. It has both post-and-lintel construction and column-and-tie-beam wooden structure, and is three rooms wide and five columns deep. The shrine in the main hall honors the Wufu City God, Sir Weiling, and the Taiwan City God. The Taiwan City God was brought by the Fujian naval officers and soldiers during the Qing Dynasty from Penghu of Taiwan during an exchange of naval soldiers. It is a historical record of the rich cultural exchanges between Fujian and Taiwan.

五福庙外观。（念望舒 摄）

Wufu Temple. (Photo by Nian Wangshu)

From the Translator

The ancient buildings of western civilization (e.g. Greece, Rome, Middle East) are very different from those of China. So let's look at the differences … identifying various aspects in the ancient buildings of Fujian in order to better understand the ancient culture of China.

So, what is the first thing that you notice about an ancient Chinese building (a temple for example)? Usually it's the roof—because the roofs of major ancient Chinese buildings are massive, consisting of an intricate system of beams, cross beams, brackets and eaves—mostly made of timber.

This points out an interesting difference from ancient western civilization, where most of the ancient buildings (those that still survive) were made of stone (or bricks); whereas in China, timber was the material most often used because it was plentiful, lighter and easier to use (although prone to fire).

The foundations of the buildings of both cultures were similar, usually consisting of massive stone foundation blocks to support the weight of the structure. There's not much to say about foundations—because they are under the ground and you can't see them but let me explain some key elements of the foundations.

Because much of China is in an earthquake area, the foundations were very important. They would hand-dig deep down usually to get to the layer of bedrock, and then they typically placed huge blocks of stone as the base, on top of which the flooring was laid. On the flooring stood the columns, holding up the massive roof.

These columns were made from huge timbers to support the massive roof—later some were made of stone. The walls were not load-bearing, which allowed for much greater wall flexibility as different needs determined, e.g. change of seasons. So, notice these elements as you wander through these buildings … the timber columns, the lighter inner walls and the massive roofs.

What one must appreciate is that the ancient artisans who built the temples and ancestral halls followed a craft thousands of years old; each aspect had meaning and relevance. If there was some deviation, they would tear it all down and redo it—I saw this actually happen once in Liancheng, Fujian at the foot of Mount Guanzhai.

Back to the roofs now. The first thing you will notice about the roofs is that the eaves project out on all sides; this is to protect the walls and wood doors from rain erosion. The early walls were made of stamped earth or clay which was susceptible to erosion from the rain. Later when bricks and other more impervious materials were used on the walls, the length of outward projection was reduced.

Additionally, the extension and raising of the eave's tip ends were designed for aesthetic reasons. Since the roofs were massive, to open up the inner space, they designed the eaves to give these massive roofs a light feel, as though flying upwards. This created a very pleasing visual impression and allowed more light to enter.

The other unique feature of the roofs is the decoration of the ridges—which were usually decorated with various animal figures representing prosperity, good health and other auspicious wishes. Some of these are carved in wood and painted or made of colorful cut-porcelain. Along the roof tops and eaves, you will often see these truly colorful ornaments, and each one has its own meaning, e.g. "good fortune", "good health", "success in the examination", etc.

There are many styles of roofs: hip roof, gable and hip roof, overhanging gable roof, round ridge roof, double-eave roof, etc. I don't think it's necessary to become a roof expert; I think it's enough to develop an appreciation for the historical and cultural aspects of the roof system as it is the most prominent part of the structure.

Another noteworthy aspect of the roof is the timber construction and how the ancient artisans achieved the projecting eaves using only wood members. If you look underneath the edge of the roof you will notice a latticework of ever larger connecting members—these bracket sets were called "duogong". To project the roof out (and support it), unique curved wood members (the "gong") were connected, one over the other (with another wood connecting piece, the "dou")—the greater the number of these members, the more the roof was able to project out. These bracket sets came into being early in Chinese history, as early as the Han Dynasty (202 BCE—220 CE).

Later when the clay walls were replaced by brick walls, and the need to project out was reduced, the size of the bracket sets became smaller but more numerous and when decorated, they became a beautiful decorative feature of ancient Chinese buildings. Another aspect of these timber roofs, as evidenced by their longevity, is their unique ability to withstand earthquakes.

The main drawback to timber structures however, is their susceptibility to fire, which was a major concern in ancient times. In many towns where the buildings were built next to each other, the builders built a raised roof wall to act as a fire wall to suppress the spread of a fire. You can see these raised roof fire walls in many ancient villages.

Rites: To the Chinese rites represent the criteria which determines human relationships in order to achieve a virtuous and benevolent life. The Book of Rites (Confucius) recorded the regulations which governed a wide range of matters, both big and small, relationships in the family and with the emperor and everyone in between. It also addressed the layout of cities and individual homes. The size and design of homes reflected the importance of the owner in the hierarchy. Obviously the emperor had the biggest house, and then the princes, and so on down.

The basic design of most buildings was in the form of a quadrangle, a symmetrical square or rectangle with various courtyards, the main ancestral hall, side living units and in the back, various storage rooms. Upon entering the main doorway, your vision is usually blocked by a screen wall to protect the inhabitants' privacy from passersby. This screen wall was often decorated with auspicious artworks.

Next there was typically a main courtyard and other inner courtyards. In one of them usually was a patio open to the sky. The patio provided much of the light to the inner rooms, and also acted as an air refresher. Around the central courtyard were the living quarters for the master and his wife, with the sons' and daughters' along the sides; in the back were the living quarters for servants, storage and food preparation.

Colors: Colors were an important part of the ancient decorations, but to understand colors first you must understand that in ancient China it was believed that the world was composed of five elements: metal, wood, water, fire, and earth. Likewise, there were five main directions: east, west, south, north and center. The five basic colors were green, yellow, red, white and black.

Many times, we see yellow rooftops and red walls on ancient buildings. Each color was aligned with different elements and aspects of ancient life, e.g. yellow was the color of the earth and also reserved for the emperor. Red is associated with fire and the sun and represented happiness and joyfulness. So, in ancient China you see a lot of these two colors on the most important ancient buildings.

Decorations with animal figures: The Chinese love to decorate their buildings by using bright colors, paintings, carvings and other ornamentation. A common motif is to use animal figures and each of them has a different (or multiple) significance.

One of the most popular animal decorations was the dragon, which was a mythologic creature possessing enormous powers. Usually as a decoration it signifies auspiciousness, prosperity, etc. In some instances, the entire dragon is carved, e.g. coiling around a pillar or on the roof lintels; or two dragons on each side with a ball between their mouths. In other cases, there's only room for the head, e.g. at rain spouts and on the ends of the ridge beams.

Aside from the dragon you can find lions guarding the entrances; typically, one has a ball and the other has one of its paws on a baby lion. Other animals include the entire range of the animal and bird kingdoms. The phoenix bird represents luck and harmony. Many of the lesser animals even adorn the buildings in the countryside.

Look at the free-standing statues and even those under the columns (usually a turtle). All of these animals have a meaning for that family, temple or ancestral hall. Even the number of animals is calculated, e.g. in the Forbidden City, there are nine dragons in various locations.

Clan ancestral halls: These were important buildings in ancient China. They served as places to honor the clan's founders but more importantly to conduct the management of clan business. In many villages the clan ancestral hall was also the place to manag the village business affairs and government functions.

Since its main function was the worship of ancestors the building was laid out accordingly, with the main hall and ancestors soul-tablets at the back with a table set before it for offerings (fruit, vegetables, candles, incense, etc.). Usually photos of the ancestors were displayed above the table on the back wall. During festivities, the long table would be moved to the center of the hall and various foods and sacrificial offerings were laid out on the table and the whole family would pay respects to the ancestors by kowtowing and burning incense.

The layout was similar to a residential quadrangle with wing rooms around the sides for meetings and other functions. Since the clan ancestral hall represented the entire genealogy of the clan, it was usually elaborately decorated in order to display the wealth, success, and importance of the clan.

In some of the ancestral halls you will find incredibly beautiful painted cut-ceramic decorations—dragons, phoenixes, tigers, lions, and even stories from the classics. Also, the wooden timbers are richly carved with animals figures and historical scenes to insure prosperity to the entire clan. Underneath the ends of the beams there was often a corbel—wood members supporting the beams—and these were often carved like lions or dragons.

Buddhist temples: The traditional Chinese quadrangle layout was incorporated into the Buddhist temples, i.e. the main arch gate, the main hall for the Buddhas, bodhisattvas, arhats, etc., the preaching hall, the sutras building, side rooms for study, etc., all according to Chinese tradition and Buddhist rules. Some of the larger temples have drum towers and bell towers.

The temples (Buddhist and Taoist) served an important purpose in the lives of the ancient Chinese. Their lives were not easy (beset by wars, adverse weather and diseases). So they often looked to the heavens/gods for blessings, fortune, longevity, happiness and many other personal wishes. Unfortunately this was not completely the Buddha's message, i.e. that relief from suffering really comes from an awareness of the emptiness of existence (there is no birth/death).

Gardens: In many of the ancient buildings, plots of land inside or adjacent to the building were set aside for gardens—and these were important elements in the desire to achieve harmony with nature. Guided by the principles of Fengshui, these gardens included rockeries, lakes, streams, plants, buildings and other "natural" elements. The "mountains and water" were the key elements and sometimes, because of limited space, the "mountains" were tall stylized rocks (usually slender with wrinkles and holes implying its age). Although the quadrangles were symmetrical, the gardens were irregular—as is nature—evoking a sense of flowing peace. The essence of the designer's spiritual ideas was also imbedded into the design of the garden.

Windows: There are many styles of windows, decorated with various designs; however, the windows that I find most interesting are the "picture windows". These are usually open with or without decorations around the frame. The most interesting aspect is the landscape view on the other side as one looks through the window ... like a beautiful picture. Different windows in the temples and halls have differing views, like natural paintings.

Paintings: I think the most important aspect of paintings is that many great Chinese artists don't just paint the object, e.g. a lotus flower or bamboo stand, but rather they paint the images of the lotus or bamboo in their mind, i.e. their impression/feelings. For example, the black-ink bamboo will reflect his feelings about virtue or benevolence. He is seeking to paint the "spirit" of the scene. Just like the great Impressionist artists of 19th century Paris.

Flowers: The choice of flowers is important both in the garden and in the artistic building decorations. One of the most commonly-used flowers was the lotus flower. It grows at the bottom of the water, in the mud, but is not affected by the mud (its environment); rather it blossoms into a pure clean radiant flower. So too, people can overcome adversities to blossom through virtue. Even in the autumn after the blossoms have all gone, the green petals remain and when it rains, they give off a pleasing sound, which stimulates one's thoughts towards nature and the mysteries of the universe.

Often as you visit these ancient buildings you may spot carvings and pictures of the lotus flower. They are there for a purpose—to instill good thoughts. And the beauty is that each person will enjoy different thoughts/emotions from the same decoration.

I hope this informal narrative will help you to understand and enjoy the ancient buildings in this book. These buildings have survived these hundreds of years because they are special, and because they have a living story to tell.

Thank you.

图书在版编目（CIP）数据

福建古厝：英、汉／中共福建省委宣传部，福建省人民政府新闻办公室编．-- 福州：福建人民出版社，2021.7
ISBN 978-7-211-08511-8

Ⅰ.①福… Ⅱ.①中… ②福… Ⅲ.①古建筑—介绍—福建—英、汉 Ⅳ.①K928.71

中国版本图书馆CIP数据核字（2020）第164872号

福建古厝
FUJIAN GUCUO

特约撰稿：卢　晶　何经平
英文翻译：Richard Howe
责任编辑：周跃进　李文淑　孙　颖
美术编辑：白　玫
内文排版：雅昌文化（集团）有限公司
出版发行：福建人民出版社
电　　话：0591-87533169(发行部)
网　　址：http://www.fjpph.com
电子邮箱：fjpph7211@126.com
地　　址：福州市东水路76号
邮政编码：350001
经　　销：福建新华发行（集团）有限责任公司
印　　刷：雅昌文化（集团）有限公司
地　　址：深圳市南山区深云路19号
开　　本：787毫米×1092毫米　1/16
印　　张：17.25
字　　数：383千字
版　　次：2021年7月第1版
印　　次：2021年7月第1次印刷
书　　号：ISBN 978-7-211-08511-8
定　　价：198.00元

和氣所舍